"This carefully compiled and outstanding resource is long-due and a timely contribution to the canon of translation education literature. It is bound to become an invaluable 'must have' and essential reading for translation and interpreting educators working in today's rapidly changing teaching environment. Its breadth and scope, including practical activities and case examples, allow for an impressive insight into teaching ethics, ethics-informed curriculum development and ethics education for different fields of translation and interpreting, also taking up pressing issues such as ethics in machine translation, post-editing, collaborative translation and research."

Sonja Pöllabauer, Centre for Translation Studies, University of Vienna

"The call for ethics to enter the classroom is not new but until *Teaching Translation Ethics*, there was not a stand-alone book fully designed to guide educators. Tipton astutely considers the place of ethics in the translation and interpreting (TI) curriculum, including when using translation technologies and throughout the research process. Her writing is engaging, and she provides useful prompts and reflection points to develop ethical sensitivity in the classroom and beyond. It is a must-read book for anyone training translators, interpreters and TI researchers."

Charlotte Bosseaux, Edinburgh University, UK

The Routledge Guide to Teaching Ethics in Translation and Interpreting Education

Routledge Guides to Teaching Translation and Interpreting is a series of practical guides to key areas of translation and interpreting for instructors, lecturers, and course designers.

This book provides university-level educators in translation and interpreting with a practical set of resources to support a pedagogically engaged approach to ethics.

Encompassing critical engagement and reflection, the resources have been designed to be easily developed and adapted to specific teaching contexts. The book promotes an integrated approach to ethics teaching. Its core goals are to improve the quality of student learning about ethics, develop confidence in ethical decision-making, and enhance a commitment to ethics beyond the programme of study.

The approach includes emphasis on problems of practice, or "ethical dilemmas", using real-world examples, but simultaneously encompasses a more wide-ranging set of ethical questions for both educators and their students. Including chapters on the ethical implications of using technology and the ethics involved in assessment and feedback, equal weight is given to both translation and interpreting.

Providing a key point of reference for information on different theories of ethics, insight into pedagogical practices around the globe, and practical guidance on resource development for classroom use and extension activities for independent learning, this is an essential text for all instructors and lecturers teaching ethics in translation and interpreting studies.

Rebecca Tipton is a Lecturer in Interpreting and Translation Studies and a researcher based in the Centre for Translation and Intercultural Studies (CTIS) at the University of Manchester. Her key publications include *Routledge Handbook of Translation and Pragmatic*s (Routledge, 2019) and *Dialogue Interpreting: A Guide to Interpreting in Public Services and the Community* (Routledge, 2016).

Routledge Guides to Teaching Translation and Interpreting

Series Editor: Kelly Washbourne

Routledge Guides to Teaching Translation and Interpreting is a series of practical guides to key areas of translation and interpreting for instructors, lecturers and course designers. Drawing on authors' expertise and experience and on documented practice from the literature of the field, the guides include: an overview of critical concepts and approaches; sample tasks and activities; instructor notes; lesson plans and teaching resources; discussion prompts for key reading; a glossary of terms. Authoritative and accessible, the guides present models of best practice in creative and intentional teaching and learning.

The Routledge Guide to Teaching Translation and Interpreting Online
Cristiano Mazzei and Laurence Jay-Rayon Ibrahim Aibo

The Routledge Guide to Teaching Ethics in Translation and Interpreting Education
Rebecca Tipton

For more information on any of these and other titles, or to order, please go to https://www.routledge.com/Routledge-Guides-to-Teaching-Translation-and-Interpreting/book-series/RGTTI

The Routledge Guide to Teaching Ethics in Translation and Interpreting Education

Rebecca Tipton

LONDON AND NEW YORK

Designed cover image by © Getty Images

First published 2024
by Routledge
4 Park Square, Milton Park, Abingdon, Oxon OX14 4RN

and by Routledge
605 Third Avenue, New York, NY 10158

Routledge is an imprint of the Taylor & Francis Group, an informa business

© 2024 Rebecca Tipton

The right of Rebecca Tipton to be identified as author of this work has been asserted in accordance with sections 77 and 78 of the Copyright, Designs and Patents Act 1988.

All rights reserved. No part of this book may be reprinted or reproduced or utilised in any form or by any electronic, mechanical, or other means, now known or hereafter invented, including photocopying and recording, or in any information storage or retrieval system, without permission in writing from the publishers.

Trademark notice: Product or corporate names may be trademarks or registered trademarks, and are used only for identification and explanation without intent to infringe.

British Library Cataloguing-in-Publication Data
A catalogue record for this book is available from the British Library

ISBN: 978-0-367-56581-7 (hbk)
ISBN: 978-0-367-56577-0 (pbk)
ISBN: 978-1-003-09848-5 (ebk)

DOI: 10.4324/9781003098485

Typeset in Sabon
by Taylor & Francis Books

Dedicated to my father

Contents

List of tables xiii
Acknowledgements xiv

Introduction 1

Who is this book for and what are its aims? 1
What are its overarching principles and themes? 1
A growing interest in ethics in TI education 3
Limited research on ethics teaching on TI programmes 3
Approach to practical activities 4
Chapter outlines 4

1 Ethics teaching and teaching ethics 9

1.1 Chapter overview 9
1.2 Ethics teaching 9
   1.2.1 Translation and interpreting theory and ethics education 10
   1.2.2 Moral philosophy 13
   1.2.3 Relativism 16
   1.2.4 Moral imagination 17
   1.2.5 Ethical competence 18
1.3 Curriculum priorities 21
   1.3.1 Ethical sensitivity 21
   1.3.2 Ethical knowledge 22
   1.3.3 Enhancing ethical judgement 24
   1.3.4 Reinforcing ethical commitment 25
   1.3.5 Priorities and pedagogies 26
1.4 Teaching ethics 28
   1.4.1 Contextual challenges for teaching ethics 28
   1.4.2 Equity/equality, diversity, and inclusion 29

        1.4.3 Aligned curriculum 32
        1.4.4 Hidden curriculum 33
        1.4.5 Assessment and feedback 34
    1.5 Chapter summary 37

2 Ethics and the translation curriculum (I)   43

    2.1 Chapter overview 43
    2.2 Ethics and the translation curriculum 43
        2.2.1 Fostering integrity and thoroughness 43
        2.2.2 Translator identity status and ethical responsibility 45
    2.3 Ethics sensitisation through pre-translation tasks 46
        2.3.1 Reading as an ethical activity 46
        2.3.2 "Being translated" 47
        2.3.3 Text profiling to determine ethical priorities 48
        2.3.4 Monolingual revision: encouraging students to notice and question 51
    2.4 Ethical competence development through literary translation 53
        2.4.1 Ethics issues in literary translation 53
        2.4.2 Speaking with and speaking for: debates on experiential knowledge 55
        2.4.3 Translators as (secondary) witnesses 61
        2.4.4 Multi- and poly-lingual literary texts to support ethical sensitisation 63
        2.4.5 Ethical topics in translating for children 65
        2.4.6 Teaching codes of ethics in the (literary) translation curriculum 69
    2.5 Ethical competence development through commercial translation 71
        2.5.1 Scoping ethics in the curriculum 71
        2.5.2 Localisation 72
        2.5.3 Hashtags in translation 74
        2.5.4 Transcreation 77
    2.6 Chapter summary 79

3 Ethics and the translation curriculum (II): Technologies in focus   83

    3.1 Chapter overview 83
    3.2 Pedagogy in the technologies-oriented curriculum: implications for ethics education 83
        3.2.1 General trends 83

    3.2.2 Developing (digital) reflexivity as a critical disposition to practice 85
    3.2.3 Digital reflexivity and pedagogical theory 88
3.3 Machine translation 90
    3.3.1 Machine translation and ethics in the curriculum 90
    3.3.2 Ethics education and machine translation: selected topics and activities 91
3.4 Post-editing 102
    3.4.1 Issues reported in MTPE student learning: implications for teaching 104
3.5 Collaborative translation 109
    3.5.1 General trends and implications for ethics education 109
    3.5.2 Labour and exploitation in online collaborative translation 111
    3.5.3 Collaborative translation in crisis situations as a support for ethics education 114
    3.5.4 Wikipedia as a support for translator ethics education 119
 3.6 Chapter summary 123

4 Ethics and the interpreting curriculum   131

4.1 Chapter overview 131
4.2 Ethics and the interpreting curriculum 131
    4.2.1 Conference interpreting 132
    4.2.2 Dialogue interpreting 133
    4.2.3 What to prioritise in interpreter ethics education? 135
4.3 Ethics education through practice 137
    4.3.1 Dialogue interpreting: frameworks to support ethics education through practice 138
    4.3.2 Role-playing and dramaturgical approaches to pedagogy in dialogue interpreting ethics teaching 139
    4.3.3 Conference interpreting: ethics education through practice 147
    4.3.4 Materials creation for targeted practice 149
4.4 Ethics education through case-based learning 151
    4.4.1 Affordances and limitations of case-based approaches 151
    4.4.2 Constructing a case 152
    4.4.3 Supporting learning 152
    4.4.4 Case examples 153
4.5 Professional dimensions of practice 157

xii Contents

        4.5.1 *Teaching codes of ethics* 157
        4.5.2 *Practical activities* 159
        4.5.3 *Self-care as an ethical commitment to interpreting: implications for pedagogy* 164
    4.6 *Social justice and ethics education* 166
        4.6.1 *Activism within ethics education* 166
        4.6.2 *Curriculum planning* 167
        4.6.3 *Practical activities* 168
    4.7 *Chapter summary* 171

5 **Teaching research ethics**   179

    5.1 *Chapter overview* 179
    5.2 *What is research ethics and why does it matter?* 179
    5.3 *Challenges of teaching research ethics on TI programmes* 180
    5.4 *Mapping and responding to change in research ethics expectations in tertiary education* 184
    5.5 *Core concepts in research ethics and some implications for TI researchers* 186
        5.5.1 *Avoiding harm* 186
        5.5.2 *Informed consent* 189
        5.5.3 *Confidentiality* 193
        5.5.4 *Data management, storage, and retention* 194
    5.6 *Ethical traditions in research ethics* 197
        5.6.1 *Consequentialism/non-consequentialism* 197
        5.6.2 *Virtue ethics* 198
        5.6.3 *Critical approaches* 199
    5.7 *An integrated approach to teaching research ethics* 201
        5.7.1 *Developing ethical reflexivity in research* 201
        5.7.2 *Integrating ethics into research methods teaching* 203
        5.7.3 *Ethics and the writing-up process* 211
    5.8 *Chapter summary* 212

Index   216

Tables

2.1 Original text producer's perspective 49
2.2 Translator's perspective 50
2.3 Text recipient's perspective 50
2.4 Planning ethics in the literary translation curriculum 54

Acknowledgements

My most sincere thanks to the series editor, Kelly Washbourne, whose own writing on ethics has been a source of inspiration for many of the ideas developed in this work, and who has given very generously of his time to comment on the work as it developed.

I would also like to thank colleagues in the Centre for Translation and Intercultural Studies at the University of Manchester and friends who have supported this project since its inception. Particular thanks to Anna Strowe, Leonie Gaiser, Maeve Olohan, Henry Jones, Silvia Terribile, Shiyao Guo, Danielle D'Hayer, and Svetlana Carsten.

I am especially grateful to Deborah Smith, Madhu Kaza, and Lawrence Schimel, and to *Latin American Literature Today* for granting permission for material to be used in Chapter 2. I also extend my gratitude to the University of Manchester for permission to use extracts from its institutional research guidance on different categories of risk in Chapter 5 on research ethics.

Every effort has been made to contact copyright-holders. Please advise the publisher of any errors or omissions, and these will be corrected in subsequent editions.

Sincere thanks also to the team at Taylor & Francis, notably Louisa Semlyen, Katya Porter, and Talitha Duncan-Todd.

A final thanks to my husband, Carl, and father, Tim, for their unstinting support and love. The loss of my father in 2022 was felt keenly as I made the final preparations, and this work is dedicated to him.

Introduction

> Something in the very nature of translation commands attention to ethics.
> (Washbourne, 2018, p. 399)

Who is this book for and what are its aims?

This book is for educators with an interest in developing translation and interpreting (TI) ethics education, regardless of programme level or structure. Its principal aims are:

- to offer a space and prompts for productive reflection on current approaches to TI ethics education at the individual and programme level;
- to foster a critical approach to established pedagogical frameworks in TI teaching in terms of their capacity to support ethics education;
- to set out practical suggestions for learning tasks to enhance ethical thinking and develop ethical competence; and
- to open meaningful debate about the ideologies shaping higher education in the contemporary age and their implications for developing and sustaining ethical teaching practice.

What are its overarching principles and themes?

A first overarching principle is that meaningful ethics education, following Floros (2011), must go beyond teaching that merely raises awareness of issues and learning that is primarily oriented to speculative thinking. It draws attention to the need for educators to focus on what it is students do: that is, how students learn to cultivate ethical thinking and ethical responsibility, whether this is conceived in relation to translation or interpreting process, academic research, interpersonal relations, or accountability to the profession and wider society. This in turn relies on "ethics work" being a constant in the curriculum. Note, however, that this book does not seek to displace current foci on programmes; instead, it supports educators to incorporate a greater ethical dimension into teaching and

DOI: 10.4324/9781003098485-1

learning in ways that are commensurate with a programme's size, shape, and learning goals, and that builds on what is currently taught.

An integrated approach is a second overarching principle, which is promoted as a means to habituate ethical thinking and maximise ethical commitment beyond a programme of study. This is ideally enacted across units of learning and through learning activities that, where possible, encompass an ethical dimension in order to generate "ethical vigilance" (noticing, observing, and questioning) and ensure students' ethical knowledge is routinely pressed into service. It is also ideally enacted at a discourse level, through a coherent programme narrative, which is reinforced through classroom interactions and in other communications with students, such as materials and tasks in virtual learning environments. In short, an integrated approach relies on distributed responsibility for ethics-related teaching.

A third overarching principle concerns purpose. Ethics education is not conceived as solely oriented to the resolution of practice-based issues, which in itself may be a misplaced goal given the porousness and contingent nature of situational dilemmas, which may have multiple solutions or none. Instead, ethics education, within an integrated vision, also extends to the (moral) development of students (capacity to empathise and reconcile other points of view), commensurate with a core goal of education, understood in its broadest sense. This brings the focus back to how students learn and the need to factor variability in ethical maturity into the planning phase. It also underscores the need to maintain a healthy level of criticality towards outcomes-based approaches to learning, which may not always be suitable for achieving some aspects of ethical development.

A concept that cuts across this book and supports the development of ethical responsibility and ethical competence is "(self-)reflexivity". The term appears in several descriptive forms (e.g. "digital reflexivity", "researcher reflexivity") as a reflection of its use in different disciplinary discourses and domains. Common to the various descriptors, as explained in Chapter 3, is a sense of folding back on something (including the self) in the moment of action, which distinguishes it from reflection-on-action as a *post-hoc* phenomenon. In short, it is the (cultivated) ability to avoid glossing over a problem or doubt as it arises in action, bringing it to consciousness to think about why it has arisen and why current personal resources and frameworks are inadequate to resolve it as a first step to taking transformative action. Reflexivity itself is not ethical, but it enhances ethical decision-making.

In the hurly-burly of academic life, finding time to reflect on one's own practice, whether individually or with colleagues, is difficult. The consequences of this vary from a diminished sense of the quality of service to others, to feelings of a lack of empowerment in reconciling personal values with changes in institutional values, or societal attitudes towards education in the modern world. Many of the activities in this book are designed to encourage educators to pause for thought about their current approach to ethics education, to the ethical imperatives raised for teaching and learning by increasing student diversity, and what enhancements to practice are feasible given the constraints on time and resources. (Self-)reflexivity and reflection are therefore integral to developing a teaching ethics.

A growing interest in ethics in TI education

The publication of this book coincides with a burgeoning interest in the topic of ethics in TI studies, mirroring developments in the scope, range, and forms of translational activities that are undertaken in on- and offline environments, and in the ever-shifting global landscape and context in which such activities take place. Students enter programmes of learning with an acute sense of the issues facing humanity "whose successful management absolutely depends on intelligently and thoughtfully devised intercultural communication" (Greenall et al., 2019, p. 642). They are also often motivated by campaigns for social justice and especially receptive to topics that enable them to unpack power relations and the social role played by translators and interpreters. The prospect of translators and interpreters taking some kind of leadership "over the hum of voices surrounding them" (Greenall et al., 2019, p. 642), and shaping public and professional discourse practices around what good translation/interpreting is or should be and what it can help to achieve, affords excellent scope to interrogate the concepts of agency, risk, and trust.

The recent *Routledge Handbook on Translation and Ethics*, edited by Kasia Koskinen and Nike Pokorn, amply evidences the breadth of theoretical perspectives on ethics in the field, and points to the considerable task facing educators in curating and prioritising topics in the curriculum, notwithstanding student choice in certain (assessment) tasks (Koskinen and Pokorn, 2020). This book does not seek to be prescriptive in terms of which topics to cover; instead, it encourages educators to think about what is feasible in the time available, and which topics (including which theoretical perspectives), modes of delivery, skills development, and tasks will best support student learning in ways that can be carried forward in the form of ethical commitment on graduation (see Chapter 1). This also requires critical reflection on some of the more commonly applied pedagogical frameworks in TI education and the extent to which they are able to develop the level of capacity for ethical thinking anticipated.

Limited research on ethics teaching on TI programmes

There is very limited empirical research on ethics in the context of teaching and learning on TI programmes, and, despite a relatively common tendency to assert that most students' ethics education concerns codes of ethics almost to the exclusion of anything else, we do not know whether this is actually the case. Johnston (2018), writing about literary translation programmes, makes the point that very few publicly available programme descriptions provide any insight into the nature of or approach to the teaching of ethics – an observation that applies beyond this specialisation. Furthermore, although the concept of ethical competence is gaining increasing prominence, *inter alia* in frameworks

4 *Introduction*

such as the European Masters in Translation competence framework, it remains under-theorised and under-investigated.

As a consequence, the suggested activities in this book are just that: suggestions and openings. They are not a definitive guide to what works, but rather what might effectively support student learning given a specific learning goal or programme ethos. The approach to activities is shaped in part by academic research from the field to demonstrate the possibilities it offers for developing praxis; as such, many activities have empirical foundations, even though the evidence for the impact on student learning remains unelucidated at the time of writing.

Approach to practical activities

The chapters include several types of activity. Some are **prompts for reflection** aimed at educators directly, whereas others are **points for discussion** that may be used in class. Still others provide **task suggestions** that may be implemented without change or adapted to the local context of teaching. Readers will note that learning aims and outcomes are indicated for some activities. This is because, despite arguing that an outcomes-based approach is not appropriate for all facets of ethics education, tasks of a more discrete and self-contained nature can be supported by predetermined aims and outcomes. They can also be adapted as needed. Additional materials can be found on the companion site to this publication.

Chapter outlines

Chapter 1 is divided into two parts: ethics teaching and teaching ethics. The first part, ethics teaching, examines the various theories students are likely to encounter in TI (ethics) education, the relationships between them, and the questions they raise for teaching and learning. Ethical relativism is also discussed in this section from the perspective of its potential to enhance the development of ethical responsibility-taking, as opposed to being viewed as something that simply closes down debate. Taking account of variability in ethical maturity among the student body, this first part also examines the concept of the moral imagination and practical steps educators can take to support its cultivation in the curriculum. The part ends with a focus on pedagogical matters. It breaks down ethics teaching into several component parts and provides a structured approach to planning, from ethics sensitisation to developing ethical commitment beyond the programme of study. The implications of student- and teacher-centred approaches for ethics education are also discussed.

The second part of the chapter, teaching ethics, is designed to foster critical appraisal of teaching practice against a backdrop of shifting values in the sector. It examines the policy agenda of equality, diversity, and inclusion (EDI) and its implications for teaching, learning, and assessment, with practical suggestions on enhancements to materials and teaching approaches. In terms of curriculum planning, this part of the chapter opens up scope for debate on the dominant paradigm of the aligned curriculum and the related outcomes-based approach to student learning, calling into question its suitability for ethics education, or at least some aspects of it. The implications for student learning of the so-called "hidden" or "informal" curriculum, particularly on programmes with large international student cohorts, are also discussed. Relatedly, the importance of developing different literacies in TI education (e.g. assessment and feedback) is brought to relief, not only as an example of good practice, but as an additional means to foster student responsibility-taking in the learning process.

Chapter 2 is the first of two chapters to explore ethics in the translation curriculum (the second, Chapter 3, focuses on technologies). The vast range of specialisations in translation and different programme structures means that the approach is necessarily selective and is why emphasis is placed on activities that can be adapted and applied to different topics and situations. The first part of the chapter explores the concept of ethical responsibility as a goal of translator education, regardless of the degree of professionalisation a programme promotes. It problematises the concepts of integrity and thoroughness from a teaching and learning perspective and recommends paying greater attention to the relationship between student and translator/interpreter identity status and its evolution over a programme of study. It emphasises that the ethical relation entailed by all translation activity does not require a professional outlook to be sustained.

The chapter then develops suggestions for enhancing ethical sensitivity in the translation curriculum through a focus on pre-translation activities. These are variously designed for students to experience first-hand the vulnerability of being a translated subject, reflect on reading as an ethical activity and its implications for translation, and identify ethical issues in different text types. Finally, the domains of literary and commercial translation are used as the backdrop for exploring different types of classroom activities (individual and group) to develop ethical sensitivity and ethical reasoning skills. In literary translation, activities are anchored around adult and children's fiction, debates on experiential knowledge and the translator–author relationship, the literary merits of "witness texts" and the complex range of ethical decision-making in their translation, and the rich potential offered by multi- and poly-lingual texts to develop ethical sensitivity. Commercial translation serves to highlight the contextual imperatives that impact on translator ethical decision-making in business terms (e.g. regulatory environments) and in terms of communication environments (e.g. multimodal, multilingual, and dynamic textual environments). Activities focus on web localisation and hashtag translation. The topic of transcreation is also included as fertile terrain for working on ethical aspects of translator education. In this regard, the experiences of one university team in developing learning projects in transcreation are examined and suggestions made for enhancements that help to foreground ethics.

Chapter 3 focuses on technologies, including those used to assist the translation process and those used to disseminate translated products in the digital environment. Although much of the content lends itself to curricula with a more explicitly professional orientation, many elements of the activities and principles discussed can be adapted to different levels and scales. The chapter emphasises the importance of cultivating reflexivity, described here as "digital reflexivity", to encourage systematic thinking and to highlight the importance of affect in interactions with different technologies as students develop skills and competence.

The chapter explores various facets of machine translation and their ethical implications, from preparation of text to evaluations of its use in situations in which people experience particular vulnerabilities (e.g. healthcare and refugee services). It also examines the potential of collaborative practice and technologies used to support translation in crisis situations, extending the discussion to volunteer translation labour in activities designed to support access to education as one example. Activities engage students in reflecting on the potential for exploitation in the platform economy, and the ethical implications of professionals and non-professionals working side by side in certain (crisis) situations. Finally, the chapter discusses the potential of Wikipedia as a learning resource and a learning environment. Activities facilitate engagement with the site's policy of "neutral point of view" and the implications of the policy for translation practice. A final section showcases an example of a university course that draws on Wikipedia as a learning environment in a collaborative learning task, promoting an emergentist (as opposed to competence-based) pedagogy, which has excellent potential to foster ethical sensitivity and skills development.

Chapter 4 is devoted to ethics education in the (spoken language) interpreting curriculum. It recognises that ethics is a topic that cuts across different modes of interpreting but maintains a division between conference and community interpreting for the purpose of developing targeted pedagogical interventions. In order to minimise potential for speculative and unstructured ethical decision-making, the chapter draws attention to the affordances of the demand control schema for spoken language dialogue interpreting, developed in the context of sign language interpreting by Robyn Dean and Robert Pollard. This is complemented by discussions on drama-based pedagogies that enable ethical decision-making to be dynamically investigated through creative teaching that engages learners in ways that do not always require an individual performance in front of peers. In terms of conference interpreting, the chapter shows how academic research in interpreting studies, particularly research that uses corpus-based methodology, can be leveraged in the creation of class materials to support ethics education.

The chapter examines the potential for both interdisciplinary and case-based learning to enhance interpreter ethics education in both subdomains. It outlines some principles of case creation to support effective learning and encourages educators to reflect on how enhancements can be made to cases they already use. The chapter also sheds light on codes of ethics in the interpreting classroom, suggesting practical activities to support understanding of how codes are created and revised, and how they may be used in disciplinary proceedings. Finally, it examines social justice and activism in interpreting teaching. Activities are designed for students to reflect on their social roles as interpreters and the extent to which they may be able to address injustices experienced by certain groups whose participation in social debate is often precluded by institutional and/or organisational language regimes, or other social and political barriers. The chapter also encourages reflection on the relationship between activism and ethics, and the implications of an activist stance for the ways we think about professional ethics.

Chapter 5 focuses on teaching research ethics in TI education. It begins by putting research ethics in the humanities into historical perspective and emphasising the influence of biomedical sciences on recent developments. It then explores concepts that are core to research ethics, such as the avoidance of harm, the importance of consent, and *post-hoc* data collection issues of data handling, storage, and sharing, recommending activities that foster social dialogue within a cohort of students through shared experiences at various stages of the learning process. Research integrity is a unifying concept in the curriculum and applies as much to research involving human participants as it does to research based on text-based sources. The chapter demonstrates various ways in which ethical theories from moral philosophy have influenced the development of research ethics. Particular attention is given to the emerging interest in an "ethic of care" in academic research, which is promoted as an alternative normative ethical theory underpinned by a relational ontology.

A significant portion of the chapter is devoted to practical suggestions for developing skills in handling ethical dimensions of common data-collection methods in qualitative research. In line with the integrated approach promoted in this book, the chapter recommends embedding certain activities into research methods training where possible. It also emphasises the importance of experiential learning and of affording scope for students to work through issues in exercises that draw on published research findings and/or on simulated activities (e.g. interviewing and focus groups), as opposed to relying solely on the supervisor–supervisee relationship for ethics-related development. A key learning goal is to activate and develop reflexive capabilities, for instance in situations in which an interviewee may make an unwarranted disclosure of a highly personal nature. Finally, attention is drawn to the importance of ethics account-giving in the writing up of academic research: that is, accounts that go beyond stating that the project has received institutional ethics approval by fleshing out key decision-making points, interpersonal tensions (e.g. with gatekeepers), and their impact on how the research process unfolded.

References

Floros, G. (2011). "Ethics-less" theories and "ethical" practices: On ethical relativity in translation. *The Interpreter and Translator Trainer*, 5(1), 65–92. https://doi.org/10.1080/13556509.2011.10798812.

Greenall, A. K., Alvstad, C., Jansen, H., & Taivalkoski-Shilov, K. (2019). Introduction: Voice, ethics and translation. *Perspectives*, 27(5), 639–647. https://doi.org/10.1080/0907676X.2019.1631862.

Johnston, B. (2018). Teaching and learning literary translation. In K. Washbourne and B. Van Wyke (Eds.), *The Routledge handbook of literary translation* (pp. 31–41). Routledge.

Koskinen, K., & Pokorn, N. K. (Eds.) (2020). *The Routledge handbook of translation and ethics*. Routledge.

Washbourne, K. (2018). Ethics. In K. Washbourne and B. Van Wyke (Eds.), *The Routledge handbook of literary translation* (pp. 399–418). Routledge.

1 Ethics teaching and teaching ethics

1.1 Chapter overview

This chapter is divided into two parts. The first part explores theories that help shape ethics education on TI programmes, their interrelations, and the questions they raise for teaching, learning, and assessment. It introduces the concept of ethical relativism and explores its potential to enhance the development of ethical responsibility-taking, as opposed to being viewed as something that simply closes down debate. Mindful of the variability in ethical maturity among the student body, this first part also examines the concept of the moral imagination and practical steps educators can take to support its cultivation in the curriculum.

It also offers guidance on developing an integrated approach to ethics education by breaking down ethics teaching into actionable components, from sensitisation to commitment beyond the programme of study, and by critically reflecting on the affordances and limitations of learner- and teacher-centred frameworks to support ethics education.

The second part places a spotlight on educators and ethical teaching practices in contemporary higher education settings, against a backdrop of neoliberal values, marketisation, and internationalisation. In foregrounding student diversity and its various definitions, it suggests practical actions that can enhance equity and inclusivity in teaching, assessment, and feedback, which include taking account of the ways in which the so-called "hidden curriculum" impacts student learning. Finally, it promotes critical engagement with a dominant paradigm of curriculum design (constructive alignment) in the context of ethics education.

1.2 Ethics teaching

This section focuses on decision-making in curriculum planning with specific reference to theory. In curricula where ethics education is typically taught as a discrete entity (perhaps a single lecture on a unit of learning, or series of lectures outside main TI teaching), educators are likely to give priority to ensuring students have some sort of grounding in ethics theories from moral philosophy,

DOI: 10.4324/9781003098485-2

perhaps accompanied by some case studies reflecting different translation and interpreting situations. The vastness and complexity of the moral philosophy literature make curating the programme of learning particularly challenging, and there is a risk that in grappling with what content to teach, the importance of *what* students learn and *how* they learn is lost; in other words, the focus is on a list of topics to "get through". This section invites educators to take a few steps back and to think about what ethics could look like in the curriculum, what sort of approaches to its teaching foster meaningful learning, and, moreover, how TI theory *combined with* theories from moral philosophy can shape ethics education.

1.2.1 Translation and interpreting theory and ethics education

Teaching translation and interpreting theory (TI theory) has considerable potential to enhance ethics education, potential which, at the time of writing, appears under threat due to the decline of theory teaching on some graduate programmes. The discussion here, though, suggests that an ethical perspective on key theoretical developments or turns in the discipline is not only desirable, but a highly productive means for students to think about the nature of these theories and their real-world implications. What is understood by TI theory varies within the discipline, however. Shuttleworth and Cowie's (1997, p. 185) definition of theory as "a specific attempt to explain in a systematic way some or all of the phenomena related to translation" is a useful way to distinguish between disciplinary theorising and the "folk" theorising that often occurs during practice. In this section, TI theory is used as shorthand for a range of disciplinary perspectives on, and ways of seeing, the activities of translation and interpreting.

A first stage in planning a coherent classroom narrative and structuring learning activities is to consider how teaching TI theory can enhance ethical thinking abilities. The list is long, chief among which is an increased capacity for abstract thinking. Theory teaching also lays the foundations for enhanced self-reflexivity – a process of conscious reflection on the self in action – which is core to ethical thinking abilities, for example by exposing students to a central ethical (and Levinasian) problem of what it means to encounter alterity. Furthermore, it opens up a range of moral vantage points, helping to avoid the reduction of ethical thinking to the rightness or wrongness of certain actions.

A second question concerns the extent to which teaching TI theory provides space for explicit reflection on ethical thinking in relation to the theories themselves. In a crowded curriculum, creating and leveraging such space requires a balance between educator-led and student-led learning, particularly if TI theory is primarily taught through didactic approaches in a lecture format. The breadth of theoretical perspectives in both fields means that a good degree of educator-led content curation is needed; and, if theory is taught as core unit of learning, a lecture format may be preferred for reasons of efficiency. The value of student-centred learning for realising the enhancements listed above should not be underestimated, however.

Short student-centred tasks can be assigned across a unit of learning in class or as supplementary exercises. Examples include guided questions inviting students – independently or with peers – to explore key concepts such as functionalism or equivalence from the perspective of their ethical validity (Floros, 2011); the implications (for developing a theory of translation and interpreting) of assuming the translator or interpreter to be a neutral figure in equivalence-based approaches and/or in interpretive theory; or the ethicality of conduit approaches to dialogue interpreting through the lens of accountability.

Students may not immediately see the value of such tasks for developing professional ethics, even viewing them as too abstract and far removed from this goal (if the goal is privileged on a particular programme). An educator's classroom narrative will be important for making explicit the connections between content, tasks, and learning goals, but so is balance. Educators may wonder whether, in the context of their programme structure and aims, a focus on the ethical dimensions of earlier theorisations in the field is a valuable use of their and their students' time. Relatedly, an emphasis on source–target text relations that are now only partially reflective of how we understand text in the digital age gives particular pause for thought as to which theoretical perspectives are promoted over others.

A final question concerns the ways in which TI theory teaching supports ethics education in broader terms and connects to ethical theories in moral philosophy. In this regard, since much TI theory concerns decision-making and navigating the entanglement of values, norms, and social conventions, following Floros (2011), its strong connections to issues of wider societal and ethical import can easily be foregrounded.

TI theory sensitises students to the fact that ethical translation and interpreting is not always about compliance, but also about disruption and transformation, especially in cases where compliance would lead to the reproduction and maintenance of inequality. A social rights-based approach to utilitarian theory, for instance, when applied alongside feminist or decolonial translation theories, may usefully ask not what a certain set of translation practices can do to make the greatest number "happy", but rather how they can achieve the greatest amount of equality (with happiness being a potential unintended consequence), thereby encouraging critical engagement with the conceptual premise of the ethical theory in question. Relatedly, Monzó-Nebrot and Wallace (2020, p. 5) make the point that, as a field, TI studies has tended to "foster consequentialism" through positing that practitioners take account of "the implications of translation options, speculate about the reception of their choices on the basis of the purpose defined by clients, usually on the grounds of hypotheses about default readers". The result of this, in these authors' view, is that "translators and interpreters have been asked to offer fit-for-purpose or functional work that aligns their production with dominant groups and ideologies, presenting themselves as neutral" – an "unduly conservative" position, in Chesterman's (2001, p. 143) view.

Educators may question the merits of including committed approaches on programmes with an explicitly professional orientation because they overly emphasise personal over professional ethics. However, this would assume that a committed approach is always translator-initiated, which is not necessarily the case. Furthermore, the incorporation of certain practices into so-called "mainstream" professional translation situations (e.g. the use of inclusive language) has its roots in committed social action (norm reformulation), which has wider social significance. Exposing students to the genealogy of certain practices through TI theory therefore has scope to support ethical thinking from multiple perspectives.

Other theoretical perspectives, such as narrative theory (Baker, 2006), show the power of translation to constitute – as opposed to merely shape – reality, through which a certain ethical vigilance is enhanced. Examining textual manipulations at different levels (including paratextual levels) also draws attention to the network of agents often involved in the production and dissemination of translated products and, hence, the importance of viewing ethical responsibility as distributed and differential. This, in turn, has the potential to open up discussions on theories in moral philosophy that place emphasis on impartiality and individuality (Kant's deontology is one example), supporting students to think about the problem of individual translators reconciling their deontic commitment to translation practice in situations when other agents – who may have competing values or different ideological agendas that can dilute or compromise this commitment in the production process – are also involved.

Finally, a translator ethics proposed by Pym (2020, p. 152) in which risk and trust (as opposed to fidelity and loyalty) are taken as "the yardsticks for assessing translators' actions", whether in relation to translation process or social relations, supports a prospective and more holistic approach (as opposed to looking backwards to the "start" text, as Pym terms it, and author) that resonates with ethical decision-making in other spheres of the social world, thereby enhancing flexibility in ethical thinking beyond the discipline.

Prompts for planning

- What are the current drivers behind the choice and sequencing of topics in translation/interpreting theory on your programme?
- How much curriculum time is devoted to theory and what learning formats are used (e.g. lectures, seminars, one or other or in combination)? How does the format impact on student learning in your view?
- To what extent does your current coverage of ethics combine theories of moral philosophy and theories of translation/interpreting, and connections between the two?
- What tasks are students asked to do in learning about TI theory and to what extent do these tasks support ethical thinking?

1.2.2 Moral philosophy

Teaching and learning primarily aim to support the development of ethically responsible and technically competent future translators and interpreters and researchers, not moral philosophers. Although this seems self-evident, it points to a tension in curriculum planning: namely, how much moral philosophy should be taught, at what point, by whom, and how much emphasis should be placed on skills development in moral philosophising? Students report being put off by content that seems too abstract and remote from the actual concerns of professional practice (Drugan and Megone, 2011). However, their perceptions may betray the fact that it is the *approach* to teaching – specifically the transition between theoretical and applied (normative) ethics – and not the *content* of teaching that is at issue.

A first point concerns expertise. Some programmes rely on teaching by members of philosophy departments as part of non-disciplinary-specific approaches to ethics education, whereas others rely on TI educators with perhaps only rudimentary knowledge of the field. An integrated approach to ethics education would help offset the downsides of both approaches. It would also ensure distributed responsibility for ethics education across a programme team, albeit to varying degrees, and encourage greater synergies between moral philosophy and TI theory.

A second and related point concerns alignment. Educators who hope that, by illuminating the complexity of certain ethical issues through moral philosophy (a "non-empirical discipline"; Fesmire, 2003, p. 2), students will be able to resolve a practice-based ethical dilemma with confidence are only likely to create frustration as this places too much onus on students to develop their knowledge and skills of moral reasoning independently. A further issue of alignment arises when TI educators do not realise that their teaching conflates theoretical ethics (based on questions such as "What should I do to lead a good life?") and professional ethics ("What do I need to do to promote ethically sound practices?") (Kermit, 2019). A failure to disentangle the two and make distinctions clear in the pedagogical narrative means that students risk adopting a pick-and-mix approach to ethical decision-making at best, and paralysis at worst.

With regard to teaching content, four macro areas are commonly distinguished within a normative ethics focus: virtue and the good; duty and responsibility; consequence of actions and utility; and justice and equality (Rudvin, 2019, p. 31). Ethical decision-making is often anchored around the categories of deontology and teleology, with the former focusing on the rightness or wrongness of actions themselves, and the latter on the rightness of an action as determined solely by its consequences. Virtue ethics is also taught as part of ethics education on some programmes of study (e.g. medicine) and considered by some to offer a productive path through the limitations of the principles-and-procedures-based approach to normative ethics, due to its emphasis on habits and character (Fesmire, 2003, p. 56).

14 *Ethics teaching and teaching ethics*

Although limited information is available on what moral philosophy is taught and how it is taught on TI programmes, there appears a marked influence of ethical theories and traditions of European heritage, among which the ideas of Aristotle, Kant, Bentham, Mill, and Levinas are prominent. Across these theoretical perspectives the typically impartial decision-making of the individual is foregrounded, suggesting scope to broaden perspectives that help account for collective decision-making. Traditions in which communitarianism is prominent, such as Confucianism or Ubuntu[1] (from the sub-Saharan intellectual tradition), are two examples. Cosmopolitanism, although considered a demanding and contentious moral position (van Hooft, 2009), also offers fertile ground for debate (Washbourne, 2013).

Conceptual comparisons across different theories will help to develop ethical thinking, but certain caveats apply. First, there needs to be clarity of purpose; too many theories risk exacerbating decision-making paralysis, especially if the distinction between theoretical and professional ethics remains unaddressed. Second, if it is assumed that a plurality of perspectives is a desired curriculum goal, privileging concepts from European or Anglo-Saxon traditions as the main comparator will undermine this goal.

Bridging the gap between exposure to different ethical theories and the development of moral reasoning skills can be achieved by various practical means, some of which are discussed in Section 1.3, below. In general terms, the teaching of moral philosophy on TI programmes ideally needs to include classroom space and guidance for students to engage critically with the key assumptions and concepts in each theoretical perspective presented. In what follows, examples of three normative theories of ethics are discussed briefly in order to highlight ways in which such engagement can be developed.

In terms of teleology, **Utilitarian ethics**, in its simplest and purest form, advocates the principle of "the right action is the one that has the best consequences" (Bennett, 2015, p. 58). Individuals and groups working to problem-solve within this perspective would be invited to consider different courses of action, and the potential costs and benefits of each. If this ethical theory – or indeed consequentialism in broader terms – is introduced in the TI classroom, students need to be sensitised to the potential for the purest form of the theory to "turn up some odd moral results" (Bennett, 2015, p. 69) due to the lack of moral limits it sets for human action, and the extent to which act- or rule-based approaches mitigate this issue.[2] Space should also be given for discussion and reflection on the centrality (and measurability) of happiness to the theory, and the contentious positioning of rights as things that are valid only "if the social practice of respecting them leads to greater happiness" (Bennett, 2015, p. 67).

In terms of deontology, **Kant's ethics** foregrounds the importance of following rules or "categorical imperatives" (e.g. "do not lie"). Absolutist interpretations of his theory, as with Utilitarianism, can generate problematic moral solutions. Bennett (2015) gives the example of a murderer turning up at the door of a house and asking if a certain person is inside (with the intention to kill them). An absolutist interpretation would result in the person who answered the door telling the would-be murderer that the person is indeed inside, and therefore respecting the categorical imperative of "do not lie". Interpreters can face analogous issues: for instance, where the inclusion of the imperative "do not give your own opinion" in a code of ethics prompts an absolutist interpretation, potentially leading to a person's safety or security being compromised. The lack of ethical maturity in some interpreting graduates has been shown to lead to such decision-making (e.g. Tipton, 2012).

Wood (2008, p. 63) argues that such absolutist interpretations largely stem from misreadings of Kant, and that Kant never asserted that moral rules should have no exceptions. He points to *Metaphysics of Morals*, in which Kant refers to the imperfection of ethical duties and the need to allow for some latitude in their application. It seems reasonable to question the extent to which this perspective is conveyed on programmes where deontology is discussed with specific reference to Kant's ethics, and whether students are sufficiently well supported to make the distinction between theoretical and professional ethics, and offered space (and alternative theoretical frameworks) to reflect on the circumstances that turn a situation into an exception in professional practice (see Subsection 1.2.3, below, for a further discussion).

Virtue ethics assumes that the right action stems from the correct motive (not its moral qualities), and that virtues are personal qualities needed to live a good life. A distinction is made between character virtues, which are considered psychological states that develop into stable, long-term moral dispositions through repeated action, such as courage, love, and temperance, and the intellectual virtues of understanding, skill, and prudence (Devettere, 2002; Seok, 2011).

Virtue ethics may be seen as a useful contrast to "impartial" Utilitarian and Kantian ethics, both of which promote the idea that all are held to be equal (Bennett, 2015, p. 93). However, unlike consequentialist or deontological ethics, both of which realise a theoretical aim of specifying "a property or properties that *make* right conduct right" and a practical aim of "discovering some form of *procedure of decision-making*", virtue ethics does not provide a "*criterion of rightness*", nor does it appear to offer guidance as to what to do in certain situations (Svensson and Johansson, 2017, p. 492; original emphasis). One of the consequences of this, as Devettere (2002) observes, is that character virtues often appear to be taken as guidelines for making decisions. Caution is therefore needed if virtue ethics are included in the curriculum to ensure these distinctions are made clear.

Prompts for reflection

- What pedagogical approaches and learning goals inform your teaching of moral philosophy and how much curriculum time is devoted to this topic?
- Is moral philosophy taught by a colleague from a philosophy department? What are the merits/demerits of such an approach in your view?
- To what extent do you make a distinction in your current teaching between theoretical ethics and professional ethics?
- How do you currently evaluate the effectiveness of moral philosophy teaching on student learning?

1.2.3 Relativism

Ethical relativism is a doctrine according to which there are no objective truths about what is right and wrong, and what is right or wrong is assumed to vary from person to person (Rachels, 1998). In cultural relativism an act is considered right or wrong in so far as it is right or wrong for a particular culture. Phrases like "Who are we to judge others?" are often used to capture a relativist viewpoint, with defenders seeing it as "a harbinger of tolerance",[3] but this has potential to lead to uncritical acceptance of ways of being and acting that, over time, can inhibit human flourishing. Cultural relativism may be seen as appealing in translation and interpreting in the context of supporting cultural diversity and sensitising students to issues that may be controversial in one context of translation but not in another (Baker, 2011, pp. 277–278). It also sensitises students to the idea of belonging to different moral communities as future translators and interpreters and how this may shape their career trajectories and decision-making.

Floros (2011) promotes the pedagogical potential of (ethical) relativism in the TI classroom, prompted by the limitations of binary thinking for student learning, through which decisions are categorised as either ethical or unethical.[4] He recasts ethical relativity using the more concrete and pedagogically useful concept of "ethical thresholds", which supports a focus on ethical stance (as opposed to translation strategy) and the reasons that give rise to different (and multiple) stances: that is, conflicting social conventions that generate norms (pp. 76–77). A key point is that ethical thresholds in translation fluctuate under the influence of different social conventions (values and narratives) and norms, all of which can change over time and in some cases lead to new ethical standards and the reformulation of norms. The concept of threshold, according to Floros, also better accounts for complex translator identities that do not align with the idealised translator commonly assumed in much TI theory.

Using ethical relativity to open up productive pedagogical space is, for Floros, "the first step towards self-reflexivity (critical reflection and possibility of contestation) and responsible action" (p. 72); however, he cautions that such self-reflexivity will not be productive if it merely leads students to think that they can do as they please. In mitigation, he proposes introducing an "ethical injunction" or "minimum level of prescription" (p. 73). Although this may seem pedagogically counter-intuitive, Floros cautions that without such an injunction, questions of undecidability can become paralysing for students. He also warns that the prescription should not be couched in terms of "universal ethical properties" and instead proposes anchoring it around a value that is common to all cultures and individuals, such as self-preservation (p. 73). This particular value is illuminated in the example translation tasks based on politically sensitive texts that Floros uses with his own students. In less sensitive contexts and texts, deriving such a common value may be far less evident; however, it does not need to be provided "top down" by educators and could form a useful part of classroom discussion.

Other, more outward-looking pedagogical approaches could involve investigating academic research and academic programme descriptions relevant to the local programme of study that focus on the ways in which different professionals navigate and are taught to navigate cultural relativism in the workplace. One example of relevance to community interpreter education concerns the primacy given to patient autonomy in many healthcare systems, which can generate cultural tension if a person is from a background in which family decision-making about healthcare is the norm. Open dialogue to encourage the expression of preference prompted by the healthcare professional, where feasible, provides a negotiated solution that respects patient values[5] and could inform the way in which an interpreter approaches certain aspects of interaction.

1.2.4 Moral imagination

The previous sections highlighted the importance of different bodies of theory in ethics education and alluded to the mediating role of self-reflexivity in critically reflecting on and discerning relevant criteria for both making and evaluating ethical decisions made by the self and others. These ongoing conversations with the self are aimed at making sense of moral experience. As such, they entail rational and reasoned thinking, but they are also bound up with less tangible, emotional, and intuitive responses that are brought to bear when imagining alternative possibilities. These are central to the work of translators and interpreters, and developing the moral imagination is integral to this work.

The concept of the moral imagination was central to John Dewey's pragmatist-inspired philosophy of learning. It has been described as a "cluster of psychological capacities" (Fesmire, 2003, p. 5), which, according to Joseph (2003, p. 29), involve a dynamic interplay of perception, reasoning, and feeling. McCollough (1991, p. 16) describes it as "a capacity to empathise with others and to discern creative possibilities for ethical action".

In a very general sense, the moral imagination is continually cultivated through our interactions with the everyday social world, in dialogue with others, and through literature, art, film, and other cultural products and activities. It is not merely a process that occurs in the mind; rather, it involves whole-body experiences of the kind that are often neglected in traditional educational environments, especially where text-based work dominates. Stimulating the moral imagination is among Callahan's primary goals of ethics education (Callahan and Bok, 1980; Washbourne, 2013, p. 43); however, until recently, the translation and interpreting studies literature has had little to say on how it may usefully be cultivated in the curriculum.

Sue-Ann Harding's (2021) work on anthropologist Tim Ingold and his concept of becoming knowledgeable through "wayfaring" offers a complementary set of ideas for thinking through the idea of the moral imagination and how it contributes to ethical ways of being in the world. Ingold's (2007) conceptualisation of living as a form of "meshwork" (of "interwoven lines of movement" and "paths of becoming" in a "continuous world") is a powerful lens through which Harding reappraises enduring dichotomies in translation and interpreting studies and associated vocabularies (e.g. source/target), and explores its pedagogical potential.

Ingold's concept of wayfaring is grounded in physical movement, emphasising its kinaesthetic potentialities. Applying this idea to translation, Harding (2021, p. 357) describes how we apprehend texts physically and literally, and make our way through them spatially and temporally. For students who, as Harding observes, often grapple with trying to impose a "pre-decided strategy" onto a text, Ingold's emphasis on "making" as a process of growth offers a useful counterpoint (p. 357). Through interactions with different materials and objects (e.g. weaving baskets), Ingold (2013, p. 21) encourages his students to move away from imposing meanings on the world and come to an understanding that what they are doing is limited to "intervening in worldly processes that are already going on" – ideas that have emerged as central to both his pedagogy and anthropology.

Although educators may not necessarily feel comfortable incorporating such experimental approaches in their teaching repertoires, instantiating a radical break with translation practice as it is more conventionally conceived in the classroom offers an opportunity for students to immerse themselves in ethical thinking through different sensory and tactual means. Michael Cronin, for instance, tasks students embarking on their translation studies to describe the scene outside of the classroom window.[6] Invariably, the students focus on the immediately obvious and visible, but through various prompts, the full scene in all of its depth and complexity is gradually illuminated in a kind of wayfaring.

> Prompts for reflection
> - What encounters with different cultural products/activities have shaped your skills of empathy and perspective-taking most vividly over your life?
> - Can you think of an example of a classroom activity (translation and/or interpreting) that could be developed to incorporate some of the ideas about wayfaring described above?

1.2.5 Ethical competence

The idea of developing competence in ethics seems counter-intuitive if it is considered in terms of mastery of something that is by nature open ended and ever evolving. The foreword to the 2022 edition of the European Master's in Translation competence framework (2023–2028) highlights ethical competence as one of several human skills that serve as a "differentiator" in a highly technologised translation market, strongly suggesting the value of its inclusion as part of a competence-oriented translation curriculum (European Commission, 2022). The word "ethics", however, appears only once in the framework (in the section on service provision), providing limited clues for educators seeking to operationalise it in the classroom.

To put this absence into context, the EMT framework needs to be read in conjunction with the outcomes-based European Qualifications Framework (EQF) for lifelong learning, revised 2017.[7] From its inception, ethical competence in the framework was positioned as a "meta-competence", which is "essential for the development of responsibility and autonomy" (European Commission, 2008, p. 8). It is not included in the EQF explicitly because it cannot "be seen separately from other knowledge, skills and competence" (p. 8), which in turn explains why it is not explicitly mentioned in other sections of the EMT framework. Meta-ethical competence is needed to navigate the complexity of a social world in which different value systems frequently clash and conflict – a complexity that varies in ethical intensity (Washbourne, 2013, p. 40).

In what follows, two approaches to ethical competence development are discussed. The first concerns "translational-ethical decision-making competence" at the level of the translation task, drawing inspiration from Zhou (2022); the second concerns ethical competence development at a more abstract level, inspired by dialogical and storied approaches used in medical education (e.g. Montello, 2014).

Zhou's (2022) model for translational-ethical decision-making competence (TEDC) is designed to develop students' intuitive and reasoning skills separately within the curriculum. It serves as a foundation for a "dual system" model of ethical decision-making, drawing on Reynolds' (2006) model in which the two are combined. Reynolds' neurocognitive model is based on two interrelated cognitive cycles that are said to operate in moral decision-making: a lower-order (reflective) cycle and higher-order (analytical) cycle. The model operates on the assumption that humans develop "ethical prototypes" through socialisation, which include "normative evaluations and prescriptive recommendations that help the individual adapt to or cope with the ethical situation" (p. 739). This means that, when faced with a moral situation, initially the lower-order reflective (and more intuitive) cycle is activated as the individual searches for experience of a similar situation to address the issue at hand. If none is available, then the higher-order cycle is activated, and analytical reasoning will be used to address the situation; the ethical prototype is subsequently modified. Reynolds developed this model in the context of ethical decision-making in business, citing situations such as fraud, bribery, and sexual harassment, which he asserts have prototypical characteristics.

Zhou (2022) does not provide examples of situations for which prototypes can be developed and suggests that, where appropriate, educators should "supply students with adequate, up to date and high-quality ethical prototypes" (p. 395), which risks perpetuating the didactic approach Zhou criticises. Although some lecturer-led ethical prototype provision may indeed be effective, especially where expert translation behaviour needs to be modelled (e.g. data security practices or translation contract negotiation regarding machine translation), scope exists for student-led prototype development for situations of lower ethical intensity. One example concerns terminological research in specialised translation situations. In the early phases of learning, students may vastly underestimate the work needed to source relevant documents, check sources, and corroborate choices (see Wakabayashi, 2003). Although such practices are not unethical, since they form part of the learning process, they can become so if applied in subsequent professional practice and lead to serious consequences.

The ethical prototype in this case cannot simply be presented by educators; instead, it is generated experientially by students applying knowledge about translation process. The decision-making process can be verbalised and reported through activities such as annotated translation assignments or commentaries, on which feedback is given. In learning terms, the ethicality of the prototype emerges as students move beyond loosely argued rationales, such as "it felt like the right term in the context", to more empirically supported statements about the relevance of the sources consulted.

The higher-order skills that shape ability to manage more complex translational situations and effective interpersonal interactions are less easily distinguished or addressed pedagogically. A storied approach to learning offers some potential and has been explored in medical ethics education since the early 2000s – a point when a narrative turn in medical ethics emerged. For Brody (2003), the approach has made it possible to bring unheard voices to the fore. Montello (2014, p. S2) writes, "Narrative offers a mode of engagement that asks different kinds of questions than those that law or philosophy might ask about moral agency, context and values." Rather than focusing on "what to do", according to Montello (2014), the approach helps clarify how a character or group "come to be where they are now in the story" as envisioned through a "mattering map" (a concept introduced by Rebecca Goldstein in her 1983 novel, *The Mind Body Problem*).

Meacham, Sloan, and Latessa (2022) adapt Montello's methodology as part of an ethics and humanism curriculum in medicine, closely tied to student experience on clinical placement. Students engage in several reflective practices (individual and collective, written and oral), including the creation of mattering maps through which they bring issues of import from their experience into the discussion. For medical students, ethical thinking is enhanced by acknowledging the whole body in different experiences (touch, smell, human vulnerabilities, among others). The immediacy of (vulnerable) others in the clinical relationship is quite different from the experiences of most translation and interpreting students, but this is not to deny that many translation and interpreting tasks evoke whole-body responses.

Returning to the work of Harding (2021, p. 358) and the concept of translation as wayfaring, she suggests, "We can also practise telling the stories of our translations and the knowledge we are growing through the making of translations, how they are coming into being and how each translation is a 'telling' of the text." Translation commentaries are a common means of encouraging students to tell their stories, but, as Harding's work suggests, they can be sites for much more than an explanation of a decision, capturing the moral imagination at work. A storied approach, then, is a way to help students understand the interconnectedness of all elements of their programme of learning (i.e. how they came to be at a particular moment of decision-making on the programme).

1.3 Curriculum priorities

This section focuses on curriculum planning and specifically on some of the organising principles that support an integrated approach to ethics education. Writing about their experiences of teaching and learning in engineering-related disciplines, Davis and Feinerman (2012, p. 352) assert that teaching ethics refers to at least one of the following: improving ethical sensitivity; increasing ethical knowledge; enhancing ethical judgement; or reinforcing ethical commitment. This list suggests an incremental and sequenced approach, although several components may overlap (e.g. developing ethical judgement may result in new insights and hence improved sensitivity). Less evident, perhaps, is which teaching practices and philosophies best support the injunctions to "improve", "increase", "enhance", and "reinforce", and what students need to do to respond effectively. Less evident still are the relations entailed by each; we may ask "In relation to what?" and "For what purpose?" The answers will vary depending on the programme aims and values but will be driven chiefly by the need to privilege an approach "most likely to result in sustained changes in reasoning and behaviours" (Romanell Report 2015, cited in Meacham, Sloan, and Latessa, 2022).

1.3.1 Ethical sensitivity

The importance of improving ethical or moral sensitivity is made plain by the realisation that translators and interpreters have the potential to put others into situations of (moral and physical) vulnerability by virtue of their decision-making. Sensitisation therefore concerns awareness of how our actions affect others (Rest, 1994). The injunction to "improve" ethical sensitivity draws attention to the fact that a student's prior life experiences serve as a springboard to discipline-specific ethical thinking. Teaching offers scope to build on these largely intuitive ethical sensibilities in order to minimise the risk of underplaying ethics as common sense, and therefore as something not requiring structured or sustained intellectual effort. In other disciplines, such as nursing and dentistry, research shows that sensitivity can be enhanced through instruction (Nortvedt, 2001).

Improving ethical sensitivity requires the formation of habits of noticing, observing, questioning, and problematising – in short, skills that align with critical thinking. Case-based learning is one of several pedagogical approaches that develop ethical sensitivity. Others include text profiling (see Chapter 2) and reflective practice (individual and group). There is, however, a risk that the degree of sensitisation is limited by the case-based method, in which the ethical issues are typically predetermined. Students would therefore benefit from exposure to situations in which they are required to identify ethical issues at stake in a process that could be scaffolded to a greater or lesser degree by the educator.

An example of scaffolding is to create a matrix to identify the characteristics of the situation, the rights and responsibilities of those involved, perceived vulnerabilities, and perceived levels of trust. This may be adapted to the type of activity, including group work towards a specific (translation) project deliverable. If used as part of an integrated approach, students should become more confident in thinking through the ethical implications of different situations independently over the programme of study. The measure of success will be determined through the range and complexity of ethical issues students are able to identify and the increasing sophistication and nuance with which such issues are described (e.g. application of meta-language).

1.3.2 Ethical knowledge

Increasing ethical knowledge is a potentially vast enterprise. How much should it be increased, and which ethical knowledge should be privileged? Section 1.2 provided some insights into different theories that may shape TI ethics education without suggesting a hierarchy. In this subsection, examples of curriculum interventions are presented to stimulate reflection on curriculum planning and intended student learning.

Activity

Consider the different levels of effort required of educators and students who adopt the following approaches to ethical knowledge, and each approach's potential impact on student learning, using the ethical theory of Utilitarianism as an example:

Delivery options

- Educator-curated content on Utilitarianism presented in a traditional lecture format, supplemented by recommended readings.
- Educator-curated reading list for students to read about Utilitarianism on their own.
- Educator selects one reading on Utilitarianism with guided questions (that will require further reading) to discuss in class.
- Group work to create wikis on the topic of Utilitarianism in a virtual learning environment.
- Pair work to plan and conduct an interview with a peer on the topic of Utilitarianism.
- Group work to write a blog post aimed at professional translators and interpreters on the relevance of Utilitarianism to each professional activity.

Questions

Which of the above approaches (or combination of approaches) to delivery do you think is likely to be most effective in terms of:

- developing student understanding of the theory of Utilitarianism;
- evaluating student understanding of Utilitarianism;
- helping students to retain information about Utilitarianism; and
- supporting students to apply knowledge about Utilitarianism to translation/interpreting situations?

In relation to your programme, which approach(es) appear proportionate to the programme learning aims and curriculum time available for teaching moral philosophy?

This activity prompts reflection on the relationship between teaching input and student learning, drawing attention to certain assumptions and gaps in the stages between content delivery, its assimilation, and its application. There is a risk, for instance, that overemphasis on teacher-led curated content on ethical theories taught in a block towards the start of a programme will limit student confidence in subsequent tasks, especially if it is not accompanied by opportunities to develop moral reasoning skills.

Section 1.2 suggested several ideas for short tasks to increase ethical knowledge through active critical engagement with key concepts in TI theory and moral philosophy. The list of content delivery mechanisms in the activity above, however, does not make any explicit connection between moral philosophy and TI theory, and privileges moral philosophy. The merits of such an approach are open to question. Bringing both knowledge bases together in planning and delivery, with short exercises to foster conceptual engagement and a greater sense of relevance to students, is therefore recommended. A final point is that increasing ethical knowledge also concerns knowledge about the self, which is emergent, but the importance of which can be drawn out in the classroom narrative.

Measuring the increase in knowledge and the extent to which this measurement is important for meeting programme aims is a further consideration. Not all teaching input requires formal assessment, but informal assessment (e.g. through classroom interactions) to gauge the extent to which certain points and practices have been retained can be useful, especially if these are to support a subsequent task. Increases in ethical knowledge will also be gauged through student performance in specific tasks designed to enhance moral reasoning, as discussed in the next subsection.

Prompts for reflection

- What kinds of ethical knowledge do you currently prioritise on course units that you teach and on the programme of study as a whole?
- Do other colleagues rely on your teaching input on ethics when developing their own curriculum interventions or vice versa?

- Are any of your approaches to teaching and learning reflected in the list above on Utilitarianism? If so, how do you typically evaluate their effectiveness in relation to the wider ecology of teaching and learning?
- How do your students respond to current teaching and learning aimed at increasing ethics knowledge (e.g. as evidenced through informal conversations and/or student evaluations)?
- How has your approach to "increasing ethical knowledge" evolved over time?

1.3.3 Enhancing ethical judgement

Approaches aimed at enhancing ethical judgement need to acknowledge that situations present different orders of magnitude due to differences in ethical intensity (Washbourne, 2013). Situations of considerable magnitude that are morally provocative may be highly engaging, but are far less likely to be experienced by students in their careers; nevertheless, certain principles can apply to lower-intensity situations, so they should not necessarily be disregarded. Consistent with the goals of this book, greater focus is placed on "everyday ethics" – that is, issues of lower ethical intensity – in order to habituate ethical thinking. Such an approach is echoed in other disciplines: for instance, Voss (2013) criticises "disaster-driven" engineering curricula that fail to equip students with the tools and frameworks they need to work through issues in their own work. Examples of lower ethical intensity issues (relatively speaking) in TI teaching include:

- interpersonal relations;
- the choice and use of materials and media;
- data handling;
- processes of research and quality assessment;
- error handling; and
- managing the degree of compatibility between skill level and task requirements.

Developing skills in moral reasoning involve activities requiring reflection-in-action (self-reflexivity during a task) and those requiring reflection-on-action (*post-hoc* reflection). The latter is supported by the ability to identify and describe relevant ethical issues in some detail using appropriate meta-language. The matrix approach proposed in Subsection 1.3.1 for identifying ethical issues could be redeployed and adapted where necessary for this analytical/reasoning stage. Students would examine the ethical situation(s) identified from the perspective of the characteristics of the situation, the rights and responsibilities of those involved, perceived vulnerabilities, and perceived levels of trust. Considering the situation from these various angles, they would weigh up the options available to all parties, taking account of how they think each came to be in that situation (mattering map). They would also be encouraged to articulate their own personal feelings and intuitive reactions to the situation in social dialogue with peers in order to address any biases or blind spots in their thinking. A key point is that several possible actions could be presented as an outcome, allowing for different situational contingencies.

Reflection on action can take place immediately after a task or at the end of the programme. Writing regular short statements to demonstrate moral reasoning in relation to specific programme tasks (e.g. in a portfolio of learning) can habituate students to reflect consciously on the importance of ethical sensitivity and develop judgement. This facilitates an ongoing conversation with educators, although it may not always be feasible to provide individual feedback. Diachronic approaches involve reflection on the learning journey as a whole, including the development of the moral imagination and translator/interpreter identity; students may also be asked to provide specific examples that demonstrate how their moral reasoning skills have evolved over the programme. The role of theory in reflective practice may need additional scaffolding, otherwise students may neglect it altogether, as seen in reports of medical students' reflections on ethical issues in clinical practice (Donaldson et al., 2010).

1.3.4 Reinforcing ethical commitment

This chapter has established that students can all too readily be turned off the value of ethics teaching if the balance of teaching input is weighted too much in favour of abstract theorising and if it is not well aligned. On the other hand, if learning about ethics becomes anchored around what Drugan and Megone (2011) describe as "bar room chat", the quality of learning will be superficial and unlikely to extend into systematic ethical thinking.

An approach to ethics teaching that is transversal (i.e. cuts across units of learning) and requires regular formal curriculum engagement, whether through written exercises or oral discussion, is more likely to habituate patterns of thinking that translate into ethical commitment beyond the programme of study. This can be reinforced in classroom narratives that help students to recognise that:

- ethical issues operate at different orders of magnitude and intensity;
- some of the ethical judgements that may have been given weight within their programme of study will become routine practices over time and be replaced by other workplace-specific or societal dilemmas; and
- professional practice requires sustained vigilance to ethical matters and confidence to assert values and principles internalised during academic study and shaped through exposure to the dynamics of the workplace.

Longer-term commitment will also be facilitated by explicitly guiding students to take stock *post-hoc* of the transformations anticipated – but not necessarily realised – by different classroom tasks in relation to ethical competence and even moral identity development.

26 *Ethics teaching and teaching ethics*

1.3.5 Priorities and pedagogies

A degree of caution is needed in ethics education when it comes to planning teaching and learning activities. For example, maintaining a distinction between "classroom" and "real world" is not always reasonable or realistic; one is not necessarily more authentic than the other. As Pacheo Aguilar (2016, p. 23) writes, translator education is about "moments in which the unforeseeable and unexpected can take place and in which both teachers and students can act authentically", which means taking risks and being alert to "the possibility of becoming someone new". In this view, the object of authenticity is not the learning experience, but the people involved.

This links to the issue of curriculum planning. Washbourne and Liu (2023, p. 177) provide a timely reminder of TI education's tendency to focus on teaching interventions – that is, being "stuck 'in the content turn'" – to the neglect of learning *as becoming*. This can be particularly detrimental when it comes to ethics education. A term such as "curriculum coverage" is salient in this regard, as it can lead to attempts to cram in certain topics and ask "What do students need to know about ethics?", obscuring the goal of student learning ("What do students need to do *to learn* about ethics?") and the wider purposes of education. Designing a curriculum around selected concepts and competencies may lead to a more enriching and meaningful learning experience (Petersen et al., 2020).

Furthermore, in ethics education, a certain resistance is needed to classroom activities oriented to hypothetical and speculative questions such as "What would you do?", since these will likely leave students wondering whether their responses are *right*. Learning is more effective if it is accompanied by different frameworks for decision-making ("What *could* you do?") that support prospective learning and the more effective projection of the self into a future scenario (see Chapter 4). Another issue concerns agency, which is more limited for students on educational programmes than it is for actual TI assignments where choice and discretion regarding whether to accept a project can be exercised; this needs to be acknowledged.

Critical engagement with the concept of situatedness is also merited. Although often viewed as a desirable element in the professionalised TI curriculum, it can be detrimental to learning if viewed monolithically. A phased approach is recommended to allow basic skills and competences to be developed before broader contextual complexities are factored into decision-making (see Miner and Nicodemus, 2021 on situatedness in interpreter education). Relatedly, students' intellectual and emotional maturity needs to be factored into learning expectations, particularly where professional discourses are invoked in relation to situated learning approaches at a point where students are not realistically able to engage with them (see Perry, 1970).

When it comes to the choice of pedagogical frameworks, the literature on TI teaching and learning reflects the strong influence of (social) constructivism in the discipline, which privileges student-centred and experiential learning

(learning by doing) in an approach that strongly resonates with Cantor's (1995, p. 1) definition: "learning activities that engage the learner in the phenomenon being studied", as opposed to simply hearing or reading about it. However, this can sometimes obscure an important distinction between the process of translating and interpreting and the process of *learning to* translate and interpret. Therefore, a number of alternative pedagogical approaches merit consideration (see later chapters).

Constructivists reject the idea of learning as something that is passed down or transmitted on the grounds that knowledge resides in the mind and learning therefore also occurs in the mind (Parson and Major, 2020, p. 19). Learning is said to be constructed in an active manner as learners assimilate and accommodate new experiences in relation to previous learning – a process enacted through what Vygotsky (1978) termed the Zone of Proximal Development (ZPD), where new potential learning takes place in collaboration with others. Within this paradigm, educators become "facilitators" and assume a less prominent role in the classroom.

Criticisms draw attention to the ethics of student-centredness. For instance, there is a likelihood that student engagement in collaborative learning – and hence depth of learning – will vary due to factors including personal effort levels, task comprehension, and (in translation tasks) confidence in using material artefacts like translation technologies. For others (Parson and Major, 2020), the approach is too unstructured, which may particularly impact students entering programmes from cultures in which teacher-centred learning and memorisation are educational mainstays. Part of the issue, as Hansen and Stephens (2000, p. 46) assert, concerns the treatment of collaborative teaching as a method, despite being "underpinned by a growth mindset". Therefore, careful attention is needed when "scaffolding" – a term that relates to lighter-touch input from educators – since it may not promote the anticipated degree of growth in learners.

A certain vigilance is required with regard to the ways in which students' self-efficacy beliefs evolve over a programme of learning, especially in cases where educators seek to privilege a constructivist approach but face institutional limitations that oblige lecture-led teaching, for example. Asking students to complete periodic short questionnaires with targeted questions (relevant to a recent topic focus) accompanied by self-efficacy scales can provide timely snapshots of learning at the group and individual level that may otherwise fall under the radar.[8]

Reflective practice is mentioned in constructivist learning as part of the process of assimilating and accommodating new experiences; however, in many accounts, it seems assumed rather than explicitly planned. In this regard, structured approaches to reflective practice deriving from Schön's (1983) account of workplace learning and other influences, such as Kolb's (1984) experiential learning cycle, support student learning and have been increasingly incorporated into TI programmes (e.g. Crezee and Marianacci, 2022). However, accounts of its implementation suggest it is very seldom used to support ethics education. Including prompts in reflective task instructions for students to bring ethical issues to the fore, articulate them using appropriate meta-language, and think about how moral reasoning was employed to overcome a particular issue is a simple way to sustain ethical vigilance and develop ethical thinking across the programme and beyond.

Didactic or teacher-centred education entails the top-down delivery of information from educator to student, usually in a lecture setting, although it is also reflected in online environments where information is simply presented to be read and absorbed without further guidance. This approach enables educators to model expert processes and articulate coherent programme narratives, including those relevant to ethics education. A dominant form of pedagogy in years past, it is now more likely to be used in combination with student-centred learning. Institutional constraints (timetabling, room availability) can impact on choice, but mitigations can be implemented, for instance using different techniques for large group teaching (e.g. polling methods, pair work, back channelling) or employing virtual learning environments (VLEs) and social media technologies to foster student-led interactions.

1.4 Teaching ethics

This section brings into focus ethical and moral questions relating to teaching practice. It has two main goals: first, to provide context and scope for structured individual reflection on what it means to be a "good" educator against a backdrop of neoliberal capitalism; and, second, drawing on social responsibility (SR) as an ethical framework, to help educators respond coherently to moral injunctions for greater equity, equality, diversity, and inclusion in higher education teaching and learning. The subsections that follow include prompts for individual reflection and guided discussion with peers. Several topics receive more detailed treatment in later chapters.

1.4.1 Contextual challenges for teaching ethics

Readers will no doubt have had occasion to consider what makes a "good" educator, in terms of both the moral and ethical responsibilities that accompany the role and specific disciplinary demands. Changes to the political and economic landscape of higher education, however, mean that external societal and institutional pressures can put the vision of the good educator into conflict with structures that perpetuate inequalities, and value systems that stress the economic benefits of a university education to the neglect of its civic role. Further, the erosion of professional discretion and judgement in the academy, for instance with regard to how the curriculum is planned – as observed by Macfarlane (2003) some 20 years ago – appears to endure. There are, however, many areas in which educators can develop counter-hegemonic discourses through critical pedagogies and reclaim educational spaces as meaningful sites of encounter with others. TI studies offers an opportunity *par excellence* to achieve just that, but whether these opportunities are fully realised at present remains open to question, due to varying levels of casualisation in the sector, among other barriers.

The subsections that follow are underpinned by social responsibility as an ethical framework to support reflection on personal duties of care to students and civic duties towards wider society. The concept of social responsibility (SR) has become something of a buzzword in the higher education sector in recent decades, particularly in Europe, where New Public Management (NPM) frameworks have required universities to demonstrate greater efficiency and relevance (social value) to public life (Godonoga and Sporn, 2023). Set against the neoliberal backdrop in which competitiveness and benchmarking are drivers of performance, however, some of the more positive intentions behind this policy can become diluted. In an attempt to reclaim some moral ground, in the following subsections the concept is underpinned by a political ethic of care (Bozalek, Zembylas, and Tronto, 2021) to develop positive action for inclusion and individual human flourishing.

> **Prompts for reflection**
> - What do you consider to be the main social (civic) and moral value of an education in translation and/or interpreting?
> - How do you view and position your role in the translation and interpreting classroom: a moral authority; a knowledgeable expert/role model; a facilitator of social justice; all of these and/or others?
> - Do you consider the delivery of moral education as part of your social responsibility as an educator? Why? Why not?
> - How would you describe the core tenets of ethical educational practice?
> - What professional and life experiences have most marked your teaching ethos and practice to date?
> - What barriers/enablers impact on your ability to realise your moral and ethical goals at the present time?

1.4.2 Equity/equality, diversity, and inclusion

The focus of this subsection – equity/equality, diversity, and inclusion (EDI) – has its roots in an explicit policy agenda that started in the UK higher education sector and now has global reach. It emerged out of the UK Advance HE 2005 Athena SWAN (Scientific Women's Academic Network) charter, which was designed to remove structural inequalities for all genders across the higher education sector and now encompasses issues impacting other under-represented groups among students and university staff, academic and non-academic.

Student diversity generates a particular set of ethical imperatives for educators. On TI programmes, diversity takes different forms depending on the local institutional recruitment policy and context; some have highly diverse cohorts due to international recruitment initiatives, whereas others largely recruit from a local population. Despite the more homogeneous cohorts in the latter in terms of language and culture,[9] institutional recruitment policy (e.g. "widening participation" in the UK) also supports diversity that inheres in differences in socio-economic background.

Diversity also encompasses physical and intellectual disabilities, whether declared or not, which also require a planned response. In this regard, it is worth stressing the dominance of biomedical models of disability in university policies and individual perspectives (Wolbring and Lillywhite, 2021), according to which disability is viewed as an inherently pathological impairment to a body system or function and as something that needs to be supported to function as "normal" (Olkin, 2002). This model contrasts with the social model of disability, developed by disabled people, which places emphasis on people being disabled by societal barriers (Disability Rights UK, n.d.).

In planning terms, diversity is intimately connected to questions of equity and inclusion; approaches to teaching in which accessibility is *anticipated*, and which assume that everyone has different needs, are becoming more widely adopted by the sector. Applying accessibility guidelines to written materials, ensuring that all instructional videos have subtitles in the same language of the presentation and are accompanied by a transcript, and paying attention to topic changes introduced in the classroom and the pace of delivery (e.g. for those who may experience sensory overload) are examples of practices that are easy to implement.

It is important to stress that, although student support has improved significantly over recent decades across the sector, specific guidance at the disciplinary level is often in short supply, and educators face pressing questions about the extent to which the learning environment supports the transition into professional practice for those with specific needs. This situation mirrors the lack of attention paid by professional associations and other stakeholders to the many ableist assumptions that underscore TI practice, suggesting greater scope for mutually beneficial dialogue on this topic.

Prompts for reflection

- What systems/policies are in place at your institution to support students with different (physical, psychological, sensory, intellectual) disabilities and medical conditions?
- To what extent are questions of ableism that are implicitly promoted in many aspects of the translation and interpreting professions reflected in and/or challenged by your programme of study?
- What accommodations (if any) have you put in place in your teaching to respond to different student needs? How effective do you think these have been from the perspectives of student experience and academic performance?

- Does your institution offer training and support to develop teaching materials that meet relevant accessibility standards?
- What assumptions underpin your programme of study in relation to student access to technology within and outside of the classroom?

With regard to inclusion, educators typically aspire to create learning environments in which all students feel involved, safe, and confident. However, what an educator believes is inclusive and how students experience it are not always well aligned. Sengupta (2022) reminds us that a policy designed to increase student diversity does not automatically foster inclusion. She points to the distinction between *accommodating* people and ensuring they are *treated* as equals, highlighting the risks in acknowledging the presence of individuals from groups occupying a marginalised position in society and denying them a right to speak or to dissent once they have entered an institution – issues that impact both staff and students.

In some educational contexts, the process of problematising inclusion has intensified as a consequence of the recent clamour for change from various social movements seeking to disrupt and challenge dominant epistemic authorities, which is echoed by large swaths of the student body desirous of educational interventions that more systematically address perceived injustices and confront oppressive ideologies. Efforts to counter heteronormative perspectives and decolonise the curriculum are examples of such interventions, which, at least to some extent, can be positioned within new pedagogical thinking underpinned by a political ethics of care and posthumanism, and through which relational ways of understanding the world are foregrounded (see Bozalek, Zembylas, and Tronto, 2021).

Policies and pedagogies encompassing intersectional and critical educational thinking and praxis offer educators a valuable foundation for reappraising current practices and assumptions and making productive educational and social change (Mahon, Heikkinen, and Huttunen, 2019, p. 464). Harmat (2020, p. 4) asserts that more intersectionally aware students "have far greater potential for success in intervention and mediation processes as well as in educational contexts, thanks to their deeper insight into the complexity of human identity and process of – often inadvertent – discrimination". Intersectional thinking extends to questions about whether learners feel their histories and lived experiences are represented in course materials (Case, 2017). This is not to suggest that all experiences need to be reflected across all materials, but periodic review of materials is recommended as the student body changes.

In addition to materials, intersectionality can be enacted through social dialogue in the classroom. For example, Harmat (2020, p. 5) writes: "When students are encouraged to share their historical narratives, backgrounds and the way they perceive their identities it legitimises who they are in regard to the learning material." A simple activity to encourage such reflection suggested by Harmat is name-sharing, which could be used towards the start of a programme. The way in which names are analysed and perceived can affect the ways in which individuals act and can "indicate the complex, multi-layered identities, hidden conflicts, ethnic and cultural tensions, and prejudices they bring with them to class" (p. 6). An openness to sharing these reflections can feed productively into later decision-making, which, in some translation situations, may be as much about responding to a client brief as to exploring the reasons why certain personal experiences lead a translator to represent others' experiences in some ways rather than others.

> **Prompts for syllabus development**
>
> - To what extent do your syllabi reflect a plurality of perspectives (epistemologies) and voices in translation and interpreting studies scholarship? Is it important to you and/or your institution that they do?
> - To what extent do the concepts of academic freedom and disciplinary integrity shape your approach to syllabus creation?
> - Do you seek to reflect your students' lived experience (of gender, race, ethnicity) in your choice of course materials?
> - Are students supported and/or encouraged to situate the histories, knowledges, and worldviews reflected in their syllabi within wider configurations of power and knowledge-building?

1.4.3 Aligned curriculum

The concept of the (constructively) aligned curriculum, introduced by Biggs (1996), is based on the principle of achieving coherence between the Intended Learning Outcomes (ILOs), Teaching and Learning Activities (TLAs), and Assessment Tasks (ATs) on a given programme of study. The approach is designed to enhance student engagement and improve learning effectiveness because it offers transparency in relation to instructor expectations, and to the purpose and goals of a unit of learning by allowing students to make connections between ILOs, TLAs, and ATs, and understand the learning environment in which they are situated (Biggs and Tang, 2007).

Curriculum alignment has been widely adopted internationally, often institutionally prescribed in a top-down manner as part of an outcomes-based approach to teaching and learning. However, it has been criticised for perpetuating instrumentalist goals of (higher) education and for being imposed by institutions for accountability purposes that can diminish its relevance as an educational tool (Loughlin, Lygo-Baker, and Lindberg-Sand, 2021). Other criticisms highlight the limits it places on professional discretion and the ways in which it obscures the many societal factors that impact on learning (race, gender, etc.) (Magnússon and Rytzler, 2022).

In the TI curriculum, aligned approaches may already be established institutional practice. However, there is certainly scope within the discipline to reflect critically on its relevance to all aspects of learning. In ethics education where meta-ethical competence is foregrounded, a learning aims and outcomes approach may not adequately capture the range of learning arising through different TLAs. In part, this is due to different temporalities operating in the learning process. The ethical maturity required of a certain task or set of tasks may develop over a longer period of time than the usual confines of a unit of learning and its assessment allow. As Crowhurst (2022) reminds us, learners are engaged in various ontological projects in addition to epistemological projects, requiring learning design to take account of the complexity of pedagogical spaces and different temporalities at play. In addition, the hidden curriculum's contribution to shaping ethical maturity should not be underestimated (see Subsection 1.4.4, below). In short, while an aligned approach can effectively support a particular vision of ethical teaching practice, it may have limitations when it comes to nurturing certain ethical skills and competences.

1.4.4 Hidden curriculum

The hidden (or informal) curriculum refers to learning that occurs outside of the formal programme of study through interaction with peers on the same and/or other programmes, self-directed investigation of topics relevant to and/or unrelated to the assigned syllabus, and involvement in extra-curricular activities. It also extends to the "hidden curriculum of place" (Winter and Cotton, 2012), encompassing interactions with spaces of learning (both on- and offline), leisure, eating on campus, and institutional messages around environmental sustainability.

Despite the many benefits of unintended learning that happens through the mechanisms outlined above, there can be a darker side to the hidden curriculum. This is due to the unspoken rules that impact on student ways of being and the way in which students execute various learning processes. It can also extend to language and discourse practices that students are assumed to know or pick up easily, which are not taught or necessarily explained. This includes assessment. Johnson (2020, p. 6), for instance, describes how written feedback on student assessment can "[encode] individual and institutional beliefs, such as about the nature of knowledge and power at the University" – beliefs that may be, in his words, "obscured by implied objectivity" in instruments like marking rubrics.

Left unchecked, academic achievement, general wellbeing, and sense of belonging can all be impacted by the hidden curriculum (Hinchcliffe, 2020). Navigating the informal curriculum can be a positive part of the individual learning experience and group identity creation on a programme of study. However, attention is needed to mitigate its more nefarious impacts on student learning, particularly in cohorts with a strong international student presence.

> **Prompts for reflection**
> - To what extent do you assume certain literacies and practices have already been developed by students prior to starting their translation programme (e.g. using a dictionary, doing internet searches), and how do these assumptions shape your approach to student feedback?
> - Do you assume students have developed reliable study practices and/or know how to access help?
> - How are students guided (if at all) to use different learning spaces to maximise opportunities for learning through social dialogue, independently, outside of the classroom?

1.4.5 Assessment and feedback

Good practice in assessment and feedback is part of the educator's professional commitment. Assessment needs to be fair, inclusive, and transparent. It also needs to be proportionate to teaching input and staff workload and time. Developing good practice requires attention to assessment literacy and inclusivity, and, for TI students in particular, underscoring the value of self-assessment as part of developing independent (ethical) judgement and responsibility. Feedback needs to be timely, useful, and carefully pitched to encourage students to engage with and act positively on it, but it also needs to be proportionate to staff workload.

Assessment literacy development involves targeted interventions to help students understand the purpose, the language, and the process of assessment (Reason and Ward, 2022), which can offset some of the disadvantages of the hidden curriculum, as outlined above. Assessment literacy makes it possible to take account of the role played by affect in assessment practices (Forsyth and Evans, 2019), as manifested, for instance, in student expectations regarding assessment types and anxiety if new types are introduced (Bain, 2023). This has resonance for the TI curriculum, in which a broad set of skills and knowledge is commonly tested, involving tasks like report-writing, brief-setting, pitching to potential clients, revising and editing, many of which will be new to students.

Developing assessment literacy will often involve marking rubrics – a set of statements about expected performance levels according to a grading band – to help students discern between performance levels and the potential weighting of components in each level. Students may even develop rubrics themselves as part of assessment literacy development, which would involve critically engaging with concepts in translation and interpreting quality assessment. On TI programmes, assessment literacy can also usefully distinguish between academic and professional expectations. For instance, educators may develop assessment criteria along pedagogical lines (i.e. anticipating a learning curve in which different elements change in weighting over a series of assessments) and/or in ways that reflect professional revisor/institutional assessor practice. A professionally oriented rubric could be used alongside an academic set of marking descriptors to provide insight into how close a piece of work is to publishable standard (translation) or acceptable public performance (interpreting), and to increase self-assessment capacity.

Inclusivity is also important in assessment. It is sometimes viewed narrowly through the prism of "accommodations" required by certain students for declared impairments (e.g. extra time for reading or an amanuensis). Emerging approaches take a more radical view of marginalised students as "fully accepted, agentic members of academic communities" (Nieminen, 2022, p. 1), informed by social models of disability. Nieminen explores the potential for combining individual accommodations with inclusive assessment design and recommends, for example, ensuring disability and neurodiversity are represented in assessment tasks and offering students scope to co-design assessments based on lived experiences, among others.

Feedback, which also carries an ethical importance in the curriculum, takes multiple forms: written, oral feedback in class or recorded, individual or group, educator-, self-, or peer-led. It is often conceived in unidirectional terms – as something handed down by educators to their students, usually in written form. By contrast, in social constructivist frameworks, self- and peer-feedback initiatives involve students more dynamically in the process, encouraging a degree of responsibility-taking (Henderson, Ajjawi, Boud, and Molloy, 2019). However, the success of such approaches relies on good feedback literacy, defined as "the understandings, capacities and dispositions needed to make sense of information and use it to enhance work or learning strategies" (Carless and Boud, 2018, p. 1316), not least because some students fail to engage with feedback at all, perhaps due to difficult prior experiences or dissatisfaction with the feedback received.

Recorded educator comments can include a summative comment and/or comments on a piece of work *as it is being marked* (i.e. verbalising the marking process), which can be an engaging way for students to hear how their instructor is thinking about their work as they read (see Carless and Boud, 2018). Feedback that is poorly articulated or ill-conceived for the task type can impact on a student's motivation to continue with their studies and/or their perceived competence levels (Pitt and Norton, 2017); in this regard, recorded feedback offers good potential to strike a conversational and constructive tone in ways that written feedback sometimes does not.

Examples of dynamic feedback include encouraging students to brainstorm in small groups with their peers to articulate what action they may take to consolidate good practice and take certain skills further.[10] Students might also be encouraged to write a paragraph at the start of the next assignment that directly responds to comments and guidance from the previous assignment about what action has been taken in the meantime and how/why the student thinks they have enhanced their approach, as a kind of rolling conversation with the assessor. In some cases, students may be asked rework an assignment based on feedback and include a comment on what they have changed in their approach. Although this might not be feasible for every piece of work, it may be an effective support for developing ethical prototypes early in the programme for basic translation processes.

Prompts for reflection

- Which approach – or combination of approaches – to feedback do you currently employ?
- Do you give space in your teaching to the development of feedback literacy? If so, which activities do you use to support this development?
- How (if at all) do you monitor the extent to which students are engaging with feedback?
- If you know you have given advice on how to tackle a particular issue and a student repeats the same mistake on the next occasion, does this impact the tone of the feedback and/or the grade?
- Which constraints and enablers impact on the amount of individual and/or group feedback given to students, whether formatively or summatively?
- If you provide written feedback to students, do you expect or guide them to take any particular action once it has been delivered?

Activity

Developing ethical feedback practice

As a support for this exercise, consult the Developing Engagement with Feedback Toolkit (DEFT) at: www.advance-he.ac.uk/knowledge-hub/developing-engagement-feedback-toolkit-deft.

1   In a translation assignment, an instructor's comments in the margin routinely contain single words followed only by a grade (and no general comment): "mistranslated", "poor target language expression", "inappropriate register". No further information is given to help the student identify what the problems are in more comprehensive terms. Imagine the work is returned to the students with the invitation to speak to the instructor individually if they have any questions. No reference translation is provided. Most students do not take up the offer to speak to the instructor. One student does take up the offer, and for each point raised wishes to know how the instructor would have translated it. The class size is 55 and the students are required to complete four pieces (500 words) that count towards their final course unit grade.

- How might the students be best supported to identify and resolve problems in their work through feedback or post-assessment class activities?
- How might the instructor best manage the single student's request for a solution to each point raised on the assignment?

> - What are the risks/benefits to student learning of providing a reference translation (or model answer)?
> - Which steps might the instructor take to mitigate the issues outlined in view of the class size and volume of assignments to grade?
>
> 2 Students in a simultaneous interpreting class receive feedback following a simulated conference led by professional interpreters who have no involvement in teaching the students in question. The event takes place towards the end of the first semester. The students are left feeling quite demoralised after receiving feedback that they felt was overly negative and did not provide suggestions for improvement.
>
> - Which actions could/should educators take to support professionals in giving feedback in such circumstances?
> - To what extent would (informal) self- and peer assessment support student learning in this case?
> - How might educators draw on professionals' feedback in subsequent classes to put it into perspective in relation to the students' learning at that point on the programme?
>
> 3 Students sit an end-of-year examination in translation involving texts taken from news sources of the kind they have worked on in class during the course. No dictionaries or other resources are allowed in the examination. The students complain that this is unrealistic and unreflective of real-world translation processes.
>
> - What information might you include in the task instructions that make the constraints imposed transparent from a learning perspective?
> - What sort of feedback would you expect to provide students following this activity that would support their skills development?

1.5 Chapter summary

This chapter illuminates several challenges facing educators in planning an ethics education on TI programmes. It illustrates the need for discernment when it comes to content choices in an already crowded curriculum and stresses the importance of not losing sight of the goal of student learning: that is, what educators and students need to do to facilitate meaningful learning experiences that will translate into ethical commitment beyond the programme of study. It encourages critical engagement with outcomes-based approaches to learning, as these are characterised by a number of limitations in relation to ethics education, not least because of the different temporalities at play in the development of moral imagination and ethical maturity. Finally, it offers practical suggestions for educators to plan approaches to teaching that take due account of the imperatives of equity, diversity, and inclusivity.

Notes

1. The status of Ubuntu as a fully fledged moral theory is much contested.
2. "Act-based approach" means that an ethical decision results in the most favourable consequences for the largest number of people in a given context; "rule-based approach" means an action is right only if it falls under a rule, the general following of which would result in greater utility than an alternative available rule (Bennett, 2015, p. 65).
3. https://plato.stanford.edu/entries/relativism/.
4. Dean and Pollard (2011, 2013) address a similar point through their Demand Control Schema, discussed in Chapter 4.
5. www.bma.org.uk/advice-and-support/ethics/medical-students/ethics-toolkit-for-medical-students/cultural-relativism.
6. Comments made at the 7th IATIS conference, Barcelona, 2021.
7. www.cedefop.europa.eu/en/projects/european-qualifications-framework-eqf.
8. For an example of a self-efficacy scale, see: www.imperial.ac.uk/media/imperial-college/staff/education-development-unit/public/Self-efficacy-in-discipline-scale.pdf.
9. Caution is needed when using the word "local", which in some contexts can encompass high population diversity.
10. This exercise would require managing in order to encourage focus on positive steps forward rather than asking students to reveal details about feedback to their peers, which may provoke anxiety if the performance was not as good as expected.

References

Bain, K. (2023). Inclusive assessment in higher education: What does the literature tell us on how to define and design inclusive assessments? *Journal of Learning Development in Higher Education*, 27. https://doi.org/10.47408/jldhe.vi27.1014.

Baker, M. (2006). *Translation and conflict: A narrative account*. Routledge.

Baker, M. (2011). *In other words: A coursebook on translation* (2nd ed.). Routledge.

Bennett, C. (2015). *What is this thing called ethics?* (2nd ed.). Routledge.

Biggs, J. (1996). Enhancing teaching through constructive alignment. *Higher Education*, 32, 347–364. https://doi.org/10.1007/BF00138871.

Biggs, J., & Tang, C. S. (2007). *Teaching for quality learning at university: What the student does*. Open University Press.

Bozalek, V., Zembylas, M., & Tronto, J. (2021). *Posthuman and political care ethics for reconfiguring higher education pedagogies*. Routledge.

Brody, H. (2003). *Stories of sickness* (2nd ed.). Oxford University Press.

Callahan, D., & Bok, S. (Eds.) (1980). *Ethics teaching in higher education*. Plenum.

Cantor, J. A. (1995). *Experiential learning in higher education: Linking classroom and community*. ASHE-ERIC Higher Education Report No. 7. Georgetown Washington University, Graduate School of Education and Human Development.

Carless, D., & Boud, D. (2018). The development of student feedback literacy: Enabling the update of feedback. *Assessment and Evaluation in Higher Education*, 43(8), 1315–1325. https://doi.org/10.1080/02602938.2018.1463354.

Case, K. A. (Ed.) (2017). *Intersectional pedagogy: Complicating identity and social justice*. Routledge.

Chesterman, A. (2001). Proposal for a hieronymic oath. *The Translator*, 7(2), 139–154. https://doi.org/10.1080/13556509.2001.10799097.

Crezee, I., & Marianacci, A. (2022). "How did he say that?" Interpreting students' written reflections on interprofessional education scenarios with speech language therapists. *The Interpreter and Translator Trainer*, 16(1), 19–38.

Crowhurst, M. (2022). *On pedagogical spaces, multiplicity and linearities and learning*. Springer.

Davis, M., & Feinerman, A. (2012). Assessing graduate student progress in engineering ethics. *Science and Engineering Ethics*, 18(2), 351–367. https://doi.org/10.1007/s11948-010-9250-2.

Dean, R. K., & Pollard, R. Q., Jr. (2011). Context-based ethical reasoning in interpreting: A Demand Control Schema perspective. *The Interpreter and Translator Trainer*, 5(1), 155–182. https://doi.org/10.1080/13556509.2011.10798816.

Dean, R. K., & Pollard, R. Q., Jr. (2013). *The Demand Control Schema: Interpreting as a practice profession*. CreateSpace.

Devettere, R. J. (2002). *Introduction to virtue ethics: Insights of the ancient Greeks*. Georgetown University Press.

Disability Rights UK (n.d.). Social Model of Disability: Language. www.disabilityrightsuk.org/social-model-disability-language.

Donaldson, T. M., Fistein, E., & Dunn, M. (2010). Case-based seminars in medical ethics education: How medical students define and discuss moral problems. *Journal of Medical Ethics*, 36(12), 816–820.

Drugan, J., & Megone, C. (2011). Bringing ethics into translator training. *The Interpreter and Translator Trainer*, 5(1), 183–211. https://doi.org/10.1080/13556509.2011.10798817.

European Commission (2008). *Explaining the European Qualifications Framework for lifelong learning*. https://europa.eu/europass/system/files/2020-05/EQF-Archives-EN.pdf.

European Commission (2022). *European master's in translation – EMT competence framework*. https://commission.europa.eu/news/updated-version-emt-competence-framework-now-available-2022-10-21_en.

Fesmire, S. (2003). *John Dewey and moral imagination: Pragmatism in ethics*. Indiana University Press.

Floros, G. (2011). "Ethics-less" theories and "ethical" practices: On ethical relativity in translation. *The Interpreter and Translator Trainer*, 5(1), 65–92. https://doi.org/10.1080/13556509.2011.10798812.

Forsyth, H., & Evans, J. (2019). Authentic assessment for a more inclusive history. *Higher Education Research and Development*, 38(4),748–761. https://doi.org/10.1080/07294360.2019.1581140.

Godonoga, A., & Sporn, B. (2023). The conceptualisation of socially responsible universities in higher education research: A systematic literature review. *Studies in Higher Education*, 48(3), 445–459. https://doi.org/10.1080/03075079.2022.2145462.

Hansen, E. J., & Stephens, J. A. (2000). The ethics of learner-centred education: Dynamics that impede the process. *Change*, 32(5), 41–47. http://dx.doi.org/10.1080/00091380009605739.

Harding, S.-A. (2021). "Becoming knowledgeable": Ingold's "wayfaring" and the "art of translation" as a politics of difference. *The Translator*, 27(4), 351–367. https://doi.org/10.1080/13556509.2021.1992890.

Harmat, G. (2020). *Intersectional pedagogy: Creative education practices for gender and peace work*. Routledge.

Henderson, M. J., Ajjawi, R., Boud, D., & Molloy, E. (Eds.) (2019). *The impact of feedback in higher education: Improving assessment outcomes for learners*. Palgrave Macmillan.

Hinchcliffe, T. (2020). The hidden curriculum of higher education: An introduction. In T. Hinchcliffe (Ed.), *The hidden curriculum of higher education* (pp. 2–4). Advance HE. www.gcu.ac.uk/__data/assets/pdf_file/0021/30873/advhe_hidden20curriculum.pdf#page=4.

Hurwitz, B. (2003). The narrative turn in medical ethics. *Lancet*, 361, 1309.

Ingold, T. (2007). *Lines: A brief history*. Routledge.

Ingold, T. (2013). *Making: Anthropology, archaeology, art and architecture*. Routledge.

Johnson, I. (2020). What hides beneath? An evidence-based take on the hidden curriculum of assessment feedback. In T. Hinchcliffe (Ed.), *The hidden curriculum of higher education* (pp. 5–28). Advance HE. www.gcu.ac.uk/__data/assets/pdf_file/0021/30873/advhe_hidden20curriculum.pdf#page=4.

Joseph, P. B. (2003). Teaching about the moral classroom: Infusing the moral imagination into teacher education. *Asia-Pacific Journal of Teacher Education*, 31(1), 7–20. https://doi.org/10.1080/13598660301617.

Kermit, P. S. (2019) Introduction. In M. Phelan, M. Rudvin, H. Skaaden, and P.S. Kermit, *Ethics in public service interpreting* (pp. 1–23). Routledge.

Kolb, D. A. (1984). *Experiential learning: Experience as the source of learning and development*. Prentice-Hall.

Loughlin, C., Lygo-Baker, S., & Lindberg-Sand, Å. (2021). Reclaiming constructive alignment. *European Journal of Higher Education*, 11(2), 119–136. https://doi.org/10.1080/21568235.2020.1816197.

Macfarlane, B. (2003). *Teaching with integrity: The ethics of higher education practice*. Routledge.

Magnússon, G., & Rytzler, J. (2022). *Towards a pedagogy of higher education: The Bologna Process, Didaktik and teaching*. Routledge.

Mahon, K., Heikkinen, H. L. T., & Huttunen, R. (2019). Critical educational praxis in university ecosystems: Enablers and constraints. *Pedagogy, Culture and Society*, 27(3), 463–480. https://doi.org/10.1080/14681366.2018.1522663.

McCollough, T. E. (1991). *The moral imagination and public life: Raising the ethical question*. Chatham House.

Meacham, K. R., Sloan, I., & Latessa, R. A. (2022). Practical tips for teaching ethics and humanism to medical students. *MedEdPublish*, 12. https://doi.org/10.12688/mep.19022.1.

Miner, A., & Nicodemus, B. (2021). *Situated learning in interpreter education: From the classroom to the community*. Palgrave Macmillan.

Montello, M. (2014) Narrative ethics. *Hastings Center Report*, 44(1 Suppl), S2–S6.

Monzó-Nebrot, E., & Wallace, M. (2020). New societies, new values, new demands: Mapping non-professional interpreting and translation, remapping translation and interpreting ethics. *Translation and Interpreting Studies*, 15(1), 1–14. https://doi.org/10.1075/tis.00046.int.

Nieminen, J. H. (2022). Assessment for inclusion: Rethinking inclusive assessment in higher education. *Teaching in Higher Education*. https://doi.org/10.1080/13562517.2021.2021395.

Nortvedt, P. (2001). Clinical sensitivity: The inseparability of ethical perceptiveness and clinical knowledge. *Scholarly Inquiry for Nursing Practice*, 15(1), 25–43.

Olkin, R. (2002) "Could you hold the door for me?" Including disability in diversity. *Cultural Diversity and Ethnic Minority Psychology*, 8, 130–137.

Pacheo Aguilar, R. (2016). The question of authenticity in translator education from the perspective of educational philosophy. In D. Kiraly (Ed.), *Towards authentic experiential learning in translator education* (pp. 13–32). Mainz University Press.

Parson, L., & Major, C. (2020). Learning theory through a social justice lens. In L. Parson and C. Casey Osaki (Eds.), *Teaching and learning for social justice and equity in higher education: Foundations* (pp. 7–38). Palgrave Macmillan.

Perry, W. G., Jr. (1970). *Forms of intellectual and ethical development in the college years: A scheme.* Holt, Rinehart, and Winston.

Petersen, C. I., Baepler, P., Beitz, A., Ching, P., Gorman, K. S., Neudauer, C. L., Rozaitis, W., Walker, J. D., & Wingert, D. (2020). The tyranny of content: "Content coverage" as a barrier to evidence-based teaching approaches and ways to overcome it. *CBE – Life Sciences Education*, 19(2). https://doi.org/10.1187/cbe.19-04-0079.

Pitt, E., & Norton, L. (2017). "Now that's the feedback I want!" Students' reactions to feedback on graded work and what they do with it. *Assessment and Evaluation in Higher Education*, 42(4), 499–516. https://doi.org/10.1080/02602938.2016.1142500.

Pym, A. (2020). Translator ethics. In K. Koskinen and N. K. Pokorn (Eds.), *The Routledge handbook of translation and ethics* (pp. 147–161). Routledge.

Rachels, J. (1998). Ethical relativism. In *Encyclopaedia Britannica*. www.britannica.com/facts/ethical-relativism.

Reason, M., & Ward, C. (2022). Improving, achieving, excelling: Developing inclusive assessment processes for a degree-level learning disability arts programme. *Research in Drama Education: The Journal of Applied Theatre and Performance*, 27(1),137–146. https://doi.org/10.1080/13569783.2021.1997581.

Rest, J. (1994) *Moral development in the professions: Psychology and applied ethics.* Lawrence Erlbaum and Associates.

Reynolds, S. J. (2006). A neurocognitive model of the ethical decision-making process: Implications for study and practice. *Journal of Applied Psychology*, 91(4), 737–748. https://doi.org/10.1037/0021-9010.91.4.737.

Rudvin, M. (2019). Situating interpreting ethics in moral philosophy. In M. Phelan, M. Rudvin, H. Skaaden, and P. S. Kermit, *Ethics in public service interpreting* (pp. 24–84). Routledge.

Schön, D. A. (1983). *The reflective practitioner: How professionals think in action.* Temple Smith.

Sengupta, P. (Ed.) (2022). *Critical sites of inclusion in higher education.* Springer.

Seok, B. (2011). Virtue ethics. In D. K. Chatterjee (Ed.), *Encyclopedia of global justice* (pp. 1130–1132). Springer Netherlands.

Shuttleworth, M., & Cowie, M. (1997). Translation theory. In *Dictionary of translation studies* (pp. 184–187). Routledge.

Svensson, F., & Johansson, J. (2017). Objections to virtue ethics. In N. E. Snow (Ed.), *The Oxford handbook of virtue ethics* (pp. 491–507). Oxford University Press.

Tipton, R. (2012). A socio-theoretical account of interpreter-mediated activity with specific reference to the social service context: Reflection and reflexivity. Unpublished doctoral dissertation, University of Salford.

van Hooft, S. (2009). Global justice: A cosmopolitan account. *Ethics and Global Politics*, 2(4), 369–382. https://doi.org/10.3402/egp.v2i4.2107.

Voss, G. (2013). Gaming, texting, learning? Teaching engineering ethics through students' lived experiences with technology. *Science and Engineering Ethics*, 19(3), 1375–1393. https://doi.org/10.1007/s11948-012-9368-5.

Vygotsky, L. S. (1978). *The mind in society: The development of higher psychological processes.* Harvard University Press.

Wakabayashi, J. (2003). Think-alouds as a pedagogical tool. In B. J. Baer and G. S. Koby (Eds.), *Beyond the ivory tower: Rethinking translation pedagogy* (pp. 61–82). John Benjamins.

Washbourne, K. (2013). Ethical experts-in-training: Connected learners and the moral imagination. In D. C. Kiraly, S. Hansen-Schirra, and K. Maksymski (Eds.), *New prospects and perspectives for educating language mediators* (pp. 35–52). Narr.

Washbourne, K., & Liu, Y. (2023). "To study is not to create something but to create oneself": An ontological turn in translator education and training. *The Interpreter and Translator Trainer*, 17(2), 177–192. https://doi.org/10.1080/1750399X.2023.2175128.

Winter, D., & Cotton, J. (2012). Making the hidden curriculum visible: Sustainability literacy in higher education. *Environment Education Research*, 18(6), 783–796. https://doi.org/10.1080/13504622.2012.670207.

Wolbring, G., & Lillywhite, A. (2021). Equity/equality, diversity, and inclusion (EDI) in universities: The case of disabled people. *Societies*, 11(2), 49. https://doi.org/10.3390/soc11020049.

Wood, A. W. (2008). *Kantian ethics*. Cambridge University Press.

Zhou, M. (2022). Educating translation ethics: A neurocognitive ethical decision-making approach. *The Interpreter and Translator Trainer*, 16(4), 391–408. https://doi.org/10.1080/1750399X.2022.2030534.

2 Ethics and the translation curriculum (I)

2.1 Chapter overview

After acknowledging that curriculum structures take many forms at both undergraduate and graduate levels, this chapter, which is the first of two on ethics in the translation curriculum, focuses on translation practice and proposes topics and activities that can be adapted for different levels and programme goals. It explores issues that impact on learning and the development of ethical responsibility in translation before considering ways to enhance ethical sensitisation through pre-translation tasks, without, however, suggesting that sensitisation is always *prior to* the task of translation.

Selected topics are then discussed in relation to two domains of translation: literary and commercial. Literary translation offers scope for sensitisation to ethical issues arising in both adult and children's fiction. It also serves as a fertile backdrop for reflecting on contemporaneous debates about experiential knowledge in translation and structural issues impacting on the distribution of opportunities to translate in the literary sphere. Commercial translation is addressed as a means to emphasise the importance of context in ethical decision-making and awareness of how multilingualism and multimodalism operate in communicative chains used to promote products and services, and their ethical implications. Attention is also given to the ethical challenges arising from transcreative approaches.

2.2 Ethics and the translation curriculum

This section seeks to stimulate productive reflection on the relationship between teaching designed to enhance ethical responsibility and implications for student learning.

2.2.1 *Fostering integrity and thoroughness*

A principal goal of many translation programmes is for students to enact professional standards of integrity and thoroughness with confidence, which requires emphasis on the ethical responsibility of the translator from the earliest phases of translator education. Although this goal is still likely to shape translation teaching and learning nearly 30 years after Andrew Chesterman first articulated it in 1997, contemporary translation situations often place radically different demands on the translator, not least due to the use of translation technologies, requiring ethical responsibility to be conceived in both individual and distributed terms.

A competence-based translation curriculum has the potential to systematise learning and skills development in ways that help foster integrity and thoroughness at the individual level by creating reliable routines in researching and revising, building confidence, and (in principle) improving the reliability and quality of the final translated output. However, its instrumentalist orientation can mask numerous issues relevant to student learning. One student's idea of thoroughness, for instance, may be far removed from another's, and not simply for reasons of personal effort. Differences in literacy development, including digital literacies, also play a part, as do highly situated tasks for which students often lack relevant external points of reference. Developing competence is therefore unlikely to occur in the linear manner perhaps anticipated and may not be significantly facilitated through collaborative learning.

All too often, pressures of time mean that an inadequate or incorrect translation solution is simply pointed out retrospectively in student feedback, meaning the important question of why errors were made in the first place remains unanswered, with students left to wonder why they were not sufficiently thorough in their approach. Mossop (1983, p. 244; original emphasis) suggests that this is rarely due to some technical incapacity but rather to students not "sufficiently [reflecting] on just exactly what it is they are *doing* when they are translating" (and, one might add, educators assuming that they are). Other factors, not least the potential impact of an outcomes-based approach to teaching and learning, may also be at play. Whether students pay attention to a list of intended learning outcomes is of course open to question, but the transmissionist epistemological assumptions that can be said to inform such an approach (Pacheo Aguilar, 2016, p. 16) risk exacerbating educator assumptions about what students think they are doing in translation and prematurely closing down openness to experimentation.

Finally, the twin psychological states of uncertainty and undecidability commonly experienced in translation require a different learning mindset in relation to integrity and thoroughness, one that is difficult to foster in a competence-oriented approach. Carving out space – whether in classroom discussion, individual reflective practice, or translation commentaries – for students to dwell on the *lived moments* of undecidability and uncertainty will help them come to terms with the different temporalities at play in the translation process and the limitations of certain sequences and practices that are effective for some translation situations but not others (i.e. critically engaging with the concept of competence). Reflection would focus on describing as precisely as possible what the nub of the issue is, what led up to that moment, what exacerbated it, why certain routines (information mining, revising, etc.) proved inadequate, and which questions, with hindsight, could have prompted a more satisfactory resolution of the problem. If students are to develop ethical responsibility and, importantly, the degree of decision-making autonomy typically expected of a professional translator, externalising and reflecting on these experiences is a first stage in transforming practice and becoming accountable to the self and others. It also resonates with the concept of the mattering map, introduced in Chapter 1.

2.2.2 Translator identity status and ethical responsibility

The degree to which ethical responsibility is fostered in the translation curriculum is connected, at least to some extent, to the development of the translator self-concept: "a mental construct that serves as the interface between the translator's social and psychological worlds" (Kiraly, 1995, p. 100). For Kiraly, its development relies on placing students in learning situations that support awareness of what it means to translate professionally (p. 114), which varies according to programme level (see Ehrensberger-Dow and Massey, 2013).

The translator self-concept starts to emerge at the point when a shift occurs between student and translator identity status, as students start to take account of situatedness and the various agents that may have a stake in and/or be impacted by their translation decisions and develop capacity to evaluate their own competence to produce and evaluate the quality of a translation. In short, this is the point when *students realise* that the act of translating puts them in an ethical relation to others and that they bear responsibility *to* other persons or entities *for* something (a translated product).

The extent to which educators are aware of this shift or actively manage it within a single unit of learning and across units of learning is open to question, especially if they have little knowledge of the evolution of self-efficacy beliefs. The transition between the student and translator identity is not necessarily linear or stable, and it might never be fully realised (e.g. on language learning majors that involve only a small amount of translation). The motivation to work as a professional translator and, hence, commitment to the translator identity status may also diminish over a programme of study, for example if the level of academic progress is lower than anticipated and self-efficacy beliefs are impacted as a result (see Contreras, 2022). It is important, however, to distinguish between translator identity and professional translator identity statuses, since the successful resolution of ethical issues in translation does not depend on the capacity to sustain a professional outlook.

> **Prompts for reflection**
>
> - To what extent do you (and your colleagues) draw on Kiraly's translator self-concept in organising the curriculum and developing your classroom discourse practices and narratives?

- Are your learning activities, task instructions, and assessments designed in ways that take account of the student/translator identity status and its evolution? Is it important that they do?
- Do you provide space for students to reflect systematically on the evolving relationship between their student and translator identity statuses? If so, do these reflections also shape your approach to teaching and feedback?

2.3 Ethics sensitisation through pre-translation tasks

This section introduces ideas to enhance student sensitisation to ethics through reading, peer translation, text profiling, and monolingual revision, all of which can be adapted to any text type. Although many of these tasks lend themselves to the early phases of translator education, they serve to consolidate skills across the programme and can be repeated and adapted as necessary.

2.3.1 Reading as an ethical activity

Conceptualising reading as an ethical endeavour is not new. Discussions at the intersection of ethics and literary practice, which have a long lineage, have much to offer translation teaching and learning in terms of their potential for shaping thinking about the relationship between self and other, different literacies and textual practices in the literary sphere, and beyond. Newton (2020, p. ix), for instance, highlights the act of reading-as-witnessing and the moral obligations that ensue as examples of the more complex ethical questions debated in contemporary literary studies, compared to earlier, narrower concerns about the extent to which individuals are morally transformed by reading.

Close, analytical reading underpins all translation activity, whether it involves a short patient information leaflet, a work of high literature, or a video game. The ability to discern different practices in reading for general purposes and reading for the purpose of translation, the connections between the two, and their respective ethical implications is an important learning goal early in a programme of study. Encouraging students to ask "Where do I stand as a reader in ethical relation to this text?" requires them to confront the different readerly positions they occupy in the translation process. That said, as a learning prompt, it would be preferable to break down the question into more concrete points for reflection, as exemplified below.

Being able to suspend – as far as possible – a translator's reading of a text (i.e. one marked by hyper-attentiveness to potential translation problems) in order to privilege "unencumbered reading", or reading for its own sake, carries important weight experientially in terms of ethics sensitisation. In other words, before imagining the ethical relation obtained between a text and its future readers in translation, students would be encouraged to work through their own ethical relation to the text as though they were the intended addressee. The value of this exercise is perhaps often assumed by educators, while the benefits are likely to be underestimated by students keen to immerse themselves in the translation process proper as soon as possible and "lose sight of the self". The following prompts help to bridge the gap between the two readerly positions.

> Reading for ethical awareness
>
> The prompts below can be adapted and used for any pre-translation exercise. As a starting point, they could be used with semi-specialised texts: for example, a short tourism-related text, a short story, a news report, or an extract from a company report. It is important for information such as original layout, colour and image use, font, and so on to accompany the text in order that students may reflect on the importance of multimodality in establishing certain ethical relations with readers.
>
> - From which vantage point(s) do I read this text (neophyte, knowledgeable amateur, technical expert, other)?
> - Does the author make a particular ethical position explicit in the text? If so, how? If not, is a position implied through language, register, genre, and/or choices made in relation to information conveyed through other modes?
> - How would I describe the ethical relation(s) the author of this text seeks to establish between readers and the text in its original version (e.g. does the author seek to effect some sort of moral transformation in readers)?
> - How does my cultural background and personal life experience influence my reading of this text?
> - How would my reading of this text differ if I were reading for the purpose of translating it? If so, how? (NB: Think also about multimodal cues present in the text environment and the intended communicative function(s) of the text.)
> - What do I start to look for in the text in my imagined role as a different reader, and how might this influence my decision-making?
> - When I imagine this text taking on a new life in translation and existing in a new intercultural space, how and to what extent might the ethical relations the author seeks to establish with the reader be transformed, and certain aspects of the relationship be prioritised over others in translation?

2.3.2 "Being translated"

Subsection 2.3.1 emphasised the importance of cultivating ethically engaged reading habits as part of developing translator responsibility. In this subsection, a pre-translation exercise suggested by Chesterman (1997, p. 154) is reprised to extend this work further. Although the original exercise was designed to trigger emotional responses in students about their own writing and "to see how one is answerable to one's own text" (p. 154), it also serves to develop sensitivity to other readers' responses to text through a direct feedback loop.

48 *Ethics and the translation curriculum (I)*

The exercise involves students working in a pair with the same language pairing. They are asked to draft a short essay in their main language on a topic of their choosing, although, for this activity, Chesterman recommends topics that encourage subjective and impressionistic approaches to writing. Students then work to translate each other's texts[1] before returning it for comment and feedback.

The potential for this activity to unsettle is not insignificant; indeed, it was designed, in part, with this purpose in mind. To optimise learning, plenary discussion is recommended to help identify what it is that students find unsettling and help build a collective vocabulary to articulate these lived experiences and what they might mean for subsequent translation practice. The exercise also has significant potential for introducing the concept of ethical responsibility experientially and activating the moral imagination, exposing students to the vulnerabilities of entrusting their writing to another reader, and experiencing first-hand the consequences of translator decisions and risk-taking.

Giving peer feedback is a dynamic process of reckoning, which involves exposing the self to another's critique; it is something that students may not find easy to embrace, particularly if they struggle to articulate motivations for translation decisions early in a programme. The exercise could therefore be repeated over the programme of study with modifications to the genre of the initial writing task and complemented by readings in translation studies (and beyond) of personal translator accounts of translating.

2.3.3 Text profiling to determine ethical priorities

A core message promoted in this book is that ethics education in translation (and interpreting) should not be viewed as a burdensome addition to an already crowded curriculum, and instead as something that can be included as an extension to regular classroom activities and independent learning tasks. Building on the suggested activities in Subsections 2.3.1 and 2.3.2, this subsection explores text profiling as an extension to text analysis in (specialised) translation preparation and as a means to build ethical sensitivity at the level of text genre. This task helps to extend attention beyond purely linguistic issues to relational ones, as well as fostering a deeper sense of text function than might be gleaned from a hypothetical translation brief alone. The concept of text profiling takes inspiration from Montalt and González Davies (2007, p. 23), who show how it may be adopted to establish ethical priorities for various text genres in the medical domain; one example is the genre of informed consent, which generates the ethical priority of clarity to enable a patient to make an informed choice.

Establishing ethical priorities presented by different text genres requires reflection on what is communicated, how it is communicated, and how it will be received and used by the target readership in ways that demand attention to the contexts of its production and reception. Health campaigning in the contemporary age, for instance, requires translators to develop a sense of how campaigns operate in the digital and non-digital worlds, and the ethical priorities associated with each. Online campaigns may involve the translation of hashtags, which requires specific planning and consultation as there is a risk that a translated hashtag may not be picked up and used by the intended audience (see Subsection 2.5.3 on hashtag translation).

These extra-textual considerations again highlight the importance of incorporating multimodal perspectives (Gambier and Munday, 2014), but they also underscore the role different literacies can play in translation decision-making. In some groups where healthcare literacy is low, clarity in a translation and even adapted (simplified) translations do not necessarily support end-user understanding; setting ethical priorities can therefore also encompass alternative communication modalities. Providing exemplars along with task instructions will help students understand the multiple ways a text can be interrogated in relation to ethical priorities.

When setting up text profiling tasks, educators will need to determine whether profiling is designed simply to identify a priority – as in Montalt and González Davies' (2007) example, above – or to identify a priority *and* prompt a certain approach to the translation process. A further consideration when setting the task parameters is agency, which may be a more productive way to approach the task than focusing solely on fidelity. Students can set ethical priorities from the translator's perspective, the potential recipient's perspective, or possibly both, while also reflecting on the ethical priorities that underpinned the drafting of the original, if these are accessible. The following examples illustrate what each agential perspective might look like in practice.

2.3.3.1 Original text producer's perspective

For this activity, it is assumed that the patient information leaflet is being produced in England in the context of the National Health Service (NHS) core principles for communication with patients.

Table 2.1 Original text producer's perspective

Genre	Ethical priorities
Patient information leaflet	• **Patient centred** – All clinical communications to patients should centre on their specific care, not internal NHS processes or systems. • **Shared decision-making** – All clinical communications to patients should enable clear, shared decision-making and mechanisms for the patient to provide a response. • **Safety reassurance** – All clinical communications to patients should reinforce that the NHS is safe and is here to care for all patients who need it. • **Deliberate language** – Language should be clear, honest and easy to understand, and tone should be active. Avoid turns of phrase which patients themselves may not identify with – e.g. 'clinically extremely vulnerable' or having 'minor symptoms'. If required, handle compassionately.

Source: Adapted from: www.england.nhs.uk/coronavirus/documents/good-communications-with-patients-core-principles/

50 *Ethics and the translation curriculum (I)*

It may not be possible for students to identify the ethical priorities underpinning a particular document as readily as in the example above. However, the example highlights the importance of students being able to search for evidence of institutional or organisational guidance on communication and employ lateral thinking if none is available.

2.3.3.2 Translator's perspective

Setting priorities here reinforces several competences: a student's knowledge about translation process and extra-linguistic knowledge.

Table 2.2 Translator's perspective

Genre	Ethical priorities
Patient information leaflet	• Ensure terminological accuracy by drawing on relevant (i.e. recent and reputable) sources, and corroborating choices through careful cross-referencing. • Identify and apply (where appropriate) current (target) cultural norms regarding the presentation of instructional information for safe and effective medication, taking into account the need to support patients in understanding the core principles and values of the NHS. • Identify means for people who do not have English as a first language to provide a response in accordance with the principle of shared decision-making.

2.3.3.3 Text recipient's perspective

Note the addition of a third column to prompt translator decision-making.

Table 2.3 Text recipient's perspective

Genre	Ethical priorities	Implications for translator decision-making
Patient information leaflet	• Accessibly written, jargon-free text • Unambiguous, authoritative information that supports safe medication-taking • Opportunity to ask questions • Presentation that is easy to follow	• Identify extent to which source text is accessibly written and the approach to specialised terms. • Identify any potential ambiguity in key messages in translation and how this might be mitigated. • Think about ways in which multilingual communication may be facilitated and advise accordingly. • Presentational issues may already be adequately addressed in the source text; if not, consider adding notes for the client with suggestions when translation is delivered.

Ethics and the translation curriculum (I) 51

There are inevitably limits on this type of activity in terms of the domain and text genre selected, with some requiring a much more comprehensive understanding of the domain. Depending on the learning goals, the text choice for the exercise will therefore need to take account of the degree of exposure to a particular domain on the programme.

2.3.4 Monolingual revision: encouraging students to notice and question

In this final subsection, attention turns to the importance of enhancing reading and research skills through monolingual revision activities as part of sensitisation to the translator's ethical responsibility. The activities focus on "textual wholes" – that is, texts of sufficient length to allow exposure to domain specificity and textual relations (as opposed to the short strings of text found in some translation environments).

Activities on monolingual revision can be introduced at an early phase in the programme of study and involve semi-specialised translated and non-translated texts (around 300 words in length as a guide), but it is recommended that non-translated texts are the initial focus. This is to ensure exposure to the technical aspects of good and ethical copywriting and copy-editing practices in the target language and culture before translation is brought into the learning frame. These activities can be supported through virtual learning environments with modelled answers if class time is limited; however, some measure of the learning derived from the activities will be needed to ensure students can make productive connections to subsequent bilingual translation practice.

A first preparatory stage is to introduce students to the basic techniques of revising and editing, ethical principles of copywriting and copy-editing, resources such as institutional style guidelines, copywriting guidance, and so forth in the target language and culture before they apply knowledge in dedicated tasks (see Hine, 2003, for an example). A twofold approach to knowledge application is suggested. The first task concerns content and students identifying the extent to which a given text meets a copywriting brief (devised by the educator). The second task introduces a range of issues (errors) for students to identify and correct at different levels of complexity and import, not unlike guidelines that might be introduced in post-editing activities (see Chapter 3):

- **Level 1 issues:** spelling (including inconsistencies in the application of certain spelling conventions), use of capital letters, commonly confused words in a language, minor punctuation errors, minor infelicities of language (e.g. grammar, syntax);
- **Level 2 issues:** inconsistencies in register, agency, and verb tense, inappropriate use of domain-specific terminology, minor errors of logic, paragraphing problems;
- **Level 3 issues:** inconsistencies in register, inappropriate use of domain-specific terminology and phraseology, more pronounced errors of logic.

52 *Ethics and the translation curriculum (I)*

Different skills of research and checking are activated at each level. As the level changes, the range of issues broadens and becomes more complex, but there should not be so many as to overwhelm students. Issues from the lowest level could still be present in the higher-level tasks. Educators may provide an indication of the number of issues per category in early iterations of this activity.

Activity

- **Topic:** monolingual revision (in the student's target language) of a patient information leaflet (low-level health issue, e.g. seasonal allergies).
- **Learning aims:** to habituate students to reading for revision purposes; to apply techniques of copy-editing and revision to monolingual texts (translated and, later, non-translated); to facilitate awareness of research processes required to support reasoned justifications for change.
- **Learning outcomes:** by the end of these activities, students will be able to: read for purpose, make and justify decisions in accordance with a brief; engage in domain-specific research (parallel texts, term bases) to check terminological and phraseological accuracy; apply relevant meta-language in the justification of changes.

Task instructions

Task 1 educator input

1 Create a copywriting brief (templates are available online). The brief could be anchored around the findings of a text profiling activity (see Subsection 2.3.3).
2 Select an extract from a publicly available leaflet for patients (e.g. on seasonal allergies), making deliberate adjustments to the text that show different degrees of misalignment with the copywriting brief.

Task 1 guidance for students

You are tasked with reviewing a text that is aimed at residents with limited [insert relevant target language] language proficiency to evaluate the extent to which you think it meets the copywriting brief. You must annotate the file to indicate where and why your think certain changes are recommended in order to fulfil the brief. Remember to support any recommendations for change with a clear rationale; you may also refer to examples of good practice found in your research in the rationale.

Task 2 educator input

Using a similar genre of text, develop three extracts (200–250 words each) for students to review and edit monolingually. Each text should reflect one of the levels below, and they should be issued in sequence to the students.

Task 2 guidance for students

In this suite of three tasks, you will work on texts on a similar topic to Task 1 independently or in groups. For each text, you must identify errors and suggest corrections using the "track changes" and "comments" functions in Word. Be aware that the errors become more complex at each level. Your suggestions for corrections at Levels 2 and 3 must be backed up by relevant domain-specific research.

As a general guide, you can expect issues of spelling, grammar, and punctuation at Level 1; issues of register, terminology, and logic at Level 2; and issues of phraseology and more pronounced issues of logic and terminology at Level 3. There may be more than one suggested solution (for this purpose, use the "comments" function in Word to annotate the text). Also note that issues from Level 1 (such as spelling) may still be present in the higher levels.

Extension: monolingual revision of translated texts

To some extent, the introduction of translated texts for monolingual editing will echo machine translation post-editing tasks; however, in this activity, students will not have access to the source text and will work solely in the monolingual mode. Educators can set up activities based on the levels described above, and incorporate common errors arising in certain language pairs covered by (at least some) students in the group. The goal is to help sensitise students to some of the features of translated text that can impact on the coherence and accuracy of content and tone not present in non-translated texts.

2.4 Ethical competence development through literary translation

2.4.1 Ethics issues in literary translation

Literary translation offers good scope to develop ethical sensitivity and responsibility, not least, as Tymoczko (2014, pp. 24–25) writes, because the cultural domain is "not generally viewed as having immediate geopolitical consequences", making it possible for ideology to be investigated in a "relatively non-controversial manner". There are, of course, cases in which literary translation can offer fertile ground for the examination of different authors' "po-ethics" as they grapple with complex entanglements of geopolitics, religion, social power relations, and national identity, among many others, and the role of the translator in navigating the resulting tensions at the level of the text. For example, Francis Jones (2010) has explored the translation of poetry in the context of conflict in the former Yugoslavia. Other, less widely researched genres are science fiction and especially social commentaries such as Mary Shelley's *Frankenstein* and Jonathan Swift's *Gulliver's Travels* (see Campbell, 2022, for further examples).

Despite offering good potential for ethics-related learning, very little is known about what literary translation programmes actually cover in terms of ethics (Johnston, 2018). Table 2.4 below provides suggested topics and question prompts to support curriculum planning.

Table 2.4 demonstrates that there is scope to develop sensitisation and ethical judgement through activities that place translation in its wider context of production. Translation practice, whether individual or collaborative, can be

Table 2.4 Planning ethics in the literary translation curriculum

Topics	Question prompts for planning
Translator competence	How is competence defined in literary translation and how can it be cultivated in the curriculum? How can students be supported to develop appropriate levels of self-awareness to decide whether they are able to take on a particular literary translation task professionally?
Quality	How does quality assessment in literary translation differ from quality assessment of other text genres? How might students be guided to reflect on the extent to which translators can improve a text?
Translator–author relations	How can students be supported to develop productive and ethical relationships with living authors, or the custodians of authors' estates where such arrangements exist?
Translator–publisher/editor relations	How can students be supported to manage relationships with publishers and editors (e.g. assert preferences in the translation process regarding how to address perceived stereotyping, gender discrimination, the use of inclusive language, etc.)?
Translator–reader relations	Which approaches to teaching stimulate productive thinking about the potential ethical relationship that the reader of the translation will have with the text?
Class, gender, race, voice, and ethnicity	How can students be supported to navigate their own biographies in translation decision-making, and understand the interrelations between these concepts and their textual manifestations?
Codes of ethics	Which codes exist, how are they created, and what pedagogical value do they offer in the literary translation curriculum?
Theoretical perspectives	To what extent is there scope in the curriculum for students to examine themes and concepts such as hybridity and hospitality? Do theories of ethics from moral philosophy have a place in literary translation teaching?

Ethics and the translation curriculum (I) 55

accompanied by supplementary tasks, such as: using the question prompts in Subsection 2.3.1 to support a piece of reflective writing; drafting communications to publishers/authors to navigate thornier ethical questions raised by the translation process; commentaries to justify translation decisions and reflect on the ethical relations between reader and text as the latter moves into a new intercultural space.

Prompts for reflection

- What balance (if any) do you seek to achieve between educator- and student-led text choices for translation purposes?
- Which criteria underpin your choice of texts and to what extent is ethics a criterion in text selection?
- To what extent does your approach to task creation draw attention to ethical dimensions of literary translation from abstract, applied, and professional perspectives?
- To what extent are you and your students able to take account of norms and expectations of the local literary translation market and/or specific publishers in the class's learning?
- Which (theoretical) ideas and perspectives are currently privileged on your programme to support students to confront different kinds of ethical issues arising from the practice and reception of literary translation?

2.4.2 Speaking with and speaking for: debates on experiential knowledge

In writing about the ethics of literary translation, Washbourne (2018) draws attention to the importance of considering "who can speak for another, how translation may speak, and whether translation is a *speaking for* or *speaking with*" (p. 399; original emphasis). These questions have come to prominence in literary translation spheres and translation studies in recent years, but also have resonance beyond literary genres. In what follows, **case-based learning** serves as a foundation for exploring experiential knowledge in translation, agency and the external forces that shape the distribution of translation opportunities, particularly in situations of inequality.

Case studies

1 The Vegetarian[2]

Overview

Deborah Smith translated South Korean novelist Han Kang's award-winning novella *Chaesikjuuija* into English as *The Vegetarian* in 2015, seven years after the original publication of the work. The English translation achieved huge success in terms of copies sold, and both Han and Smith were awarded the

Man Booker International Prize in 2016. At the time of translating the work, Smith had been learning Korean for only three years; she was a Korean studies scholar and a self-taught translator. However, she was able to maintain close contact with the author, who speaks English, and accessed advice from a native Korean language speaker throughout the translation process.

Early reviews of the translation (e.g. Yu, 2017) highlighted what were perceived as serious failings, from mistranslations to over-embellishments. In response, Smith worked closely with the author and publisher to these correct errors in subsequent editions.

This case provides support to debate and examine ethical decision-making during translation, self-assessing competence to take on a particular translation task, the motivations for pitching a translation to a publisher, the ethics of reading, and the ethics of relationship management (with the author, publisher, and audience). Students starting out on their careers are likely to ask many of the same questions that Smith navigated as she worked on this publication, which means it will resonate with their stage of learning. Furthermore, the case can usefully be read in the wider context of Smith's translator development and critical engagement with the literary translation sphere: she went on to found Tilted Axis Press with the express intention of exploring alternatives to phenomena such as language hierarchisation and the commercialisation of literary translation.[3]

The following suite of activities may help to stimulate discussion of the case within the classroom.

1 **Suggested prompts for student discussion** (following an introduction to the case and public debate):

- Which criteria best support an evaluation of Smith's initial decision to pitch the translation to a publisher? To what extent might a consequentialist ethical standpoint support the evaluation?
- Which criteria do you think shape a publisher's decision to go ahead and contract (a self-taught translator in this case)? To what extent is your reasoning influenced by consequentialist and/or virtue ethics (or other ethical theory)?

2 **Translator–audience relations.** Read Smith's response to criticism of her translation, which appeared in the *LA Review of Books* in 2018:

For a first-timer, being bombarded with mistake-listing articles and emails left me pretty shaken. Was it true that I'd betrayed Han Kang's work through negligence or arrogance? Not consciously, because I love her to the point of reverence and think her work is stone-cold genius, but by daring to translate from a language I hadn't yet mastered? It's now four years since I translated *The Vegetarian*, seven since I started learning Korean, and I understand now what I didn't then: that learning a language is not a progression toward "mastery", and that nothing teaches you to translate like actually doing it. I'm glad to have brought the work of a brilliant writer to an international audience, in sufficiently faithful a way for a qualitatively, if not quantitatively, similar reception. Some people tell me I ought to be proud, but to be honest I'm happy to feel conflicted – such an attitude is more useful for those of us in positions of privilege, encouraging us to act responsibly and generously towards texts, authors, and other translators.

(Smith, 2018)

Question: What are the ethical implications for the translator, the translation process, author and audience of the assertion "nothing teaches you to translate like actually doing it"?

In the same interview, Smith reflects on inherent tensions in the translation process:

[I]f source language conventions are transferred just as they are, they will likely be mistaken for authorial idiosyncrasy, or worse, simply bad writing.

(Smith, 2018)

Question: Can you think of any occasions when you have come across this tension in your own literary translation work and/or in translation criticism you have read in literary reviews? Which steps (if any) can/do translators (and/or other relevant agents in the translation production network) take to reconcile this tension?

3 **Translator–author relationship management.** In an earlier interview with the *Guardian*, Smith asserted:

When I began I didn't know what the usual author–translator relationship was, whether you were supposed to get in touch, or even if Kang spoke English. So I just went ahead and translated the whole book, sent it in with a list of questions, and waited.

(Kang and Smith, 2016)

In the same interview, the author, Han Kang, claimed:

I was very happy when it was translated into English because it is my only other language, and reading through Deborah's translation, and her notes and questions, it was fascinating to ponder on the subtleties and possibilities of language.

(Kang and Smith, 2016)

Questions:

- What, if anything, do these two descriptions reveal about the ways in which: i) the translator thought about how to establish an ethical relationship with the author; and ii) the author responded to the translator's correspondence?
- If you were in Smith's position, would you adopt the same approach to establishing translator–author relations? Why? Why not, and what might you do differently?
- How do you think you would react if an author was not interested in responding to your questions or engaging with the translation process?

4 **Insider knowledge.** Compare Smith's account above with Madhu Kaza's reflections on the curation and editing of *Kitchen Table Translation* (Kaza, 2017b):[4]

Kitchen Table Translation extends from [my] personal experience to a greater curiosity about how immigrants, children of immigrants, or people who identify as part of a diaspora might bring a particular set of concerns to the task of translation distinct from the mainstream of literary translation in the United States. When the movement of texts (translation) is linked with the movement of bodies (migration), issues of language and culture necessarily collide with questions about politics, history, race and imperialism – the very contexts of migration and diaspora ...

For me, with all its predicaments, all the violence it may carry on its back, translation is an act of hospitality. Hospitality, conceived not as charity, not as condescension or even merely tolerance. A hospitality that recognizes both the dignity and the difference of the other. In this model, translation is not about assimilation – of the other language or the other body. The impossibility of any particular translation is not a difficulty to be overcome, just as the difference of an immigrant, a refugee, or anyone deemed other is not a difference to be overcome, but rather greeted with care.

(Kaza, 2017a)[5]

Complement Kaza's reflections by reading Nike K. Pokorn and Kasia Koskinen's "The ethics of linguistic hospitality and untranslatability in Derrida and Ricœur" in *The Routledge Handbook of Translation and Ethics* (Pokorn and Koskinen, 2020).

Question: Thinking about the different subject positions occupied by Deborah Smith when she first tackled *The Vegetarian* and Madhu Kaza (and the contributors to *Kitchen Table Translation*), what might you identify as the particular "set of concerns" each brings to the literary translation process and the ethical priorities they generate?

2 The Amanda Gorman case

Overview

Amanda Gorman is an American poet and activist who came to global prominence for her poem *The Hill We Climb*, written for and performed at the inauguration of President Joe Biden on 20 January 2021. The poem, which has since been translated into many different languages by both individual translators and teams of translators, has generated intense debate about representation, experience, and opportunity in (literary) translation. The translation into German, for example, was undertaken by a team of three translators who were specifically tasked with making the political and social significance of the poem clear and avoiding excluding, as far as possible, any marginalised groups. Although the use of gender-neutral language was one strategy considered to support inclusivity, it was eventually rejected by the team (Marshall, 2021).

Particular controversy ensued after the publisher Meulenhoff selected a white person to translate the poem into Dutch. The translator in question, Marieke Lucas Rijneveld – an award-winning author in their own right (Booker International Prize) but not a published translator and, by their own admission, not proficient in English – subsequently withdrew from the project.

Amanda Gorman has never publicly commented on issues concerning the translation of her work.

This case supports teaching and learning in relation to a different set of ethical questions from those raised in the first case study, including: the degree of diversity in the literary translation sphere; the opportunities available to translators from various backgrounds; and the influence of identity politics on translation practice. In pedagogical terms, student learning will be optimised if the Gorman case is used to explore these and other related questions, as opposed to simply debating the perceived "rightness" or "wrongness" of the publisher and/or translator decisions.

A potential stimulus for classroom debate is Susam-Saraeva's (2021) provocation piece and responses to it published in the Taylor and Francis journal *Translation Studies*. Susam-Saraeva poses the question as to whether translators (and interpreters) need to have analogous life experiences (experiential knowledge) to those of source authors or speakers. Her article draws on key concepts of "secondary witnessing" – a reference to Deane-Cox's (2013) work on Holocaust memoirs and testimonies in translation – and "debriefing", which is defined as a process of self-reflexively acknowledging the baggage one brings to a particular situation to prevent it from unduly influencing another's experience of a similar situation.

The published responses to the provocation piece, two of which are discussed here, serve as useful additional supports for students to think through Susam-Saraeva's starting question. Moira Inghilleri's (2021) response draws attention to the potential ethical benefits of collaboration and the importance of fostering shared agency as a means to offset perceived undue emphasis on the individual translator (or interpreter). Inghilleri cites the example of Omid Tofighian's translation of Iranian Kurd Behrouz Boochani's account of detention in an Australian offshore prison, sent via thousands of text messages and published in English as *No Friend but the Mountains* (Picador, 2018).

The second response, by Haidee Kotze and Anna Strowe, draws specifically on the Gorman case. These authors support Susam-Saraeva's call to debate "who *can, may* or *should* translate" and stress the importance of discussing "the structural elements of societies and institutions that facilitate those modalities" (Kotze and Strowe, 2021, p. 351; original emphasis). Their article brings together a series of interconnected questions concerning the way in which a translator's ability to carry out a task is assessed, the extent to which different forms of knowledge are valued, and the way in which translation tasks are allocated, distributed, and recognised (p. 352), all of which, they argue, requires engagement with the external social, economic, political, and institutional forces that shape these decisions.

A classroom activity based on the Gorman case might proceed as follows:

1 Introduce the Gorman case and debates about it within and outside translation studies. (Students might be encouraged to research the case independently and share sources with peers.)
2 Drawing on Kotze and Strowe's (2021) response to the provocation piece, students discuss the following statement in small groups:

[T]he suggestion that there is knowledge that cannot be acquired intellectually through research, but must be experienced or embodied, may be viewed as an affront.
(Kotze and Strowe, 2021, p. 351)

3 Students then discuss another of Kotze and Strowe's assertions from the perspectives of the Gorman case and their own local context of translation:

Representativeness needs to be considered as much as representation, and the question who *should* translate needs to be seen not only as a reflection of the ethical imperatives of responsibility towards the text, author, client, and audience at the local level, but also as a reflection of the ethical imperative to establish a more equitable and representative translation and publishing industry, in contexts characterised by inequality.
(Kotze and Strowe, 2021, p. 353; original emphasis)

The group will need to become acquainted with the local context in terms of potential structural inequalities, so the discussion might usefully involve a wider group of stakeholders invited into the classroom or as part of an extra-curricular event.

4 Students could complement their in-class discussion with further reading of different translator accounts in which questions of experiential knowledge are prominent. Examples include works by Carolyn Shread (on translating the Haitian author Marie Vieu-Chauvret)[6] and Carol Maier (Shread, 2011; Maier, 2006).
5 Finally, the students undertake an individual translation task.

Activity

1 Each student selects an extract (poetry or prose) authored by a living person. The person should be someone whose life experience and identity are deemed central to their work but whose experience is very different from the student's. The student then produces a translation independently.
2 Students present their translations to their peers and talk through selected decision-making points and the extent to which their lack of shared experience impacted on the translation process, including how they mitigated/accommodated this. This activity may be complemented by reading Määttä, Puumala, & Ylikomi (2021), who explore how a lack of shared experience between an interpreter and an asylum client can create vulnerability in the asylum procedure.
3 Students also reflect on what they believe would be gained in the process through active collaboration with the author and how they might approach the author of their selected extract to set up a dialogue for creative exchange and developing shared agency.
4 Finally, students consider a situation in which they pitch their translated extract to a publisher but are turned down on the grounds that they are not perceived as appropriate for the task. How would they feel? What counter-arguments might they make in response?

2.4.3 Translators as (secondary) witnesses

The concept of the translator as "secondary witness" was mentioned above in the context of Susam-Saraeva's (2021) provocation piece on experiential knowledge, in which it was attributed in particular Sharon Deane-Cox's work on the translation of memoirs and accounts of the Holocaust (e.g. Deane-Cox, 2013). Many texts on this topic may fall outside of the literary genre yet still have strong literary merits, and therefore usefully extend debate about ethical translation practice.

Exploring the interface between translation and Holocaust studies, Peter Davies (2014) explains how what is commonly termed the "witness text" raises thorny questions of ethics and representation. He expresses some concern that discussions about which methods should apply to the treatment of such texts in translation risk narrowing swiftly to matters of proscription and prohibition (p. 206). As a counterpoint, he highlights fidelity as a central ethical concern in this type of text, which can take multiple forms: the person of the witness; the text as it stands; the ethical concerns that motivate the translation; the demands of historical accuracy; and the needs of the victim community more generally (p. 211).

To complement Davies's perspective, preparation for working with witness texts can be supported by Deane-Cox's (2014) examination of Alison Landsberg's (2004) concept of "prosthetic memory", which Landsberg describes as a memory that "emerges at the interface between a person and a historical narrative about the past" (p. 2), the experiential conduits of which are things like films, museum exhibits, and audio guides. Reprising the concept of "wayfaring" and the kinaesthetic experience of engaging with a text (see Chapter 1), educators can take inspiration from Deane-Cox's application of Landsberg's concept to the study of translation practices at the Oradour-sur-Glane visitor and interpretation centre in Limoges, France.[7] In addition to reflecting on the challenges certain witness texts pose for translators, students can be encouraged to reflect on the impact of different media on the reception of translation in different spaces of memory, and the extent to which they help people to have "a more empathic and ethical response to ... events encountered by another" (Deane-Cox, 2014, p. 272).

Activity

Voice in witness texts and the task of the translator

Task

1. Educators or students identify one "witness text" – for example, a published memoir or a contribution to a collection of accounts – either in book form or from an online source. The text may relate to any kind of event. (NB: Choosing a text raises a number of ethical issues. For example, the act of searching, and scanning texts for extracts, may provoke a strong emotional reaction, so it can be a useful to allow space to address this process as a group. An educator may have a text ready to use with students that is fairly conservative in terms of the detail provided to minimise the risk of emotional trauma. However, the group discussion may lead students to want to explore their own ideas. They could be given the option of working with the educator-selected text or finding their own, as long as appropriate support is provided.)
2. Drawing on Davies (2014), students examine their chosen text independently and come together to discuss how they might tackle the translation, supported by the following question prompts. (The text for this activity could range from a single page to a whole chapter, and students might opt to create a hypothetical brief to shape their thinking.)

Ethics and the translation curriculum (I) 63

- Does the text contain any historical or grammatical inaccuracies? If so, would you seek to correct them in the translation?
- Do you think that your translation should seek to preserve the literary quality of the text or do you think that it is ethically more important to prioritise the use value of the text as a potential documentary source? (NB: To address this question, it may be helpful to consider a hypothetical brief.)
- Can you identify specific aspects of the text that represent its "truth" and may pose particular translation challenges?
- How might you establish a hierarchy of fidelity in planning the translation (e.g. fidelity to the author, the text, the audience, the translator, and the wider victim community)?
- How does the text shape your understanding of yourself as a (secondary) witness and your relationship to the person who wrote the account?
- To what extent does the degree of distance in terms of time, geography and even age of the witness impact on your thinking as a translator?

3   As an extension activity, students could be tasked with translating an extract from their text (approximately 500 words) and presenting it in accordance with the brief (e.g. a recording could be made if it were to feature in a museum audio guide). A second classroom discussion could then be held in which they reflect individually on the extent to which their initial reflections influenced their approach to the translation and any additional considerations that arose in the process.

2.4.4 Multi- and poly-lingual literary texts to support ethical sensitisation

Multi- and poly-lingual texts offer valuable sources of material for (literary) translator ethics education. Due to the often radically disruptive impact on reading and sense-making, they serve as a useful point of entry for educators seeking to develop ethical sensitivity through practices of observing, noticing, and questioning – skills that are transferable to other text genres. Educators can select examples from a wide range of cultural locations, literary movements, and historical periods; examples may also reflect different varieties of the same language used within a single work for particular aesthetic, narrative, or political effect, and as a display of a certain "writerly ethics" (Alexandrova, 2020). The examples below draw on three very different literary texts to illustrate the range of discussion points multi- and poly-lingual texts can generate: James Joyce's *Finnegans Wake* (1939), S. Qiouyi Lu's short story "Mother Tongues" (2018), and Monica Ali's novel *Brick Lane* (2004).

Finnegans Wake, written within the modernist tradition of multilingual writing that was prominent in the early part of the twentieth century, is not an obvious choice for the translation classroom due to the vast complexity of its narrative layers, cultural associations, and inter- and intra-textual references (Alexandrova, 2020). It is recommended here not as a "start text" (Pym, 2020) for translation practice *per se*, but rather as a means to sensitise students (specifically graduate students) to the ethical questions arising from the multilingual position and positioning of the writer, reading as a bodily activity, and its ethical implications.

Multilingualism takes many forms in *Finnegans Wake*, from what might be described as baby talk to borrowings (e.g. from Italian) that are distorted through a character's mispronunciation, giving the work the character of what Alexandrova (2020, p. 208) describes as a "living organism". Even the text's so-called "majority language" does not always exhibit the level of stability or boundedness students might expect from a source language, presenting an ethical injunction to the reader (translator) to read differently, move beyond binarist thinking in the translation process, and accept the discomfort that some texts are more "ungovernable" than others (but not untranslatable, as Alexandrova observes).

Students could explore short extracts of the text that illuminate the issues mentioned above as well as accounts by various translators and examples of translation criticism to understand the spectrum of ethical responses generated by this hugely complex text, and reflect on the value of translation criticism more broadly for developing translation practice. Alexandrova, for instance, highlights the approach adopted by translators Robbert-Jan Henkes and Erik Bindervoet for a Dutch edition of *Finnegans Wake* in 2002. Drawing on archival evidence of Joyce's writing process, the two translators developed a means of domesticating the multilingualism and poly-referentiality of the text "without assimilating it into an oppressive monolingual regime" (Alexandrova, 2020, p. 138). Archives may not be available to students during their studies, but exposure to their potential support for decision-making sheds new light on what it means to be thorough.

Turning to examine the potential of more contemporary examples of multilingual fiction for developing ethical sensitivity, Pym (2020) reminds us that approaches to ethics that draw on the philosophical dialogue tradition and foreground encounters with an Other reflect social and historical contexts that are very different from many modern-day situations in which the Other is no longer separate (or separated) from the cultural sites of production. These situations find ample expression across the international literary sphere, which abounds in multilingual fictionalisations of authors' migrant experiences. These are examples of what Rebecca Walkowitz (2015) terms the "born-translated" novel: that is, a work in which translation is a condition of its production.

The act of translating multilingual fiction positions the student at the heart of the ethical encounter as a learning experience that may enhance the moral self through engaging the moral imagination while also developing certain translation competences. Kaza's (2017a) assertion that "The impossibility of any particular translation is not a difficulty to be overcome, just as the difference of an immigrant, a refugee, or anyone deemed other is not a difference to be overcome, but rather greeted with care" may prompt students to consider what this might look like when enacted in a textual response, and how this injunction can be read, for example, alongside Venuti's (1998) ethics of difference.

S. Qiouyi Lu's "Mother Tongues" is one example.[8] The story focuses on an attempt by the central character, Jiawen Liu, who has immigrated to the United States, to monetise her second language (English) to help pay for her daughter's college education. The work is written primarily in English but includes sections in Mandarin and Cantonese Chinese – languages that operate as a site of intergenerational struggle between Jiawen Liu and her mother. If the text is used as the basis for classroom activities and discussion, students can also explore the author's personal website to learn more about their motivation to write and reflect on how this could inform translator decision-making in this case.

Finally, Monica Ali's *Brick Lane* tells the story of a Bangladeshi woman's journey to London aged 18 for an arranged marriage and her subsequent life in the city. The novel is written solely in English, with readers invited to imagine conversations in Bengali through this "novelistic lingua franca" (Cormack, 2006). Hence, the central character's struggle to learn English is depicted entirely in that language. Cormack (2006) highlights the narrative device of letters written by the main character's sister in Bangladesh and the fact that the reader does not know whether these are "inept attempts at writing in English" or "a free translation from illiterate Bengali". The work therefore supports productive reflection on the implications of its monolingualism in translation for the reader's ethical relationship to the text.

2.4.5 Ethical topics in translating for children

Despite presenting particular vulnerabilities as a social group, in terms of translation practice, translating children's fiction has much in common with translating for adults. Ethical decisions taken on the basis of subjective assumptions, as opposed to empirical evidence, can undermine author–reader relations, skewing the reception of a particular author's work in its new cultural context. One example concerns misplaced assumptions about the need for simplification, based on the view that children have "only limited capacity to understand texts" (Stolze, 2003, p. 209). Simplification diminishes exposure to features that may be difficult, foreign, challenging, or mysterious (Stolze, 2003). Empirical research, albeit on a small sample, has shown that children (e.g. aged 10–11) are able to assess the implications of some translation strategies on a more abstract level and are not discouraged by unfamiliar (foreign) words (Joosen, 2019).

> **Activity**
>
> *Comparative analysis of translated children's fiction*
>
> Task
>
> As a preliminary task to translation, students can be encouraged to investigate contemporary examples of children's fiction in translation for a particular age group.
>
> 1. Students select up to three works in translation, all aimed at the same age group but by different authors and translators.
> 2. Prior to starting the analysis, students explore resources that provide information on general reading levels for their chosen age group. One such resource is the Oxford Levels: https://home.oxfordowl.co.uk/reading/reading-schemes-oxford-levels/oxford-reading-tree-levels%20/.
> 3. Students analyse each work, identifying the general translation strategies used by the translators in each case, the range of ethical questions (e.g. decisions to simplify, exposure to foreignness, stereotyping, moralising) posed by the source text, and the translator's response.
> 4. Students present their findings to their peers in small groups and discuss what (if anything) the activity has taught them about how they view their moral responsibility as a translator for children and which factors are likely to influence their translation decision-making in the future.
> 5. Extension activity: students can repeat the activity by exploring more morally challenging texts written for children (e.g. about experiences of conflict, loneliness, death, relationships, race, etc.).

It is not uncommon for some children's literature to incorporate a didactic and/or moralising element or perspective that may be more or less pronounced in different country contexts (e.g. see Mdallel (2003) for a discussion of didacticism in children's literature in the Arab world). The diachronic study of moralising elements in children's fiction is one way to draw attention to changing social conventions and their implications for translator decision-making.

> **Activity**
>
> *Retranslation and didacticism*
>
> Task
>
> 1. Educators (or students) identify a piece of children's literature in translation that is well known within the literary canon of a

> relevant country context and language combination, and one that has been translated several times.
> 2 Several passages from the translations are selected for comparison, with a focus on the pedagogies at play in each, based on Stolze's (2003) point that pedagogics is often an overall goal of text production when translating for children.
> 3 Students explore the observed translation choices and degree of pedagogic manipulation before discussing which approach they would take if they were tasked with translating again for audiences today.

As a support for decision-making in translation, students may also find it helpful to develop their thinking by drawing on publications in which writers and translators discuss their work and relationships with other stakeholders in the process. As an example, the rest of this subsection focuses on three extracts from Arthur Malcolm Dixon's (2023) interview with the bilingual poet, author, and literary translator Lawrence Schimel, who discusses the translation of his own fiction into various languages and touches upon some of the (ethical) issues raised by various translators.[9] The first extract concerns the translation of a rhyming story for children that Schimel wrote in Spanish:

> For a long while the biggest objection to the books was the margarine; I hadn't thought twice about rhyming "margarina" with "cocina" in Spanish, especially as both my husband and I are dairy-free. But some of the editors had moral objections (for instance, in Switzerland, where it was a matter of national pride for it to be butter instead of margarine) and some translators asked if they could change it to butter because margarine is so polysyllabic and didn't fit the meter or the rhyme well. In Israel, to avoid issues of kosher dietary laws (and because margarine in Israel comes in bars, not round containers), we changed it to hummus and actually named the cat Hummus, too, which worked out quite nicely.
> (Lawrence Schimel quoted in Dixon, 2023)

Schimel's interview is an example of a publicly available resource through which students can access first-hand accounts of author interactions with translators. For instance, educators can work such interactions into a sample brief to support a translation task. They can also serve as a means for students to interrogate some of the meta-language encountered in the TI literature and compare it to its use by a practitioner. For instance, Schimel's reference to being "faithful to the spirit of the work" in the first of the two extracts below is an interesting angle through which to explore concepts of fidelity and loyalty, compared with the editorial position-taking in relation to a nation's dairy industry and dietary laws in the earlier passage. As with the Smith case study above, both of the following extracts may help students to understand the basis on which an ethical relationship with an author can be established:

[S]ince I both write in multiple languages and translate primarily from and into two, I fully understand and appreciate how flexible one needs to be sometimes – or how many liberties a translator may need to take – in order to be faithful to the spirit of the work ...

I've regularly talked with a lot of the translators, and helped supply them with some of the various existing versions, in case those might help aid or inspire solutions for their languages. I tell the translators to take whatever liberties they need to recreate the books, which should be fun, rhyming adventures. Since they can't change or contradict the art, they can be as free as they need to with the plot, if doing so helps them be more faithful to the text, if that makes sense.

(Lawrence Schimel quoted in Dixon, 2023)

Activity

Simulating translator–client negotiations

Tasks

1 A previous client, a language services provider, has contacted you to translate a work of fiction aimed at children aged between five and seven. The text is accompanied by lots of images that you feel reinforce unhelpful stereotypes, some of which are also reflected in the text itself. Draft an email to the client setting out your concerns and your suggested changes.

2 In 2023, the publisher Puffin announced that it had made a number of edits to works of fiction for children by the British author Road Dahl (1916–1990) in order to remove language and references it deemed offensive and/or inappropriate. For example, two historical figures with a reputation for promoting racist views were expunged from *Matilda*.

Original version:

> She went on olden-day sailing ships with Joseph Conrad. She went to Africa with Ernest Hemingway and to India with Rudyard Kipling.

Edited version:

> She went to nineteenth-century estates with Jane Austen. She went to Africa with Ernest Hemingway and California with John Steinbeck.

Imagine that you have been contacted by a publisher who wishes to commission translations of several of Dahl's works. In small groups:

- Discuss the *Matilda* edit in relation to the target language and culture into which you would be working. What (if any) are the implications of the changes for the target culture audience in terms of how they might be received compared to the original references?
- Consider how you would approach negotiations with the publisher regarding which version of the works (original or edited) you think should be used as the basis for the translation.

2.4.6 Teaching codes of ethics in the (literary) translation curriculum

Anecdotal evidence suggests that, within the TI curriculum, many students' first encounter with ethics is through the theoretical prism of deontology and the textual artefact of a code of ethics. While this plays an important role in sensitising students to expected professional behaviours and the source(s) of professional authority, if the topic is positioned towards the end of a programme of study, it can lead to students viewing ethics as relevant only as they are about to embark on their professional careers.

As with all planning for teaching and learning, when codes of ethics are introduced to the curriculum, educators need to be clear as to what kind(s) of knowledge they are seeking students to privilege. For instance, are codes used with the aim of supporting a critique of deontology as it is presented in various moral philosophical accounts, or evaluating others' translation decisions drawing on the provisions of a code to determine adherence or breaches, or something else?

A phased approach in which codes are examined in their own right prior to their application in the evaluation of a piece of translation might be viewed as logical. However, another set of questions should be asked:

- What would an educator expect a student to be able to do with the knowledge they have learned from such an exercise?
- Is it reasonable to expect students to check all subsequent translation tasks against a particular code prior to submission?
- How does the ethical knowledge developed through this approach to learning fit with translator/translation ethics discussed in the curriculum from a non-deontological perspective?

Pre-set cases, such as those discussed earlier in this chapter, can serve several pedagogical purposes and support different skills development. Case design – discussed in more detail in Chapter 4 – is important since cases that are highly decontextualised or in which ethical issues are always predetermined in advance by educators can limit learning; decontextualised cases in particular can encourage students to think that there is a single "right" answer, diminishing the scope for discussion of "how a person came to arrive in a set of circumstances", which is central to narrative approaches to ethics (see Chapter 1).

If time allows, encouraging students to investigate the range of codes available in the local translation market (generalist and specialist), who created them, how often and how they are revised will provide a sense of where the deontological authority lies in the translation community they will enter on graduation. Asking students to create a code from scratch can also be an effective means to engage them with the conceptual, professional, and contextual imperatives that shape codes and think about their overall purpose and function. Lewis's (2019) study of literary translators' perceptions of Professional Translation Association codes sheds important light on different potential hierarchies at play in decision-making and the implications for ethical responsibility; it inspires the prompts for analysis in the following activity.

Activity

Analysing codes of ethics for literary translators

Task

1. Students gather examples of different professional (literary) translation associations' codes of ethics.
2. First-stage analysis: general comparison of the codes in terms of layout, scope, language, and purpose.
3. Second-stage analysis. For each code:

    - Identify the way in which the professional translator association in question articulates hierarchies of loyalty to publisher, audience, and author in the code.
    - If the publisher, as the "client", is positioned as the principal focus of translator loyalty within a service-oriented ethical framework, what implications might this have for translators seeking to privilege representational models that emphasise author and audience? In other words, what is the deontological force of the hierarchy presented in the code?
    - Are there any clauses in the code for which you think exceptions may be made?
    - Does the code take account of the ethical issues arising at different phases of the translation process (e.g. initial draft, redrafting, etc.)? Are translators clear on their level of ethical responsibility in later phases of the process? (NB: Think about publisher marketability decisions and how these may conflict with a translator's decision-making.)
    - Does the code assign ethical responsibility for the translated product to the translator or is it distributed across various agents, such as editors and publishers?
    - Which aspects of the code do you think would benefit from review? For what reason?
    - To what extent do the provisions of this code overlap or diverge from a code that you have drafted from scratch prior to this exercise?

2.5 Ethical competence development through commercial translation

This section draws on translation in commercial contexts to explore approaches to sensitisation and ethical judgement through comparative analysis and experiential learning with an emphasis on collaborative learning tasks.

2.5.1 Scoping ethics in the curriculum

Commercial translation encompasses a broad range of situations, modalities, and text genres – from advertising materials to patent translation and multilingual customer online chat – so it is likely to be a major component in a translator's portfolio over a professional translation career, especially for freelancers. Although not all programmes include commercial translation as a stand-alone unit of learning, many incorporate at least some exposure to topics in this subfield from a practice and/or research perspective. This domain opens up myriad ethical questions about the role of translation in globalisation, sustaining hegemonies and inequalities, and perpetuating harms, as well as topics such as the potential for the translation of user-generated content to challenge or renegotiate power relations in transnational commercial spheres.

A significant focus of commercial translation teaching will be on communications designed to build and sustain a commercial relationship with individuals and groups, and the ethical implications of decisions taken by translators and a wide network of other agents. The words "text" and "relationship", however, can take on very different forms in the commercial world, particularly in online environments (hashtags and hyperlinked content are two examples), and present ethical challenges not typically encountered in other translation situations.

Some exposure to the porousness of online social media environments, their (visual) grammar and interactivity, will be of value to students who may be assigned, for instance, to curate, translate, and monitor online social media accounts for commercial enterprises; however, a strong multimodal dimension to teaching and practice will be required for the ethical implications to be addressed. Further, the increasing appeal to transcreation in the commercial sphere is likely to feature significantly in teaching and learning, especially on more professionally oriented and practice-focused programmes of study; however, the creative freedom entailed by the activity also has ethical implications. Both of these topics are developed in the suggested activities in this section.

Unfortunately, the lack of academic research on commercial translation generally, and ethical matters in commercial translation specifically, means that educators have few points of reference to plan their teaching other than their own experience, where relevant (notwithstanding the fairly large body of research on translation in tourism and advertising). In one of the few publications to address the topic of ethics in commercial translation directly, Feng and Yang (2018) focus on the translation of brands and the names of commercial organisations and materials into Chinese. Their discussion is couched against a regulatory shift according to which all overseas organisations need to observe a strict phonetic translation of the original name, so that all organisations are placed on a level playing field. This draws attention to the importance of contextual awareness in fostering ethical responsibility that goes beyond developing effective research skills, as is illustrated below through a focus on localisation and transcreation.

2.5.2 Localisation

This subsection examines the potential for the study and practice of website localisation to enhance sensitisation and ethical judgement. Web localisation is understood broadly as a process of "[adapting] digital content on the web and through mobile applications or software applications to meet the cultural, linguistic and legal and other requirements of a target market where it will be deployed" (Benmamoun, Alhor, Ascencio, and Sim, 2020, p. 216), and operates on a spectrum from standardised to full cultural adaptation. Here, the focus is on digital content. Nguyen (2021) identifies five main approaches across this spectrum:

- **standardised** – a monolingual site that is used by a company for all countries;
- **semi-localised** – a site where some elements are translated, mainly to facilitate online shopping;
- **localised** – a translated site is created for each country in which a company seeks to promote its presence, and most content pages are also localised;
- **highly localised** – content and structure are localised, and some companies may also use a country-specific URL; and
- **culturally adapted** – users in the target locale are provided with a fully immersive experience; site content and structure will take account of highly specific phenomena, such as symbolism and perception.

Guided comparative website analysis is recommended for sensitising students to ethical issues such as representation (of local values, approaches to otherness and voice) and user experience (including unintended harms) prior to undertaking more hands-on localisation activities.

Activity

Comparative analysis of localised websites

Task

Working independently or in small groups:

1   Choose one or two sectors as a focus and select criteria for identifying a number of websites (six–eight) for analysis, such as: the scale of commercial operation (large multinational, small/medium-sized enterprise), and geographical coverage (companies operating in one region, e.g. Asia-Pacific, or a region within a single country, e.g. Andalucía in Spain).

2   Once a small sample of sites has been selected, the analysis can take several directions. For example, students may reflect on:
    • the language ideology at play in a particular corporate entity's approach to localisation, particularly if different variations of one language are present within a single country context (e.g. French and Maghrebin French in Metropolitan France);
    • the coherence of site visitor's reading experience, a sense of the extent to which a particular sector invests in appropriate language support in developing websites (e.g. comparing those that include only a translation widget with those that invest in more sophisticated localisation strategies); and
    • corporate attitudes to otherness and intercultural encounters evidenced through localisation practices.

3   Example:
    Sector: higher education. Analysis of a selection of (private/public) university websites that have been localised (not necessarily to the same extent) as part of international student recruitment initiatives.

    Suggested topics for analysis: extent of localisation on the site; quality of target language copy (evidence of revision?) as a reflection of the level of care these entities give to translation practice as part of maintaining their public face and reputation; ethical issues for prospective students (accuracy of information, extent to which foreign students can have confidence that academic and non-academic services will meet their needs).

    Suggested approaches to analysis: risk (e.g. of partial localisation); consequences (for students of unclear information); accountability (opportunities for site visitors to interact in their own language).

4   Extension activity: the exercise is repeated for social enterprises (non-profits). There is limited academic research on the ways in which social enterprises engage with web localisation, but there is some evidence to suggest that they are starting to appreciate the benefits of a planned strategy (Benmamoun et al., 2020). Web localisation for social enterprises presents an interesting context for translation teaching and learning due to the differences in funding structures and barriers to growth, some of which may be values-based when compared to for-profit entities (Benmamoun et al., 2020).

5   Suggested post-activity reflection prompts:
    • Which ethical issues in localisation are you likely to have overlooked before completing this exercise?
    • What have you learned about the ethical issues in localisation specific to the sector(s) and websites you have studied?

- What (if anything) has this exercise helped you to understand about the impact of different ideologies, attitudes, and translation practices on for-profit and not-for-profit relationships with potential audiences and consumers?
- What sort of advice might you now give to the site owners in your sample on how to improve their approach?

2.5.3 Hashtags in translation

The translation of hashtags may seem an unusual area of focus within commercial translation teaching and learning, as it is not a task in which professional translators regularly engage. Yet, it offers a level of complexity that supports ethics sensitisation and judgement in commercial translation situations, and even beyond, in relation to empathy, transparency, critical engagement with questions of coherence (i.e. of readers' and users' experiences), operation of monolingual norms, and accessibility.

Hashtags have been described as technologies for meaning-making (Zappavigna, 2018), often emerging from "folkonomy" and developed by users themselves, but corporations also create their own (Laestadius and Wahl, 2017). As a resource, they are multifunctional, fulfilling a technical purpose as meta-data and performing an indexing function, while also serving as a semiotic resource. This multifunctionality leads Desjardins (2017, p. 52) to "new ways of thinking about equivalence", which also has ethical implications. She writes:

> Translating a hashtag is not just a matter of translating only the signifier or only the signified (or even the sign as a whole), it is a matter of understanding why specific hashtags are chosen over others and how they associate seemingly disparate [user-generated content].
>
> (Desjardins, 2017, p. 49)

Drawing on examples of hashtag creation and usage following the election of Donald Trump in 2016, Zappavigna (2018, p. 30) shows how hashtags perform various types of meaning, such as indicating the semantic domain (#Trump), linking a post to a meme (#TinyTrump), reappropriating a political slogan (#Maga), and making meta-comments. They vary in their positioning within a post (e.g. initial, integrated, or culminative) and their organisation serves to attract attention in different ways (e.g. to be more visible in users' streams), which can be important when the goal is to achieve some type influence. In some commercial examples, multilingual captioning in a post is accompanied by a hashtag in English, which Desjardins (2017) describes as evidence of a clear international strategy.

The translation of hashtags demands cognisance of a wide range of contextual factors, requiring a different kind of research from that which is commonly undertaken for other translation tasks. It also demands knowledge of particularised (ethical) reading practices, digital literacies, and visual grammars.

Desjardins (2017), for instance, highlights the importance of taking account of indexing practices and topic popularity in the translation process. She further stresses that a translated hashtag that does not have the equivalent reach of the source for the target audience (e.g. because it embeds a post in a contrasting set of posts) may have significant commercial consequences. The dynamic nature of the hyperlinked text of the hashtag also creates additional issues for translators to address. Drawing on the example of Instagram, Desjardins (2017) highlights the problem of disconnect between some hashtags and the linked content, which may be unrelated.

Awareness of cultural difference in hashtag use also forms an important part of translator research and ethical sensitisation. As an example, using Hofestede's cultural dimensions framework, Sheldon, Herzfeldt, and Rauschnabel (2020) suggest that hashtag use in the United States, which tends towards individualism, is generally oriented towards a documenting function, whereas there is a greater tendency to the non-functional use of hashtags (e.g. the "inspirational hashtag") in countries with more prominent collectivist values. However, this very broad-brush assessment may mask certain realities on the ground. Students should therefore be encouraged to explore the range of cultural perspectives and experiences of communities at a more granular level, if possible.

In teaching and learning terms, students need to build knowledge of the hashtag as one part of the intercultural encounter, and develop greater empathy with users' movements through social media environments and the ways in which they use hashtags to engage with and shape them. In short, a new ethics of reading is required. A starting point could be to ask students to explore:

- the way in which hashtags are used to explore a particular topic in different cultures and languages (on one platform or across several platforms, including some in different country contexts, if possible);
- the sort of information a particular type of hashtag returns (evaluative or factual, or other);
- the way in which different clusters of hashtags are used by different user types (including commercial entities);
- the configuration of hashtags in posts with a commercial focus or influence; and
- the extent to which corporate-created hashtags for particular commercial campaigns are adapted by users.

Educators could then ask students to translate a set of hashtags drawn from a variety of contexts and campaigns, including commercial ones. Students share their ideas and rationales before researching online to see whether the translations are already in use and the contexts in which they are being used. This will sensitise them to the prospect that their translation choices may not achieve the desired level of reach or indeed that they link to content and posts that deviate from the source reference in ways that may be damaging (e.g. to image, reputation, truth, etc.). These preparatory activities lead to tasks that encourage students to apply their knowledge in a hypothetical situation in which the goal is to advise different types of entity (e.g. for-profit and social enterprise) on a strategy for hashtag translation/multilingual content for a particular campaign. Two examples are provided below.

Activity

Scenario 1

A commercial company that is new to the market wishes to promote a sustainable fashion campaign on social media to appeal to potential customers in different countries. The company hopes to achieve several goals through the use of hashtags: raise brand awareness across languages and cultures; promote a new line of products; foster debate about social change in the fashion industry; and promote ethical values of production internationally.

Task

Students ideally work in multilingual/multicultural groups. The goal is to provide a short report to the company on potential strategies and platforms that should achieve the desired level of reach and engagement in the targeted countries. The task involves copywriting in the source language of the group (i.e. creation of hashtags for translation) and consideration of these creations for translation purposes. This can be broken down into four sub-tasks.

SUB-TASK 1: FINDING OUT WHAT WORKS

Investigate and evaluate examples of similar campaigns on several social media platforms (to include corporate posts, use of hashtags, degree of multilingualism in a single post, user-generated posts promoting the concept and reusing/creating new hashtags, and popularity of certain hashtags compared to others).

SUB-TASK 2: EXPLORE OPTIONS FOR SOCIAL MEDIA PLATFORMS AND STRATEGIES ACROSS PLATFORMS

As above, this involves researching similar campaigns across several platforms.

SUB-TASK 3: ENCOURAGE USER-GENERATED CONTENT BASED ON THE COMMERCIAL ENTITY'S HASHTAG STRATEGY

As above, students investigate examples of user-generated content, patterns, and trends in other campaigns.

SUB-TASK 4: ENCOURAGE INTERCULTURAL EXCHANGE TO DEVELOP AN INTERNATIONAL COMMUNITY OF USERS

As above, students explore how international communities of users develop and the strategies that prompt the highest levels of engagement.

Scenario 2

A non-profit organisation wishes to launch a public health campaign. In determining the best type of campaign, students may take inspiration from UN awareness days or other high-profile campaigns (e.g. Movember, Stoptober).

2.5.4 Transcreation

Debates in translation studies in which transcreation was considered a mere rebranding exercise have given way to a more service-oriented outlook, in which the translator assumes a more prominent co-authoring role (Katan, 2021). Although some connection is observed with the discourse of localisation and translation, Pedersen (2014) asserts that transcreation is distinguished from this domain as a service relating to the production of persuasive texts specifically in the advertising and marketing sectors, with many transcreators coming from copy-editing as opposed to translation backgrounds (Katan, 2021).

Transcreation applies to two different conditions: the creation of new copy based on a brief in which no translation is involved; and the creation of copy based on a source text, part of which may be translated or adapted, with the incorporation of new text elements (Morón and Calvo, 2018). In translational terms, it offers a high degree of scope for innovation and individual input, placing the translator at the freer end of the "literal–free cline" (Gaballo, 2012). One focus of student learning will be to reach an understanding that such creative freedom is bounded by commercial and ethical imperatives.

Although not couched in terms of ethics education, Morón and Calvo's (2018) report on a simulated project (TeCreaTe) with final-year undergraduate students at the Universidad Pablo de Olavide (UPO) in Seville, Spain, offers excellent potential for developing ethical judgement and responsibility through collaborative learning. Over an eight-week period, the students were able to experience more than one role (translator/transcreator, reviser, and project manager) in assignments requiring transcreation where a source text was presented under one of two conditions: i) translate from scratch with a brief; or ii) review and improve on a low-quality source text with a brief. A second activity involved no source text and a brief to produce copy from scratch. Finally, students were required to identify realia and culturally bound variables in a text before discussing how they might handle these in a client report.

The simulated project focused on the fashion industry and specifically on campaigns launched by Topshop and Primark. The texts were approximately 650 words in length and included a range of text types, such as slogans and hashtags. Student work was assessed on the basis of the extent to which the work met the specifications of the brief and the spirit of the brand and campaign, the overall consistency of the transcreation decisions, and the extent to which marketing and trading policies may be compromised by certain decisions.

The educators in this case were struck by the difficulty many students experienced in understanding and accommodating the constraints imposed by the transcreation brief, despite the preparatory training they received. (There is an interesting parallel here with post-editing guidelines and student performance, discussed in Chapter 3.) Elements such as corporate identity and brand, and the nature and spirit of the fashion collections in the campaigns were often not taken into account as anticipated. This was indicated through the high number of substitution strategies employed over approaches such as explicitation and explanation or omission. Furthermore, decisions were often implemented without communicating with the "clients" (the instructors in this case). The educators sought to mitigate some of these issues by inviting students to a round-table discussion on transcreation and international copywriting with industry experts and freelance transcreators, and providing relevant supporting documentation ahead of the assignment.

It appears that students found it difficult to absorb commercial and business-related knowledge and developing international copywriting literacies in this front-loaded approach, whereas they displayed more confidence in linguistic aspects of the project, which is consistent with experiences reported in other research (e.g. Wakabayashi, 2003). In addition, they may have experienced difficulties in the ethical nature of relationships with the instructors (who played the role of hypothetical clients), deciding not to engage due to fears of appearing insufficiently independent.

Unfortunately, we do not know whether the decision to put more resources into the activity and involve experts led to any improvements. The lack of student exposure to commercial practices at that point in their lives means that it is very difficult to enact prospective learning based on such a highly situated activity. The relevant external points of reference are not in place and it is difficult to "wayfare" a path through. Therefore, an increase in scaffolding for the various components may be necessary, and students could be encouraged to submit short interim reports (either written or video presentations) for formative feedback. Teaching input could be adjusted at these points. Such reports, which could be couched explicitly in terms of ethical competence development, would enable students to reflect on the maturity of their "ethical prototype development" for the various technical and relational aspects of the task.

Student prompts for interim report-writing

- **Language:** provide one or two examples of terminological and phraseological research, and outline your group's approach to revising and checking supported by reference to relevant resources.

- **Meta-language:** pay attention to the language used to describe translation problems in your report and agree as a group on the application of concepts and ideas derived from different theories of translation.
- **Society and culture:** provide one or two examples of transcreative solutions proposed in the project so far and justify your approach, drawing on your research and knowledge of relevant societal and cultural norms and practices.
- **Commercial imperatives/international copywriting literacies:** provide a short (200-word) summary of your group discussions on the importance of brand identity and other contextual information to your group decision-making and any resources consulted in developing copywriting practices.
- **Relational ethics:** each member of the group should write a short (up to 200-word) paragraph describing:
  - the general approach to communication adopted in the different roles;
  - the level of formality present in group communications (i.e. the general informality of student-to-student communication or the greater formality of a business-to-business communication);
  - whether any conflicts have occurred, how they have been resolved, and what could be improved; and
  - the quality and quantity of communication with the "clients".

2.6 Chapter summary

This chapter encourages reflection on the development of ethical responsibility in the translation curriculum by critically engaging with the concepts of competence-based curricula and learning outcomes. It offers practical suggestions for ways to enhance ethical sensitivity in processes of reading, text analysis, and translating. It also suggests ways to embed ethics-related work across the translation curriculum through practical exercises relating to the literary and commercial domains of translation, many of which can be adapted to other domains. Finally, it foregrounds wider disciplinary and societal debates about hierarchies of knowledge and structural inequalities that can limit opportunities for some translators.

Notes

1 In Chesterman's description of the activity, students work into their non-native language, but if there is a mix of students with the same combination but a different main language, then students could translate into their main language.
2 The author acknowledges Deborah Smith's kind support for the inclusion of this case study.
3 www.tiltedaxispress.com/about.
4 Kaza emigrated from India to the United States as a child.
5 The author gratefully acknowledges Madhu Kaza's permission to use these excerpts.

80 *Ethics and the translation curriculum (I)*

6 Shread (2021) refers to this earlier translation work in her own response to Susam-Saraeva's (2021) provocation piece.
7 The Second Waffen SS Panzer Division massacred 642 inhabitants of Oradour-sur-Glane on 10 June 1944 by. The ruins of the village are accessed through the visitor centre.
8 Available on S. Qiouyi Lu's personal website: https://s.qiouyi.lu/resource/reading-guide/.
9 The author gratefully acknowledges Mr Schimel and Mr Dixon's kind permission to reproduce these excerpts.

References

Alexandrova, B. (2020). *Joyce, multilingualism and the ethics of reading*. Palgrave Macmillan.
Benmamoun, M., Alhor, H., Ascencio, C., & Sim, W. (2021). Social enterprises in electronic markets: Web localization or standardization. *Electronic Markets*, 31(1), 215–231. https://doi.org/10.1007/s12525-020-00430-7.
Campbell, I. (Ed.) (2022). *Science fiction in translation*. Springer.
Chesterman, A. (1997). *Memes of translation: The spread of ideas in translation history*. John Benjamins.
Contreras, N. S. (2022). The development of translator identity: An interpretative phenomenological study of Chilean translation students' experiences amid local and global crises. Unpublished doctoral dissertation, University of Manchester.
Cormack, A. (2006). Migration and the politics of narrative form: Realism and the postcolonial subject in *Brick Lane*. *Contemporary Literature*, 47(4), 695–721. https://doi.org/10.1353/cli.2007.0014.
Davies, P. (2014). Translation and Holocaust testimonies: A matter for Holocaust studies or translation studies? In J. Boase-Beier, A. Fawcett, and P. Wilson (Eds.), *Literary translation: Redrawing the boundaries* (pp. 204–218). Palgrave Macmillan. https://doi.org/10.1057/9781137310057_13.
Deane-Cox, S. (2013). The translator as secondary witness: Mediating memory in Antelme's *L'Espèce humaine*. *Translation Studies*, 6(3), 309–323. https://doi.org/10.1080/14781700.2013.795267.
Deane-Cox, S. (2014). Remembering Oradour-sur-Glane: Collective memory in translation. *Translation and Literature*, 23(2), 272–283. https://doi.org/10.3366/tal.2014.0156.
Desjardins, R. (2017). *Translation and social media: In theory, in training and in professional practice*. Palgrave Macmillan.
Dixon, A. M. (2023). Lawrence Schimel: "It is important for all of us to remember that children live in the world with us". *Latin American Literature Today*, 25. https://latinamericanliteraturetoday.org/2023/03/lawrence-schimel-it-is-important-for-all-of-us-to-remember-that-children-live-in-the-world-with-us/.
Ehrensberger-Dow, M., & Massey, G. (2013). Indicators of translation competence: Translators' self-concepts and the translation of titles. *Journal of Writing Research*, 5(1), 103–131. https://doi.org/10.17239/jowr-2013.05.01.5.
Feng, D., & Yang, F. (2018). Negotiating boundaries: Ethical issues in commercial translation. In J. Bian and K. T. Çalıyurt (Eds.), *Regulations and applications of ethics in business practice* (pp. 3–12). Springer.
Gaballo, V. (2012). Exploring the boundaries of transcreation in specialised translation. *ESP across Cultures*, 111, 95–113. https://edipuglia.it/wp-content/uploads/ESP%202012/Gaballo.pdf.

Gambier, Y., & Munday, J. (2014). Conversation between Yves Gambier and Jeremy Munday. *Cultus*, 7, 20–36. www.cultusjournal.com/files/Archives/conversation_gambier_munday_3_p.pdf.

Hine, J. T., Jr. (2003). Teaching text revision in a multilingual environment. In B. J. Baer and G. S. Koby (Eds.), *Beyond the ivory tower: Rethinking translation pedagogy* (pp. 135–156). John Benjamins.

Inghilleri, M. (2021). Response by Inghilleri to "Representing experiential knowledge". *Translation Studies*, 14(1), 95–99. https://doi.org/10.1080/14781700.2020.1846606.

Johnston, B. (2018). Teaching and learning literary translation. In K. Washbourne and B. van Wyke (Eds.), *The Routledge handbook of literary translation* (pp. 31–41). Routledge.

Jones, F. R. (2010). Poetry translation, nationalism and the wars of the Yugoslav transition. *The Translator*, 16(2), 223–253. https://doi.org/10.1080/13556509.2010.10799470.

Joosen, V. (2019). Children's literature in translation: Towards a participatory approach. *Humanities*, 8(1), 48. https://doi.org/10.3390/h8010048.

Kang, H., & Smith, D. (2016). It is fascinating to ponder the possibilities of language. *Guardian*, 21 May. www.theguardian.com/books/2016/may/21/my-writing-day-han-kang-deborah-smith.

Katan, D. (2021). Transcreation. In Y. Gambier and L. van Doorslaer (Eds.), *Handbook of translation studies*, Volume 5 (pp. 221–226). John Benjamins.

Kaza, M. H. (2017a). Editor's note: *Kitchen Table Translation*. *Aster(ix)*, 9 August. https://asterixjournal.com/note-translation/.

Kaza, M. H. (Ed.) (2017b). *Kitchen Table Translation*. Blue Sketch Press.

Kiraly, D. C. (1995). *Pathways to translation*. Kent State University Press.

Kotze, H., & Strowe, A. (2021). Response by Kotze and Strowe to "Representing experiential knowledge". *14*(3), 350–354. https://doi.org/10.1080/14781700.2021.1988338.

Laestadius, L. I., & Wahl, M. M. (2017). Mobilising social media users to become advertisers: Corporate hashtag campaigns as a public health concern. *Digital Health*, 3. https://doi.org/10.1177/2055207617710802.

Landsberg, A. (2004). *Prosthetic memory: The transformation of American remembrance in the age of mass culture*. Columbia University Press.

Lewis, D. (2019). The development of translation-specific ethical codes and the practice of literary translation. Unpublished master's dissertation, University of Manchester.

Määttä, S. K., Puumala, E., & Ylikomi, R. (2021). Linguistic, psychological and epistemic vulnerability in asylum procedures: An interdisciplinary approach. *Discourse Studies*, 23(1), 46–66.

Maier, C. (2006). Translating as a body: Meditations on mediation. In S. Bassnett and P. Bush (Eds.), *Translator as writer* (pp. 137–148). Bloomsbury.

Marshall, A. (2021). Amanda Gorman's poetry united critics: It's dividing translators. *New York Times*, 16 March. www.nytimes.com/2021/03/26/books/amanda-gorman-hill-we-climb-translation.html.

Mdallel, S. (2003). Translating children's literature in the Arab world: The state of the art. *Meta*, 48(1–2), 298–306. https://doi.org/10.7202/006976ar.

Montalt, V., & González Davies, M. (2007). *Medical translation step by step: Learning by drafting*. St Jerome.

Morón, M., & Calvo, E. (2018). Introducing transcreation skills in translator training contexts: A situated project-based approach. *Journal of Specialised Translation*, 29. www.jostrans.org/issue29/art_moron.pdf.

Mossop, B. (1983). The translator as rapporteur: A concept for training and self improvement. *Meta*, 28(3), 244–278. https://doi.org/10.7202/003674ar.

Newton, A. Z. (Ed.) (2020). *Ethics and literary practice*. Multidisciplinary Digital Publishing Institute.

Nguyen, N. (2021). The 5 levels of website localization. University of Strasbourg. https://mastertcloc.unistra.fr/2021/09/02/levels-of-website-localization-for-translators/.

Pacheo Aguilar, R. (2016). The question of authenticity in translator education from the perspective of educational philosophy. In D. C. Kiraly (Ed.), *Towards authentic experiential learning in translator education* (pp. 13–32). Mainz University Press.

Pedersen, D. (2014). Exploring the concept of transcreation. *Cultus*, 7, www.cultusjournal.com/files/Archives/pedersen_5_p.pdf.

Pokorn, N. K., & Koskinen, K. (2020). The ethics of linguistic hospitality and untranslatability in Derrida and Ricœur. In K. Koskinen and N. K. Pokorn (Eds.), *The Routledge handbook of translation and ethics* (pp. 87–98). Routledge.

Pym, A. (2020). Translator ethics. In K. Koskinen and N. K. Pokorn (Eds.), *The Routledge handbook of translation and ethics* (pp. 147–161). Routledge.

Sheldon, P., Herzfeldt, E., & Rauschnabel, P. A. (2020). Culture and social media: The relationship between cultural values and hashtagging styles. *Behaviour and Information Technology*, 39(7), 758–770. https://doi.org/10.1080/0144929X.2019.1611923.

Shread, C. (2011). On becoming in translation: Articulating feminisms in the translation of Marie Vieux-Chauvet's *Les Rapaces*. In L. von Flotow (Ed.), *Women and translation: Returning to feminist theory in translation* (pp. 283–303). University of Ottawa Press.

Shread, C. (2021). Response by Shread to "Representing experiential knowledge". *Translation Studies*, 14(1), 104–108. www.tandfonline.com/doi/full/10.1080/14781700.2020.1850333?src=recsys.

Smith, D. (2018). What we talk about when we talk about translation. *LA Review of Books*, 11 January. https://lareviewofbooks.org/article/what-we-talk-about-when-we-talk-about-translation/.

Stolze, R. (2003). Translating for children: World view or pedagogics? *Meta*, 48(1–2), 208–221. https://doi.org/10.7202/006968ar.

Susam-Saraeva, Ş. (2021). Representing experiential knowledge: Who may translate whom? *Translation Studies*, 14(1), 84–94. https://doi.org/10.1080/14781700.2021.1863633.

Tymoczko, M. (2014). Why literary translation is a good model for translation theory and practice. In J. Boase-Beier, A. Fawcett, and P. Wilson (Eds.), *Literary translation: Redrawing the boundaries* (pp. 11–31). Palgrave Macmillan.

Venuti, L. (1998). *The scandals of translation: Towards an ethics of difference*. Routledge.

Wakabayashi, J. (2003). Think-alouds as a pedagogical tool. In B. J. Baer and G. S. Koby (Eds.), *Beyond the ivory tower: Rethinking translation pedagogy* (pp. 61–82). John Benjamins.

Walkowitz, R. L. (2015). *Born translated: The contemporary novel in an age of world literature*. Columbia University Press.

Washbourne, K. (2018). Ethics. In R. K. Washbourne and B. van Wyke (Eds.), *The Routledge handbook of literary translation* (pp. 399–418). Routledge.

Yu, C. (2017). You say melon, I say lemon: Deborah Smith's flawed yet remarkable translation of "The Vegetarian". *Korea Exposé*, 2 July. https://koreaexpose.com/deborah-smith-translation-han-kang-novel-vegetarian/.

Zappavigna, M. (2018). *Searchable talk hashtags and social media metadiscourse*. Bloomsbury Academic.

3 Ethics and the translation curriculum (II)

Technologies in focus

3.1 Chapter overview

The centrality of technology to current translation practice means it inevitably cuts across the two chapters devoted to translation teaching and ethics in this volume. Chapter 2 briefly alluded to the role technology plays in skills such as information mining and the dissemination of translated information. This chapter addresses a different set of technology- and ethics-related questions for translator education, foregrounding the role of assistive technologies in translation production and the role of online environments and ideologies that shape translation workflows. The suggested activities are designed to sensitise students to the importance of digital ethics in developing professional responsibility (Mitchell-Schuitevoerder, 2020), the social consequences of certain computer-assisted translation solutions, and the ethical implications of engagement in various forms of online collaborative translation.

At a broader level, the chapter encourages approaches to teaching and learning that draw out some of the implications of technology for intercultural encounters and the ways in which the "other" is perceived through and as a consequence of human–machine interactions. It also examines shifts in attitudes to technology-assisted translation among the general population and the implications for the professional translator self-concept. Digital reflexivity is viewed as a critical disposition to translation practice and the development of self-efficacy beliefs in the digital era, and is promoted as a supporting skill in developing ethical responsibility.

3.2 Pedagogy in the technologies-oriented curriculum: implications for ethics education

3.2.1 General trends

What to teach and which pedagogical approaches to privilege are questions that take on an ethical and moral dimension in the technologies-oriented translation curriculum. A key driver for many programmes in terms of curriculum design is the increasingly pluri- or trans-disciplinary role profile of language professionals, which, for Ginovart Cid, Colominas, and Oliver (2020, p. 171), oblige the

DOI: 10.4324/9781003098485-4

incorporation *inter alia* of CAT tools, translation memory, and machine translation into the curriculum, with a concomitant emphasis on declarative and technical knowledge.

Multi-componential approaches to curriculum design, based on the principle that certain topics and skills need to be included if graduates are to find a good job (Pym, 2003), appear increasingly unrealistic due to the proliferation of roles in translation production networks (Moorkens, 2020), the pace of technological change (O'Hagan, 2020), and the heterogeneity of the translation market (Rothwell and Svoboda, 2019). Although such approaches could be seen as morally consonant with contemporary student employability agendas, as Pym (2003) observes, they may not align with students' expectations and aspirations for what a translation curriculum should contain. This is less true of programmes that are explicitly translation technology-focused, although these too must address issues of scope.

Uneven institutional access to resources can also impact curriculum planning. Aside from issues of staff expertise, there are significant gaps in the availability of training data for neural machine translation systems, which means that, for many language pairings, rule-based, statistical machine translation or human translation are the only options (Melby, 2020; Esqueda, 2021). Beyond the classroom, geographical location may also impact the ability of institutions, companies, and freelancers to leverage certain technologies due to cost or political control (Zetzsche, 2020). While these issues present limitations for some course providers, they risk engendering an unhelpful deficit mindset in terms of curriculum planning: see Desjardins (2017, p. 69) on the tension between translator education and the problem of the "military-industrial-academic paradigm". To an extent, this can be addressed by fostering critical debate among the student body on topics such as the relationship between technologies, linguistic diversity, and hegemony (Bowker, 2020; Sin-Wai, 2016), and fair access to information (Nurminen and Koponen, 2020).

The versatility required of new translation graduates places a considerable burden on educators to determine a knowledge agenda around technologies that supports a broad foundation for learning. Such an agenda is likely to combine, to varying degrees, technical and soft skills development with awareness of the social, cultural, economic, and political contexts that influence the development of technologies and their use. There is a growing consensus around the need to extend technologies teaching beyond instrumentalist and transmissive approaches, which have largely dominated due to the didacticism of CAT tools teaching, to a focus on developing critical and informed users (Bowker and Buitrago Ciro, 2019). This outlook offers scope to incorporate ethics as a cornerstone of professional responsibility, and serves to engage students in broader agendas of social responsibility (Drugan and Tipton, 2017).

Approaches in which technical and declarative knowledge are privileged have received critical attention with regard to the extent to which they restrict student ability to develop adaptive expertise and overemphasise "[preparing] graduates for an immediate placement in a stratified market that will only absorb those that conform" instead of encouraging transformative thinking that will lead to "new solutions for translation problems that are situated within uncharted or lesser-known challenging social contexts" (Neves, 2022, p. 468). Part of the reason for the emphasis on the former to the neglect of the latter, in Neves's view, is the focus on pedagogy that seeks to bring the real world into the classroom – for example, through simulated project tasks that reflect dominant industry processes (see Chapter 1 for further discussion of this topic). There is no suggestion that the approach be sidelined, although it merits greater critical scrutiny in terms of what constitutes "real" and the extent to which it is compatible with assessment goals (see Willbergh, 2015). It does, however, leave scope to explore alternative or complementary perspectives (see Pietrzak, 2022, for further discussion of employability as an objective of translation education).

Discussion points

Reviewing your translation technologies curriculum and the place of ethics within it:

- What range of translation-related technologies are most commonly taught on your programme?
- Do you operate a stand-alone unit on technologies or embed their use across the curriculum? Which factors shape your approach?
- Which educational philosophies inform your teaching and learning in the translation technologies curriculum? Are there any changes that you would like to implement?
- Which ethical topics relating to technologies (if any) does your programme currently include?
- If you do include ethics, is it a topic that tends to be incidental to the core curriculum or do you take a planned approach?
- To what extent do you incorporate formal reflection or other assessment strategies in translation assignments relating to ethics (individual and/or group work)?
- Which resources might you draw on (and signpost students to) when exploring ethics-related topics and technologies?
- What do you consider the most important ethical issues students need to address at BA and MA level in relation to translation technologies, given the scope of this topic on your programme?

3.2.2 Developing (digital) reflexivity as a critical disposition to practice

In terms of ethics education, teaching and learning do not need to be wholly anchored around the human–machine interface. Important social questions around the neutrality of technology (Kenny, 2017), technological determinism (Olohan, 2017), environmental sustainability (Cronin, 2020), and the consequences of employing technologies in a range of translation situations, from trade to immigration and healthcare (Drugan, 2019), among many others, serve to complement a focus on hard skills, or may form a stand-alone unit of learning with a social responsibility orientation. However, since a large number of programmes do incorporate some hard skills development, helping students to achieve at least a degree of "interactional stability" with the material agents of translation technologies and to reconcile processes of resistance and accommodation (following Olohan, 2011) within the learning experience can be viewed as one goal of ethics education in the technologies-oriented curriculum. In what follows, the process of reconciliation is considered to rely, to a large extent, on (digital) reflexivity[1] as a critical disposition to translation practice in the digital age, which requires cultivating through dedicated pedagogical intervention.

(Digital) reflexivity captures more than the general process of trial and error, and the internal conversation that accompanies this process, common to student learning. It speaks to deeper questions of agency and the struggles to assert agency over digital technologies, especially when accompanying levels of digital literacy are at various stages of development and in situations where a complex set of (translation and learning) technologies is implemented in a single learning task.[2] When viewed from the perspective of "reflection-in-practice" (Schön, 1983), reflexivity involves a conscious process of calibration and recalibration of technical competence and understanding in the moment of action. This requires vigilance regarding the extent to which current personal resources are adequate for the task and the changes needed to transform the learning situation, which may be determined collaboratively. However, the struggle to assert agency also involves judgements about the rightness or wrongness of certain choices and their consequences, highlighting the importance of viewing (digital) reflexivity as a critical disposition to learning and not simply part of the dynamics of knowledge creation. As such, reflexivity is defined as the ability to bring to consciousness a source of difficulty or problem in the external environment, evaluate the adequacy of personal resources and moral frameworks to resolve it, and enact appropriate strategies to bridge gaps. It is an action involving "folding something back upon itself" and "pointing to or reflecting upon oneself" (Kadiu, 2019, p. 10). For Kadiu, these actions can be labelled "reflexivity" and "self-reflexivity", respectively, which emphasises the concept's slipperiness.

Although it has elements in common with paradigms of reflective practice widely applied in education in disciplines with a human service element, the development of reflexivity as a critical disposition does not necessarily require spending time on formal post-activity reflection. In what follows, emphasis is placed on educators scaffolding effective decision-making *in the moment of action* – for instance, through a structured approach to defining problems and the provision of sufficient contextual information to support students to ask relevant questions of themselves and their approach, particularly in collaborative learning tasks.

In technologies-oriented learning, problems of a technical nature are commonly resolvable by accessing relevant manuals and technical guides, along with hands-on practice to address questions such as "How does this work?" and "How do I achieve x in this interface?" However, the block or problem may relate to a hypothetical stakeholder or client expectation that is less easy to envision and define. It may also relate to an emotion or feeling generated by the complex configuration of material and non-material interactions and intellectual expectations: "Why does this system expect me to work in this way?" and "Why am I reacting so negatively/positively to x?" When students ask these questions of themselves, they are less likely to bring them into the open to avoid feelings of inadequacy, underplaying their significance in the learning process as a consequence. Resistance to and accommodation of different materialities and practices in later professional life are arguably shaped by the extent to which these (inter)personal questions are attended to in learning. Empirical research is needed to determine connections between enhanced scaffolding for reflexive thinking and the development of self-efficacy beliefs, but the basic idea that having greater awareness of how a critical disposition can be embodied and activated through reflexivity is a theme that has achieved increased prominence in the TI education literature (see Pietrzak, 2022, on self-reflection as a strategy in metacognitive translator training).

A critical disposition is promoted to support student engagement with the wider social context in which their learning takes place. At the time of writing, student anxieties about increasing automation and depersonalisation, and what these mean for their professional prospects, are still hovering in the background. There is scope to address such matters constructively – for example, by encouraging discussion about the creation and implementation of technology that may have a dehumanising effect (O'Brien, 2012, p. 109) and how informed users and experts in the field might effectively counter or renegotiate this issue. Further, as Vieira (2020, p. 2) reminds us, many of the automation challenges impacting on the language services industry are present in other economic activities, too, and therefore need to be couched against the broader social backdrop.

(Digital) reflexivity can also help mitigate what might be termed "cognitive shock", triggered by exposure to translation environments in which text integrity at the syntagmatic level is radically disrupted (Pym, 2011); in other words, environments where text is reduced to short, decontextualised strings. This is not to diminish the ability of students to adapt, but the potential to unsettle may go unnoticed by educators and impact the degree of general translation competence developed over time. At a broader level, text fragmentation is increasingly echoed by task fragmentation in the wider language services industry, which means students will often work on only a portion of a project (Moorkens, 2020, p. 12). It will be almost impossible for students to begin to reconcile such fragmentation during their programmes of study, but there is arguably an ethical imperative for educators to help them anticipate what this will entail during their working lives: that is, they should be encouraged to think about the impact on personal levels of satisfaction of working regularly with text in decontextualised strings and/or undertaking only a portion of a translation project.

3.2.3 Digital reflexivity and pedagogical theory

As a critical disposition to practice, (digital) reflexivity is consonant with the constructivist-inspired view of cognition as a process of "organising and reorganising one's own subjective world of experience" (Sumara and Davis, 1997, quoted in Kiraly, 2015, p. 20) and therefore with the idea of learning being more of a process of constructing the self. Constructivist-inspired pedagogies emphasise the importance of embodied action as the basis for learning, which, for Kiraly (2006; 2015), underscores a dynamic view of knowing and the importance of collaborative opportunities for learning. Collaborative learning, in which individually acquired skills are deployed in group tasks that simulate professional translation projects and increasingly draw on social learning opportunities (Marczak, 2018), is now a common feature of translation programmes (Bowker and Marshman, 2010). It helps to embed technologies across units of learning (Mellinger, 2017), extending to cross-institutional transnational initiatives that promote intercultural learning and exchange (Monk et al., 2015), and often supported by partnerships with a number of technology providers (Guerberof and Moorkens, 2019; Shuttleworth, 2017).

Although often centred on a clearly delimited (project management) task, collaborative learning does not necessarily proceed in a sequential manner. Students will grapple individually and collectively with material agents in the translation process and engage in interpersonal communication to problem-solve and refine translation outputs with varying degrees of success. Learning can be disrupted by variability in commitment, effort, self-efficacy beliefs around the use of technology, and the extent to which there is agreement about the attainment of project milestones and final deliverables at the required level. In short, there will be many learning outcomes among the group (including ethics-related learning), not all of which will necessarily have been predictable from the start.

It is this openness to so-called "emergent competence" that Kiraly (2006; 2015) has sought to develop through an approach to teaching that is underpinned by a post-positivist epistemology. Through this approach, although the emphasis remains on embodied action, there is a displacement of the educator as an epistemic authority. Instead, they become a co-learner with their students, "occasioning" learning; the scaffolding for reflexivity mentioned above can be seen as an example of this occasioning. The implications of this approach for ethics education in the technologies curriculum have yet to be empirically researched, and there is evident nervousness in Kiraly's and others' work (e.g. Calzada Pérez, 2019) with regard to the level of "chaos" such approaches may produce in the classroom. However, if programmes are to bring some of the real world into the learning environment, and that world is characterised by (text and task) fragmentation and technological complexity, then such an educational philosophy may be considered ethically viable in the digital age.

The box below presents an indicative list of topics that support a focus on ethics in the translation technologies curriculum. It takes inspiration from a wide range of translation studies literature and professional translator concerns.

Several of the topics are developed in subsequent sections through suggested classroom activities relating to machine translation, post-editing, and online collaborative translation.

Topics in ethics and translation technologies (an indicative list)

- **(Cognitive) ergonomics.** What are the challenges for translators when handling complex platforms and software and how are they impacted as individuals in terms of affect, stress, and support? What sort of bodily stress do different technologies generate for translators?
- **Interpersonal relations.** How do project managers use technologies when communicating with translators, and are there any ethical issues arising from their use? How do the various situations in which collaborative translation is undertaken impact on the nature of ethical issues and the strategies employed to address them?
- **Quality.** What does translation quality mean (e.g. in machine translation post-editing) and how do different client quality expectations impact on post-editing and revision processes?
- **Fairness.** What should professional translators expect as a fair price for translation work involving different types of technology? What impact does technology have on individual productivity and how can translators manage expectations about fairness in terms of workflow and delivery?
- **Accessibility.** Which questions do different translation platforms raise in terms of accessibility and adaptability for individuals with different needs? What are the implications of machine translation for fair access to information?
- **Data security and privacy.** Which issues arise for freelancers as compared to language services providers? Which ethical questions do individual freelance translators and language services providers need to consider in terms of the portability of translation memories?
- **Intellectual property and copyright issues.** What are the implications for freelancers in relation to the fair attribution of rights in agreements with language services providers?
- **Professional and personal concerns.** What are the implications of different technologies for translators' job satisfaction, professional identity, and self-worth?
- **Technoneutrality.** What are the risks for translators and various translation processes in assuming technology is neutral?
- **Environmental sustainability.** Which factors govern the relationship between translation and environmental sustainability? Which mitigations might freelancers and language services providers implement to minimise environmental impact from a technologies perspective?
- **Artificial intelligence.** What are the implications of the fact that there is little likelihood of human agents tracing and understanding decisions taken in AI-based systems?

3.3 Machine translation

This section briefly introduces machine translation and salient developments before examining some of the ethical implications for users (translators) and consumers of translated products produced solely through machine assistance.

3.3.1 Machine translation and ethics in the curriculum

Machine translation (MT) – which Christensen, Bundgaard, Schjoldager, and Dam Jensen (2022, p. 22) define as "an umbrella term covering a wide range of paradigms such as rule-based MT, example-based MT, open-source or generic MT, pragmatic-based MT, statistical MT and neural MT" – is an established and expanding sector in the language services industry. Viewed as both a tool and a service (Mellinger, 2017, p. 290), MT's ubiquity in the modern world raises questions for educators about the extent to which it influences, or should influence, teaching and learning (Rico and González Pastor, 2022) in terms of both technical and critical skills development.

Several scholars (e.g. González Pastor and Rico, 2021; Mellinger, 2017) advocate a cross-curriculum and goal-oriented approach to MT to avoid an overemphasis on tool acquisition (instrumentalist approaches) and facilitate modelling of expert behaviour. Although many staff members may have had some interaction with an online machine translator, either professionally or personally, inconsistencies will inevitably arise if lay knowledge is relied upon in the classroom. This was highlighted in Rico and González Pastor's (2022) audit of staff at the Universitat de València (17 participants) prior to a short course on MT and post-editing, in which considerable variability in knowledge and expertise emerged. Transversality as a curriculum goal is likely, therefore, to require investment in staff skills development.

Sycz-Opoń and Gałuskina (2017, pp. 196–197) discuss MT's potential to "sabotage the learning process" if introduced without sufficient prior preparatory work. This points to a need to plan a balance between translation from scratch and MT within a programme, and the extent to which both are developed in tandem or in sequence. Translation from scratch will likely involve some machine-translated text (Nitzke, 2019), through access to online resources, but educators may seek to develop certain translation competences through a phased approach in which different constraints on assistive technologies apply. Once students are exposed to the fact that in open systems translations are likely to have been proposed by "the crowd", as opposed to experts in a particular field (Moorkens, Castilho, Gaspari, and Doherty, 2018), they will understand the need to develop a certain vigilance with regard to the appropriateness of a proposed translation solution and engage in detailed checking processes.

In terms of preparatory work, some academic programmes devote considerable curriculum time to developing competence in translation memory creation, terminology management, and MT engine creation (Shuttleworth, 2017), fostering practical and connective knowledge to support understanding of how systems work and their limitations. However, neural MT systems employ a connectionist approach (i.e. they use neural networks to learn from existing translations and their own translated output), drawing on large amounts of data, and are difficult to train (Forcada, 2017), limiting scope for engine building as an experiential focus of the curriculum.

Machine translation carries particular risks for translators and wider society and, as such, merits ethical scrutiny. Canfora and Ottmann (2020, p. 59) summarise these risks as the generation of typical translator errors that may cause damage in safety-critical situations; liability (i.e. if errors occur in neural machine translation (NMT), who is to blame?); and cyber-risk (particularly if using free online engines). A curriculum that encompasses competence in MT quality assessment (Way, 2018), error detection, and the risks of using neural MT in high-stakes situations (Ragni and Vieira, 2022) will help to develop sensitivity to these matters and strategies for mitigating risk.

A further ethical issue concerns the use and reuse of data to train machine translators (Moorkens, 2022). Sensitising students to such issues as they arise in translation contracts (e.g. in relation to the reuse of a translator's data for human and MT workflow) and allowing scope for reflection on the problems of individual translator control over how their data is (re)used falls within the development of good digital ethics practice. As Moorkens (2022, p. 130) explains, "For those who are not aware of the variable ways MT may be used within professional workflows, the decision to accept or not accept may be difficult, particularly if the agency has not been transparent."

Finally, the use of MT within the programme of study more generally raises ethical issues for both educators and students. For instance, educators may need to reflect on advice they give to students in international cohorts working in a second or third language who wish to use machine translators to facilitate their learning (e.g. by translating translation studies literature). They will also need to manage the use of MT in assignments where the learning goals are premised on limited or no MT input through effective task design to stop students taking short cuts and maximise engagement with the learning aims.

3.3.2 Ethics education and machine translation: selected topics and activities

This subsection examines selected MT topics for teaching and learning purposes. It proposes a range of classroom activities to support critical engagement with MT, foster good digital ethics practice, and stimulate structured reflection on the moral implications of MT in a range of social situations. The activities are couched within a learning outcomes framework, as opposed to an emergentist framework, as they are principally oriented around short, discrete tasks with pre-definable goals.

3.3.2.1 Preparing texts for machine translation

The quality of raw machine-translated output is impacted by the quality of both the MT system and the source text (which may require some pre-editing to optimise the raw output). The advent of neural MT has impacted pre-editing practices used in older, rule-based and statistical MT systems, with some becoming redundant (Sánchez-Gijón and Kenny, 2022). However, in terms of teaching and learning, it can still be instructive for students to familiarise themselves with pre-editing for several reasons: first, as a general means to enhance writing skills and the ability to follow guidelines; second, to learn about the impact of pre-editing different text genres on raw machine-translated output; and third, to gain a sense of which types of text present the greatest challenges for NMT systems. From an ethical perspective, the ability to follow guidelines supports good ethical practice in related areas of post-editing where this attribute is required and serves as a further support for discussions about quality as an ethical issue in translation process and product.

Activity

Pre-editing texts for neural machine translation

- **Learning aims:** to introduce the concept of controlled natural language; to sensitise students to the resources available to support the editing of texts; and to support the application of guidance to sample texts and generated machine-translated output.
- **Learning outcomes:** by the end of this activity, students will be familiar with relevant definitions and guidelines applicable to pre-editing; after applying these guidelines to a short text, they will have explored the outcome in a machine-translated version and compared versions with their peers.
- **Recommended reading:** Marzouk and Hansen-Schirra (2019).

Task

1   The task assumes that students have previously been introduced to machine translation and understand its potential to impact the quality of raw output. The educator should introduce students to the concepts of pre-editing rules, controlled natural languages, and clear writing guidelines, and the similarities between them. They should then provide examples of edited texts. A set of guidelines, CLOUT (Controlled Language for Optimized Uniform Translation) rules, devised by Uwe Muegge, is available (in English) at: https://works.bepress.com/uwe_muegge/88/. Online readability checkers, such as www.online-utility.org/english/readability_test_and_improve.jsp (English) and https://cental.uclouvain.be/amesure/ (French), may also be introduced.

2   Students select a short text (or text extract) to which they will apply the CLOUT (or other) guidelines as an individual practical exercise (e.g. approximately 200 words). For this exercise, a short instructional text is recommended, such as the following on the subject of fire safety: www.westsussex.gov.uk/media/17778/wildfire-leaflet_res.pdf.

> 3 Working in small groups, students pass their versions through a selected online neural machine translator and compare the outputs, reflecting on the extent to which the raw machine output requires post-editing.
> 4 The exercise is repeated with a text proposed by the educator, such as (following Sánchez-Gijón and Kenny, 2022) one that has multiple communicative functions and/or specific features like a complex, ambiguous structure or extra-textual referents that may be only implicit in the text. The selected text should help students engage with specific features of a particular source language, including formulations that the neural MT system might find difficult to handle. Sánchez-Gijón and Kenny (2022) suggest invisible plurals in English or the expression of negation in some languages, which can lead to ambiguity.
> 5 Students discuss their findings with their peers and in guided plenary with their educator.

3.3.2.2 Social bias in machine translators

Algorithmic bias concerns the idea that the amplification of human biases is common to many machine learning algorithms due to the fact that systems are trained using texts that are inherently biased (Farkas and Németh, 2022). The consequence is that problematic social asymmetries relating to age, race, ableism, and gender, for example, are perpetuated (Prates, Avelar, and Lamb, 2020, p. 6363). Tomlain et al. (2021) draw attention to debates over "debiasing" – for instance, whether it should happen upstream, before the system is trained, or downstream, once the system has been trained.

Students may be interested in debating the prescriptivist assumptions underpinning this debate – that is, whether should be removed if it is reflective of the "distinctive skewings that are present in the general population" and the extent to which they believe that developers of AI-based systems have a democratic and ethical obligation to be as open and positive as possible (Tomlain et al., 2021, pp. 422–423). These authors also draw attention to the different conceptualisations of bias, not all of which are encompassed in MT, which has led to a focus on "representational harms" like stereotyping (p. 420), to the neglect of others.

> **Activity**
>
> *Sensitising students to bias in machine translation using gender as an example*
>
> - **Learning aim:** to conduct a small case study to investigate manifestations of bias in a freely available online machine translator.
> - **Learning outcomes:** by the end of this activity, students will be able to: articulate approaches to research on the topic of gender bias;

reflect on other types of bias and their textual manifestations; conduct a small-scale study of representational bias through MT.
• **Recommended reading:** Prates, Avelar, and Lamb (2020).

Task

1 Students independently identify and read a selection of literature on machine bias, and find examples of how it manifests in different types of text.
2 The educator leads students in discussing their readings and examples, before exploring with students some of the challenges in analysing gender bias in MT.
3 Students and/or the educator select a sample of text extracts (different genres and functions) in which gender is salient.
4 Working in small groups, students select a freely available online machine translator to experiment with several different text sources and evaluate the machine's handling of the selected gender issues.
5 Students select another category of bias, alternative conceptualisations of gender bias, or other forms of bias and repeat the activity with other text extracts. They may be interested to explore issues concerning challenges to the Western gender binary and the extent to which this is accommodated in current online machine translators. They may also extend their research to explore other settings in which bias has been identified as a salient issue, such as video-game localisation. Recommended reading: Rivas Ginel and Theroine (2022).

3.3.2.3 Digital ethics: developing good practice

The term "digital ethics" encompasses issues of data management, privacy, and security. There have been ethical questions about ownership of translation data and data sharing since translation data (aligned source-and-target pairs) were first harvested for reuse in the 1980s (Moorkens and Lewis, 2020, p. 469). In the 1990s, such questions coalesced around the use of translation memories; more recently, the advent of data-driven MT and the concomitant need to repurpose data for testing and training have generated the pressing issue of the assignation of rights to use data for MT training (Moorkens and Lewis, 2020). These authors assert that the attribution of copyright and the reuse of translation as data are currently "subject to conflicting and inconsistently-interpreted laws and conventions" (Moorkens and Lewis, 2020, p. 478).

Supporting students to navigate contractual demands around data production and data sharing is therefore a desirable curriculum component within an ethics education, but subject to rapid change. For instance, less than a decade ago, Moorkens et al. (2016) recommended using translation memory (TM) meta-data for assigning or limiting usage rights in situations where a translator is worried it might be reused to train MT systems; however, the rapid increase in the use of neural MT and the scale of data required for training now make it almost impossible to trace an individual translator's input (i.e. their intellectual and creative contributions).

Drawing attention to the limitations of individual translator agency to influence certain data-sharing practices and the extent to which they have control over others, the potential risks for clients of data sharing, and the need for vigilance in quality assessing machine output will help students to ask relevant questions before committing to a situation that may challenge their personal values and sense of professional integrity. Mitchell-Schuitevoerder (2020, p. 120), for example, points out that Google differentiates between Google Translate and Google Cloud Translation, with the former storing text to train the system and the latter being ISO 20718 compliant (an international standard of practice for protecting publicly identifiable information in public cloud services), only storing data for a short period until the translation is completed. However, this short storage period means that some clients and language services providers prefer not to use it, and Mitchell-Schuitevoerder warns that some of the latter will state this in their contract terms.

The following activities are designed to encourage skills development and understanding of good digital ethics practices, focusing on honesty, data security and protection, and copyright.

Activity

(Trainee/professional) honesty and integrity in the use of machine translation

- **Learning aims:** to sensitise students to the ethical issues of using MT as a potential short cut to practice in academic and professional spheres.
- **Learning outcomes:** by the end of this activity, students will be able to assess the consequences of poor time management and the risks to self and others of having recourse to MT.
- **Recommended reading:** Sakamoto (2019a).

Task

1 Group discussion: students read and reflect on two scenarios in small groups.

- Scenario 1: Imagine that you have been tasked with producing a translation from scratch for an assignment on your programme in which the task instructions explicitly state that you may use electronic resources (termbases, online dictionaries, and parallel texts) to support your translation, but no MT engine should be used. One of the goals of the exercise is to test research and data-

96 *Ethics and the translation curriculum (II)*

mining competences and students' ability to edit/revise their own work. Several students who are running behind with their assignment preparation use a freely available machine translator and do a few light edits prior to submission. (Note that the instructor intends to use this source text for future translation activities on the programme.)

- Identify the ethical issues that arise in this scenario for the instructor and the students concerned, and what risks might the practice generate more widely? (NB: The group can discuss this scenario in relation to various text types/genres. In this scenario, literary MT serves as a fruitful prompt for discussions around moral rights in addition to copyright.)
- Scenario 2: A freelance translator accepts an offer of work from a regular client even though they are not entirely familiar with the subject area. They sign a contract that includes a clause forbidding the use of freely available online machine translators in the workflow. After starting the job, feeling under pressure to meet the client's deadline, the translator decides to speed up the process by putting sections of the text through a freely available online machine translator.
- Aside from breach of contract, what other ethical issues are evident in this scenario?

2   Students share their discussion points with the wider group in a plenary.
3   The educator supports students to draft time management plans and develop strategies for effective communication with clients regarding potential delays to delivery.

Activity

Understanding the language of data security and protection

- **Learning aims:** to familiarise students with professional discourse on data security and protection; to foster technical understanding of key concepts.
- **Learning outcomes:** by the end of this task, students will be able to: articulate conceptual knowledge relating to the field of data security and protection; evaluate professional discourse about and offers of data protection in leading MT services; hypothetically plan ahead for freelance work and decision-making about which level of service they may need for working with different types of text and client.

Task

1   Students select one online MT platform to explore the scope of data protection offered by free and subscription (or "pro") versions.

2   They then create a glossary of key data protection terms and research data protection standards at national and international levels: for example, personal identifiable information, TLS encryption, persistent storage, ISO 27001, certified data centre operator.
3   Students discuss the degree of prominence of information on data protection for free versions of a platform on the website and make a list of key points/risks that they would need to consider as a freelance translator when setting up.

Activity

Developing digital ethics awareness and planning for freelance work

- **Learning aims:** to engage students with professional translator discourse about data protection and security; to plan and draft a data protection and security statement.
- **Learning outcomes:** by the end of this activity, students will: demonstrate awareness of current issues in data protection impacting professional translators; identify sources of information relating to current legal provisions impacting their local context of work; apply knowledge about data protection and security to a draft statement for public viewing; engage in a hypothetical exercise to ascertain the most appropriate online services for secure document transfer.

Task

Following on from the previous task in which students familiarised themselves with the language and standards of data protection relating to the use of machine translators, the aim of this activity is to increase their knowledge of data protection more broadly.

1   Students explore (individually or in small groups) discussion threads in translator forums relating to the protection of client data for translation assignments.
2   Students imagine setting up a website as a freelance translator and include a section on how their client's data will be protected. They then draft a statement that reflects the relevant data protection laws at the time of writing.
3   Students explore best security practices for freelance translators, starting, for example, with a discussion of the items listed at: www.proz.com/securepro/security-practices/list. As a follow-up, students discuss the perceived benefits of the SecurePRO^{TM} scheme (or other

schemes relevant to the students' local context), available through Proz, in terms of the reassurance it provides to clients.
4 Students then imagine a scenario in which they (as freelance translators) need to discuss options for clients to send documents to them. Discussions could be anchored around: which email providers offer the most secure services; which other file-sharing services and cloud services could be considered; and how files will be backed up securely.
5 The outcome of these discussions could be written up as a hypothetical email setting out the options to the client.

Activity

Copyright issues in different jurisdictions

- **Learning aims:** to sensitise students to the concept of copyright; to stimulate reflection on translator agency in relation to translation memory (TM) ownership and portability.
- **Learning outcomes:** by the end of this activity, students will be able to: articulate what copyright is and how it might impact their professional work; situate their reflections in the context of professional translator experience; plan ahead for interactions with language services providers regarding TMs.
- **Pre-task reading:** Park (2023); Basalamah and Sadek (2014).

Task

1 Students read Park (2023) before undertaking some research into the concept of "works made for hire" and establishing whether provisions exist in the country in which they plan to work.
2 In class, an invited speaker with expertise in copyright provides an overview of the concept and its operationalisation in the country in question.
3 Park introduces different philosophical perspectives through which to consider the question of translator rights. In small groups, students discuss the following statements, focusing on the concept of agency and imagining in each case how they might make the case to relevant others (language services providers, commissioners) to assert their view:

- Translators have the right to determine how to use or manage the TMs in which their translations are included, and other parties to the translation service contract have a duty to respect their choices.
- Translators are often compelled to sign over the copyright of the TM to the language services provider, which serves to advance the interests of the language services provider and clients. Translators

are treated only as a means, and their translations are exploited without their consent.
- Reusing translations in the form of TMs amounts to the creation of secondary work, and should earn translators licence fees (e.g. under a collective licence regime). However, the likely small volume of TMs for individual translators under a collective regime might make such a system not worth the investment.

4 Students exchange ideas in a plenary on the points above.
5 Student reflections are discussed by an invited professional translator/representative of a professional translator association, who is invited to share anonymised experiences of TM ownership in their professional practice.
6 Extension activity: students are given examples of contract terms regarding copyright to analyse and compare across different translation domains (literary, commercial, legal) within a single country context. The findings could also form the basis of discussions with an invited professional translator.

3.3.2.4 Accessibility

Accessibility in the field of machine translation encompasses several subtopics, including the accessibility of MT globally (e.g. limitations on language pairs available) and fair access to information. Asscher and Glikson (2021, p. 5) are among a growing number of researchers to explore the moral and practical implications of using (online) MT in a wide range of social situations in which power imbalances often obtain. The admissibility of machine-translated content as evidence in a court of law and its use in public health contexts (Vieira et al., 2020) and the ethical implications of using MT to support participation in various aspects of civic life (e.g. Nurminen and Koponen, 2020) are other examples. This research opens up fertile ground for students to engage with concepts of agency and power within an ethics-oriented approach to translation, and also has the potential to shape student skills in advising.

Asscher and Glikson (2021) explore end-user perceptions of machine and human translation, based on a scenario of an immigrant worker who has been wronged and needs to have an official complaint translated for submission to the local authorities. In this study, participants (university students and professional translators) were invited by means of an online questionnaire to evaluate the translation, which was ostensibly produced by one of two means: machine translation or human translation. In reality, the two types of translation (from English to Hebrew) were identical as they were both generated using Google Translate. The evaluation was anchored around accuracy, reliability, ability to convey cultural and emotional otherness, and the translation's assumed functional effectiveness in helping the immigrant. The findings show that the lower evaluations given for the translation labelled "MT" gave rise to a desire to introduce changes to the text to support the immigrant in ways that deviated from the source. The following suggested activity is derived from this research.

> **Activity**
>
> *Accessing institutional authorities through machine translation*
>
> - **Learning aims:** to encourage reflection on the social consequences of machine translation in situations of power and resource imbalance.
> - **Learning outcomes:** by the end of this activity, students will have: directly engaged in a translation task with a stated social purpose; developed empathy with users of open machine translators who have limited recourse to funding for professional translation support and elicited views on the potential pitfalls of the former approach for achieving the desired social goal; and, drawing on these findings, applied new knowledge to an advising task in the context of a local charitable organisation working with multilingual service users.
>
> *Task*
>
> 1. The educator develops a letter based on a fictitious scenario. They could use the scenario outlined in Asscher and Glikson (2021) or a different one, such as: writing to the local council to request assistance due to the poor state of housing; requesting help to manage a debt from a local government department due to a change in circumstances; or seeking advice from a driving licence authority in relation to a health condition.
> 2. Each student produces a translation of the letter from scratch.
> 3. The educator then gives the students a version of the letter that has been translated using an online machine translator.
> 4. Working in small groups, students discuss the differences between their translated letters and the version produced using the automated translation process. The evaluation should be multi-layered, taking account of completeness, accuracy, communicative effectiveness, and other criteria that can be determined in advance by the group within a student-centred learning framework.
> 5. Each group sets aside the automated version and produces a single version of the text based on their own translations of the letter.
> 6. Students next approach peers outside of the programme of study to elicit views on both texts from the perspective of general readers. They should draft a list of criteria prior to approaching others for comment on the texts.

Ethics and the translation curriculum (II) 101

7 The findings of this activity and the different sets of criteria used by each group are discussed in a plenary.
8 Extension activity: students devise a short set of guidelines for a charity organisation (or advocacy group) that is thinking of using MT to help its clients liaise with local institutional authorities, outlining potential pitfalls and benefits.

Activity

Machine translation, access to information, and participation in electoral cycles

- **Learning aims:** to explore the concept of linguistic justice and the potential of machine translation for different text types, events, and communication needs across the electoral cycle.
- **Learning outcomes:** by the end of this activity, students will have: developed familiarity with the communication needs of a multilingual electorate in a typical electoral cycle; experienced the outputs of MT from various event types and text types in the cycle from the position of a hypothetical voter; and reflected on opportunities for participation in the various stages supported by MT before applying new knowledge and empathic skills to suggest ways in which the process may be enhanced.
- **Recommended reading:** Cabrera (2022); Nurminen and Koponen (2020); Van Parijs (2011).

Task

1 Students are tasked with exploring the relevant literature on and definitions of linguistic justice.
2 Students reflect on communicative events that typically occur during the voting cycle and the potential uses of MT throughout the cycle (e.g. from written and spoken media information and debate to communicating with candidates and understanding voting instructions on ballots). They gather text examples representing different stages in the cycle. These could include audiovisual sources with speech-to-text translation enabled.
3 Students select up to three freely available online translation platforms through which all texts will be processed, ending up with three sets of texts for each platform.
4 They then examine the output in accordance with a set of criteria determined by the whole class in advance. An assumed level of language proficiency and personal biography also need to be established

> for the imagined voter to support understanding that not all limited language proficient voters necessarily have a migrant background.
> 5 In a plenary, groups share their findings and reflect on strategies that could be implemented to support better participation in the various stages of the voting cycle.

3.4 Post-editing

Post-editing (PE), understood broadly as "the correction of raw machine translated output by a human translator according to specific guidelines and quality criteria" (O'Brien, 2011, pp. 197–198), has grown significantly in recent years as a consequence of the explosion in digital content – growth that has been steadily reflected in translator education. For example, in 2017, the European Master's in Translation (EMT) network incorporated post-editing into the list of core competences on master's-level programmes in a learning statement that also alludes to related topics in digital ethics: "Apply post-editing to MT output using the appropriate post-editing levels and techniques according to the quality and productivity objectives, and recognise the importance of data ownership and data security issues" (European Commission, 2017, p. 8).

PE commonly takes one of two forms: light post-editing for documentation that will not enter the public domain, which involves making a text understandable; and full post-editing for texts that will be published. It involves a "spectrum of agency" (Vieira, 2019), from no human involvement to high levels of involvement, for instance with MT suggestions being made as a text is being translated.

Post-editing now has its own ISO standard (ISO 18587), which has led some scholars, such as Nitzke, Hansen-Schirra, and Canfora (2019), to advocate the development of a specific PE competence model in recognition of the additional competences post-editors need to acquire. Although these authors do not advocate a strict separation of PE and translation in the curriculum due to the considerable overlaps, they stress that the former role warrants new self-perception and professional ethics.

PE also highlights the porousness of the boundaries between different translator tasks and technologies, which requires a high degree of versatility and, hence, advanced skills in (digital) reflexivity. To illustrate this porousness, O'Brien (2022, p. 106) describes translator work environments that combine translation memory, terminology management, and machine translation, asserting that they often involve a translator moving from editing a sentence (e.g. a fuzzy match), translating the next one from scratch, and then post-editing the one that follows.

O'Brien (2002) was one of the first scholars to suggest what a dedicated PE course might look like. This template has since been complemented by scholarship on course implementation in different countries, which describes the challenges and student outcomes in assessment, and provides fertile ground for understanding the ethical issues students are likely to confront during their learning. Examples include Flanagan and Christensen (2014) in Denmark, Kenny and Doherty (2014) in Ireland, Guerberof and Moorkens (2019) in Spain, Yamada (2019) in Japan, and Konttinen, Salmi, and Koponen (2020) in Finland. In a recent survey, Ginovart Cid et al. (2020, p. 299) ascertained that the most commonly privileged topics on academic programmes in which PE is taught the are:

- PE levels (light and full PE);
- PE guidelines (exhaustive list and examples in the relevant language pair);
- PE attitude (decide when to discard and translate from scratch);
- MT systems (rule-based, example-based, statistical, hybrid, or neural);
- PE risks (under-, over-, and pseudo-editing where students introduce errors into a segment rather than editing);
- integration between CAT tool and MT systems;
- PE techniques and strategies (shift, replacement, addition, deletion); and
- practical PE exercises in the relevant language pair.

The combination of lectures and practice-based seminars to contextualise the activity within the translation workflow is common to the courses reflected in the literature above. MT is often taught either in parallel with or prior to PE knowledge and skills development, and assessment commonly includes the creation of a post-edited product (a light or full post-edited text) and reflective commentary on the process. In the literature and survey cited above, the ethical aspects of PE are not explicitly mentioned in either the course content or assessment tasks, with the exception of the programme at Dublin City University, Ireland, described by Kenny and Doherty (2014). However, issues around attitudes, professional integrity and identity, trust (of data), risk, productivity, and fair remuneration are thrown into sharp relief in all phases of MTPE, all of which take on ethical importance to varying degrees. Students also need to develop confidence in discerning MT quality, the relevance of MT output for certain text types, and the need for domain expertise in PE over generalist translator input.

The relationship between emergent professional translator self-concept and differential quality and productivity expectations in MTPE also merits attention. O'Brien's (2012) assertion that translators who are used to producing high-quality (publishable) translations, whether from scratch or through full post-editing, can feel professionally affronted if tasked with producing anything less than this standard (i.e. translation that is "good enough") is echoed in more recent surveys of professional attitudes (e.g. Sakamoto, 2019b). Post-editing of machine-translated output differs from revising a suggestion by a translation memory (Moorkens and O'Brien, 2017), and some of the reluctance expressed by professional translators concerns the extent to which MTPE boosts productivity, as compared to editing translation memory (Sánchez-Gijón, Moorkens, and Way, 2019). Exposing students to (freelance and language service provider) professional discourses of accommodation of and resistance to PE-related practices provides important context for student learning and forms the basis of the next activity.

3.4.1 Issues reported in MTPE student learning: implications for teaching

Under-editing seems to be a common outcome in reported student performance in MTPE, in contrast to over-editing (or "preferential changes"), which has been observed in professional translator outputs, although both may occur across these groups. Reports include perceptions that many students see the activity chiefly as a lexical task (Daems et al., 2017) and often fail to adhere to or fully understand PE guidelines, despite the provision of what educators consider clear task instructions. For instance, students in Depraetere's (2010) study failed to spot omissions, did not sufficiently correct errors, and neglected to amend suggested terminology even when a better solution was available. This strongly suggests the need for greater scaffolding early in the task in the form of a detailed checklist, which can be gradually faded as students engage in subsequent iterations.

As Flanagan and Christensen (2014) point out, student performance in Depraetere's study may have been influenced by the list of "dos and don'ts" issued as part of the task. Yamada's (2019) experiment, which used Google's Neural Machine Translation tool to replicate a 2014 experiment using Google's Statistical Machine Translation tool, found poorer error correction in neural MT plus PE.

Sycz-Opoń and Gałuskina (2017) attribute some of these issues to the multi-layered nature of the PE task, particularly in terms of the number of potential categories of errors. It appears that students struggle with the open-ended nature of the task and become overwhelmed by the process of error spotting. This suggests a phased approach might benefit student learning to build up reflexive thinking incrementally (i.e. build up a prototype of problem triggers, their manifestations, and solutions). It also suggests that the error-spotting approach does not adequately encourage connections between general competence development in translation (i.e. from scratch), checking, revising and editing, and discernment in the options presented by the machine translator and/or translation memory.

Several alternative approaches may be considered. First, a tandem approach in which from-scratch translation precedes an MTPE exercise. This can be a phased approach anchored around a spectrum of agency, from a radical "trust nothing/check everything" starting point to a more informed approach to (MT output) data trust as skills develop. To encourage rigour in checking, texts for this type of activity should be short (up to 250 words). The goal is to build up reference points that enhance reflexive thinking and improve error-detection rates over time. In this approach, students are not instructed to follow any PE guidelines.

Educators can then start to build guidelines into subsequent light or full PE activities as they gauge the degree to which students are making productive and active connections between their translatorial agency (i.e. knowledge of the translation process, confidence to make decisions based on domain specificity relating to terminology, phraseology, etc.) and scrutiny of machine-translated output. If these guidelines are not consistently followed as anticipated, it may be that the nature and range of the errors in the text need some manipulation by the educator to build up student confidence slowly. Educators may also consider providing worked examples and/or an indication of how many improvements are required in different categories (terminology, syntax, etc.). For information on guidelines for different levels of post-editing, see, for example, the Translation Automation User Society (TAUS) guidelines.[3]

The following activities, which support the development of ethical competence in the PE curriculum, should be implemented alongside the general PE curriculum structure, described earlier. By contrast, some activities may be used as stand-alone tasks for students who receive only a brief introduction to the topic as part of their translator education.

Activity

Resistance to and accommodation of post-editing

- **Learning aims:** to put student learning about post-editing into context by exploring the impact of the activity on professional translators' self-concept.
- **Learning outcomes:** by the end of this activity, students will be able to critically evaluate the parameters used by professionals in assessing and expressing their degree of resistance to and/or accommodation of MTPE in their workflow.
- **Recommended reading:** Sakamoto (2019b).

Task

This task assumes that students have been introduced to the concept of MTPE, but direct experience of post-editing is not required.

1. Working in groups of four to five, students gather examples from industry blogs and professional publications of discourse about PE over the last five years (freelancers and staff translators).
2. Students share their examples on a platform such as Padlet and review each other's contributions.
3. Each group categorises the examples by year, translator status (freelance/staff), attitude (broadly positive, broadly negative, neutral), and type (MTPE as part of a translator's workbench, MTPE of raw output by a machine translator (open/proprietary)).
4. The examples are examined for patterns in language use (e.g. resistance, accommodation), critical moments that led to a shift in attitude/use, and the extent to which MTPE impacts on the translator's professional identity/self-concept. Students discuss their own attitudes to the phenomenon and the extent to which these have been confirmed or challenged by their findings.

5 Students share their findings in a plenary or create a short video in which they present the key points from the exercise to share in a virtual learning environment or on a video-sharing site (subject to local university regulations).

Activity

Sensitisation to user needs in MTPE

- **Learning aims:** to introduce students to different levels of MTPE in a given scenario.
- **Learning outcomes:** by the end of this task, students will be able to evaluate different levels of MT output and human translation from scratch in relation to a specific social situation in which the needs of multilingual communities have not been duly addressed.
- **Recommended reading:** Bowker and Buitrago Ciro (2015).

Task

Bowker and Buitrago Ciro (2015) conducted a study in which end users (a group of newly arrived Spanish-speaking immigrants) were invited to evaluate different machine-translated versions of a text (e.g. raw MT output, rapid PE output, maximally edited machine-translated output and human translation). The study found that rapidly post-edited machine-translated output suited their needs best.

1 The class is presented with a hypothetical scenario: a local environmental organisation is seeking advice on whether MT might suit their needs in communicating with members of different communities about a new transport scheme that is likely to impact the local area significantly over the next ten years. There will be regular updates on the scheme and invitations to attend meetings and ask questions.
2 In small groups, students draft three short notices about this scheme (approximately 250 words, intended for a literate adult audience) for translation (e.g. information about a planning application; invitation to a "town hall" meeting with developers; information about proposed changes to the scheme; information about potential compulsory purchase of properties; information on the scheme's environmental impact).
3 Each group creates a portfolio of the three texts in translation. For each text, they produce: raw MT output, rapid MTPE output, full MTPE, and a human translation from scratch.
4 Each group recruits an evaluation panel. This could be formed of student peers from other classes who are asked to put themselves in

the position of a member of a minority-speaking group or peers from the same class.
5 Prior to the evaluation session, each panel is provided with a supporting "evaluation sheet" to help the evaluators decide which type of translation best suits their needs. It may be that different types are relevant to different types of communication.
6 The various groups report back on their evaluation sessions, highlighting key points from the discussion and the range of justifications made for the approaches to translation preferred by the group. The discussions are commented upon by the students to compare the extent to which their own views (which are informed by prior study and familiarity with the MTPE literature) were reflected or challenged by the peer evaluation.

Activity

Negotiating the use of MTPE with a client

- **Learning aims:** to plan and carry out research to advise a client on the potential use of free MT in a commercial setting.
- **Learning outcomes:** by the end of this task, students will be able to: devise a set of questions, plan, and carry out a review of options for a hypothetical scenario involving MTPE; collaboratively test ideas as an evidence base for making recommendations; and apply knowledge about MT security and data issues.

Task

1 The class is presented with a hypothetical scenario: a small but highly innovative fashion brand hopes to increase its international appeal by translating product descriptions into 15 languages. The brand is seeking advice as to whether MTPE using a free online translator system would be viable for extensive product descriptions and some promotional campaigns; and, if so, what level of post-editing would be required to meet their needs and boost their international reputation.
2 In small groups, students draft a list of questions they need to address in order to advise the company and produce a project plan. As a guide, they should think about:
  - data security and confidentiality issues;
  - the time-bound nature of texts (is MTPE viable if texts are regularly updated?);

108 *Ethics and the translation curriculum (II)*

- the potential value to the business of them investing in their own system that can be trained in domain-specific texts; and
- the extent to which MTPE that uses a freely available machine translator is (ethically) viable for translating a creative promotional campaign.

3 The groups work through their questions and plans by creating and testing some hypothetical texts as an evidence base to support their recommendations.
4 Each group produces a short report including this evidence to justify their recommendations.

Activity

Interpersonal communication and negotiation of MT use[4]

- **Learning aim:** to consider strategies for effective interaction with a client who may have used an MT platform prior to sending the output to the translator to post-edit.
- **Learning outcomes:** by the end of this activity, students will have: reflected on the nature of translator agency in this scenario and options available to assert professional knowledge and responsibility; planned how to request fairer remuneration and articulated that request in a draft email; reflected on the wider implications of the practice for other translators.

Task

1 The class is presented with a hypothetical scenario: a businessman operates a specialist holiday facility aimed at elderly tourists with mobility problems. They have used a CAT tool to translate a promotional brochure and offer a freelance translator the job of post-editing the text. However, they are only prepared to pay the price of a fuzzy match for machine-translated segments (partly of poor quality). A section of the MT output is sent to the translator to help them decide whether they wish to accept the job.
2 Students are asked to identify the ethical and financial issues in this scenario for the client and the translator.
3 Students discuss possible approaches to a dialogue in which the translator attempts to persuade the client that the fee offered is unreasonable for MT segments that require major revision and proposes one that ensures fairer remuneration for the work required. They then draft an email that sets out the translator's position and recommendation.

4	The educator informs the class that the client refused to increase the fee on the grounds that other translators had accepted comparable remuneration in the past.
5	Students discuss their reactions to this response and what action (if any) they might be able to take to ensure greater consistency of practice for the profession.

3.5 Collaborative translation

This section focuses on collaborative translation in a range of settings, paying particular attention to the potential for exploitation, the ethical implications arising from situations in which professionals and non-professionals work side by side, and the potential of Wikipedia for fostering ethical sensitivity and developing skills in ethical reasoning.

3.5.1 General trends and implications for ethics education

As discussed in the previous section, collaborative working in translator education has become widely embedded in pedagogical approaches that promote situated learning and simulate real-world tasks. However, in accounts of these learning situations, ethical competence development appears to be largely incidental and unplanned, emerging out of interpersonal interactions. In this section, the proposals for developing ethics education engage more directly with models of collaborative translation in both the for-profit and the not-for-profit sectors, which have evolved rapidly since the early 2000s in tandem with developments in the online platform economy (Cordingley and Frigau Manning, 2017; McDonough Dolmaya and del Mar Sánchez Ramos, 2019). The ethicality of such models and their impact on working practices, individual translators, and wider society (e.g. Piróth and Baker, 2020) merit some attention within the curriculum, not least because many translation students are attracted to volunteer initiatives as part of their general skills development.

Crowdsourced translation is one such model that appeals to virtual "crowds" online to generate translation content (O'Hagan, 2011, p. 14; Jiménez-Crespo, 2017), and its use is also reflected across sectors. Although most crowdsourced translation concerns unpaid contributions through wide recruitment appeals, in some contexts paid professional translators may be involved in this activity under a closed recruitment process and vetting of interested parties (García, 2015). The shift to this model of translation production has shone a spotlight on issues of process and motivation, both of which have ethical implications.

In terms of process, some crowdsourced approaches challenge the traditional linear model of translate–edit–proofread (TEP) as they usually entail translators working with advanced translation memory tools, checking and correcting each other's work as the project progresses (DePalma and Kelly, 2011, p. 382). In terms of motivation, translators working in highly specialised domains are able to share expertise and knowledge in dynamic ways, whereas others are attracted by the ideals of online communities collaborating to achieve social justice goals or promote a favourite product.

Kang and Hong (2020, p. 55) highlight the increasing difficulty of distinguishing between volunteer and crowdsourced translation due to the degree of overlap in their characteristics, such as the frequent lack of financial compensation and drive to participate, which is often influenced by affect. Over a decade ago, Pym (2012, p. 4) drew attention to the fact that translators are interested in and motivated by value exchange of a social, symbolic, and cultural kind, not just an economic kind. This observation still resonates at the time of writing, not least due to experiences of Covid-19 and the many examples of violent conflict and population displacement in the contemporary world.

Collaborative translation in online environments is promoted in this section as a lens through which students can sharpen their critical faculties and develop ethical reflexivity in order to identify and plan responses to the use of technology and technology-mediated practices that are shaped by particular ideological formations. As such, the section focuses on educator input and student-centred activities that foreground intersections between agency, discourse, ideology, practice, identity, and community. The examples chiefly concern volunteer translation activities outside of commercial spheres, in part because it is likely to be beyond the resources of programmes to simulate more advanced, commercially oriented collaborative translation experiences. A focus is placed on:

- (translation) labour and its conceptualisation in the online platform economy;
- the ways in which labour and expertise are used (and potentially abused) in these environments;
- what engagement in collaborative working means for online working relationships (between professionals, and between professionals and non-professionals), the translator self-concept, and self-worth; and
- how collaborative practices are evaluated in terms of their outcomes for individual translators and wider society.

A phased approach to collaborative translation is anchored around the following:

- open discussion of prior knowledge and experience;
- exposure to the experiences of others through analysis of translator accounts of volunteer and remunerated collaborative translation work;
- sensitisation to the ideological formations in which different collaborative translation platforms and initiatives are located, and to the risks and benefits to the individual;
- socialisation to collaborative translation initiatives in which non-professional and professional translators work side by side; and
- experience of translation practice in a real-world online collaborative translation environment.

Activity

Open discussion of prior knowledge and experience of online collaborative translation among students

Class discussion prompts:

- Have you come across or searched for opportunities online to collaborate on translation projects, whether for payment or for altruistic reasons?
- Have you been involved in any collaborative translation work directly? What motivated you to get involved and had you received any translation training prior to starting?
- What support (if any) was offered by the organisation or group with which you engaged?
- Have you ever been involved in user-generated translation projects – for instance, have you supported the dissemination of products of popular culture to transnational fan communities? If so, how would you describe these experiences (in terms of collegiality, time commitment, personal satisfaction, risk)?
- If you have experience of collaborative translation work, did you encounter any ethical issues while doing the work that might dissuade you from doing any more in the future?
- If you have no experience of collaborative translation, which ethical issues do you think you might encounter, and might these deter you from participating in such activities?
- Once you are working as a professional translator, do you think it will be important to offer some *pro bono* services for causes that would benefit from a professional level of input?

3.5.2 Labour and exploitation in online collaborative translation

Many students entering translation programmes are likely to lead very full lives in the digital sphere, which may include informal translation activities as part of their online cultural and leisure interactions as committed and interested linguists. However, the boundaries between personal and professional activities involving translation can be fairly porous and risk generating vulnerabilities. The potential for exploitation is ever present (Zwischenberger, 2021).

Writing on this topic more than a decade ago, McDonough Dolmaya (2011) acknowledged that some translators may not even think they are being exploited due to the fact that they have been taken in by the rhetoric and marketing devices of for-profits that promote such activity as part of their business models. These include appeals to values such as equal opportunity, global connectedness, universal access to information, and to affect such as an individual's enthusiasm for a particular product or technology (Kang and Hong, 2020, p. 54). This is another example of where the development of (digital) reflexivity, which translates here into an ability to comprehend the tensions between personal motivations and third-party interests, can support a critically informed approach to personal decision-making and evaluation of the consequences of certain practices.

Educators may consider the potential of adopting a case-study approach to a selected online platform (owners, funding, goals, ideology, use of translated data), the hierarchies and practices embedded within it, and, by extension, a critical appraisal of the outcome of the labour given by translators over time. Following Zwischenberger (2021), students might also be encouraged to think about how the profits and benefits that translators help to generate are distributed, the extent to which they benefit from them directly, and the ramifications for individuals and wider society of exploitative practices, using a consequentialist lens as a supporting theoretical framework.

Activity

Evaluating crowdsourced translation in for-profit educational course providers (also known as massive open online course providers – MOOCs)

- **Learning aims:** to explore the organisation and its use of volunteer translation in a for-profit online setting; to sensitise students to the ecology of practice in such settings and variability in ecology between platforms; to consider the ethical issues for paying users of platforms that come to rely on translated content.
- **Learning outcomes:** by the end of this activity, students will be able to: identify ecologies of volunteer translation practice in for-profit settings; apply knowledge of translation quality assessment and assurance in a critical evaluation of the outcomes of this practice; discern ethical issues for paying customers and the long-term sustainability of the ecology of translation practice.
- **Recommended reading:** Kang and Hong (2020).

Task

1   The educator ensures that the class understands that large online educational course providers often rely on crowdsourced translation to make materials available across languages and cultures. For example, in discussion forums, many (non-professional) translators express a desire to see their language represented among those offered in the hope that this will empower others in their language community by providing them with access to more educational programmes, adopting a type of "pioneer" role.
2   Students explore the for-profit educational provider Coursera (or another provider) in relation to the role of translation in its course provision.

3 In small groups, students discuss the following points (or others for different platforms):

- Are you in favour of the democratic principle of allowing users to suggest and support the addition of new languages? Why? Why not?
- Can you find examples where this model is used by for-profit, education-oriented organisations and supported by a wider infrastructure of mentors, moderators, and quality-control checkers?
- What are the ethical implications of the model for those paying to access materials where such an infrastructure is in place and in cases where it is not?
- Is the model sustainable? If not, what impact might this have on the organisation (in terms of public trust, reputation, etc.) and users in the longer term?

Activity

Exploring the concept of labour in online (volunteer) collaborative translation initiatives

- **Learning aims:** to introduce students to different concepts of labour in the online digital (platform) economy; to facilitate examination of the language and discourse practices different platforms use to conceptualise translation labour and motivate participation; to sensitise students to the potential for exploitation in online collaborative translation.
- **Learning outcomes:** by the end of this activity, students will be able to: define different concepts of labour relating to online collaborative platform working and situate concepts in the context of translation labour; identify discourse practices used to motivate participation in online collaborative translation; and discern the longer-term value attached to contributions as well as the traceability of potential benefits.

Task

In this task, students are invited to research and discuss different conceptualisations of labour in the context of volunteer collaborative translation and critically engage with the language platforms use to appeal to volunteer translators.

1 In small groups, students discuss concepts like "prosumer", "playbour", "contributor", "pool of workers", and "empowerer" in relation to different types of online collaborative and crowdsourced translation initiatives that they themselves have identified or that have been

presented in class. They also consider the relationship between these concepts and "autonomy" and "dependence" in online collaborative translation. They determine which concepts most adequately capture the nature of labour required of translators on the selected platforms, acknowledging that more than one may apply.

2   Each group then selects several crowdsourced translation platforms to examine the **language** they use to **appeal** to volunteer translators and the **initiatives** they have designed to **motivate** commitment and continued involvement. The group should also reflect on the ways in which they might be able to trace or identify the potential benefits of their contributions in the future. Suggested platforms include:

- Ted Talks: www.ted.com/about/programs-initiatives/ted-translators
- WordPress: https://make.wordpress.org/polyglots/handbook/translating/expectations/
- Translators Without Borders: https://translatorswithoutborders.org/meet-the-twb-community
- PerMondo: www.permondo.eu/volunteers/
- Global Voices: https://globalvoices.org/global-voices-translation-services/

3   Sample questions (vis-à-vis Global Voices) to stimulate discussion:

- Which rhetorical devices does the platform use to encourage individuals to join its community of translators?
- What evidence is there of how the organisation articulates the relationship between its more commercially oriented translation work (for which it pays translators a "competitive rate") and volunteer work?
- Is it clear how translators might gain access to the organisation's paid translation opportunities?
- Which ethical practices (if any) does the site promote in translation and/or project management?

4   In a plenary, students present key points from their group discussions. Extension discussion points may include: reflection on the extent to which their perceptions (and potentially motivations) remain unchanged or have been transformed by their investigations and discussions; the implications of physical distance and fragmentation (of tasks/involvement) for the translator's sense of self-worth and personal development.

3.5.3 Collaborative translation in crisis situations as a support for ethics education

The deployment of technological solutions to support professional and non-professional multilingual communication in the provision of assistance and aid to stricken individuals and communities has demonstrated that the power of the "crowd" can be rapidly and effectively mobilised, with non-professional or "citizen" translators and professionals often working in tandem (O'Mathúna, Escartín, Roche, and Marlowe, 2020). Experiences of crowdsourced translation following the Haiti earthquake in 2010 (Munro, 2010; 2013) and during the Covid-19 pandemic (Zhang and Wu, 2020) provide insights into how various solutions and technologies were pressed into service and what they entailed for those involved.[5]

From an ethics perspective, there are many challenges at the organisational level for authorities on the ground, developers of translation products, and the sustainability of initiatives in general terms (Hunt, O'Brien, Cadwell, and O'Mathúna, 2019), which are beyond the scope of translation programmes to address directly. Nevertheless, there are many aspects of research on crisis translation, not least the findings of the International Network on Crisis Translation (INTERACT),[6] that serve as a useful backdrop for ethical competence development in online collaborative translation as well as other translation situations, particularly in relation to community- and capacity-building. The rest of this subsection focuses on interactions between citizen translators and professional translators in collaborative translation initiatives in crisis situations, and the development of the translator self-concept in these moments of vulnerability and uncertainty.

Collaborative translation in a crisis situation is one of the few occasions when non-professional (or "citizen") translators and professionals work together. In such situations, productive working relationships need to overcome potential inter-group tensions in order to achieve desired goals. They also need to take account of the context and potential psycho-social vulnerabilities of all members of the volunteer collaborative translation initiative, given that they, along with the intended recipients of the translation, are themselves victims of the crisis. The concept of the "other" collapses, at least to some extent, bringing into sharp relief the question of partiality and how this is navigated by the group.

O'Mathúna et al. (2020) propose a virtue ethics framework to support analysis of and sensitivity to the complexities of intra-group communication in situations (in this case humanitarian response) where ethical decision-making can be fraught and in which deontological codes devised for stable moral environments can prove inadequate. However, virtue ethics, as an approach rooted in Western philosophy, merits further critical attention (from educators and students) in terms of its role and function in an applied approach to practice.

Educators can encourage students to research the extent to which a virtue ethics framework accounts for cultural diversity, and how and whether hierarchies of virtues operate at different phases of an initiative. Frameworks from other ethical traditions, such as those that emphasise collective decision-making and community wellbeing, also merit consideration (see Pym, 2020). Furthermore, students may wish to explore the relationship between deontology and collaborative practice in situations in which professionals and non-professionals work side by side as well as the temporal and environmental factors that shape attitudes to what practice should look like over time. Despite the impossibility of bringing the "real world"

116 *Ethics and the translation curriculum (II)*

into the classroom for such activities, a well-contextualised case-study approach with practical tasks anchored around specific ethical problems can support student skills development and learning.

A final consideration concerns the ways in which students are supported to conceptualise the formation of the temporary translator community of practice and their own place within it in a crisis situation. In this regard, O'Mathúna et al.'s (2020) aforementioned study invokes Ricœur's (2007) concept of linguistic hospitality and the emphasis placed on translation as a form of ethical engagement and a place of meeting. For O'Mathúna et al. (2020, p. 27), Ricœur's articulation of linguistic hospitality suggests important considerations that may not be immediately apparent in humanitarian situations: that responders from outside a community are guests as well as helpers (who need food and shelter themselves); that communities have resources that responders may lack (e.g. capacities in local languages, cultural expertise, understanding of local geographies and customs); and that mutual exchange is both possible and necessary as a basis for respect and trust.

Activity

"Drawing a crowd": understanding the factors impacting crisis translation initiatives

- **Learning aim:** to identify examples of collaborative translation initiatives in crisis situations and the ways in which the voices of interested parties are represented.
- **Learning outcomes:** by the end of this activity, students will be able to: identify accounts of real-world approaches to crisis translation; distinguish voices within those accounts to evaluate how and the extent to which different constituencies are represented; ascertain the extent to which machine translation solutions are present and how they impact crisis communication.
- **Recommended reading:** Zhang and Wu (2020).

Task

1 Students are invited to explore initial communications between interested linguists (including professional translators) during the Covid-19 pandemic, the conflict in Ukraine, or another crisis situation of their choosing as a starting point for considering the ethical obligation for translation in such situations and selected ethical aspects of the collaborative process.
2 Students map responses across social media, mainstream media, educational providers, charities, and local authorities.
3 Individually, students search for examples of crowdsourced translation initiatives, focusing on the ways in which volunteers advertised

Ethics and the translation curriculum (II) 117

their services and coordinated translation services, and the different technologies and digital communication platforms they used.

4   After pooling their findings with a small group of peers, students reflect on:

- whose voices are prominent in the examples (non-professionals or professionals) and how their experiences are represented;
- the extent to which there is a sense of people trying to reinvent the wheel and neglecting to refer to what worked in previous situations (with reference to the uniqueness of different situations);
- the extent to which and how technologies (including translation technologies) were used;
- the extent to which the voices of recipients of translations are present; and
- the extent to which people use machine translation independently, as opposed to looking for sources of information produced by other translation means.

5   Whole-class discussion to share findings and reflect on the potential risks of individuals relying on machine translation solutions in certain circumstances.

Activity

Setting up community practices and intra-group support for a mixed professional and non-professional cohort of volunteer translators in a crisis situation

- **Learning aims:** plan technological and communication approaches to facilitate translation in a health crisis situation; develop strategies for key intra-group tensions involving perceived issues around professionalism, technical skill, and religious convictions.
- **Learning outcomes:** by the end of this activity, students will be able to: articulate the communicative and technological needs of a mixed professional and non-professional group of translators working in a crisis situation; formulate arguments and strategies to address intra-group tensions; articulate the psycho-social aspects of crisis translation and questions of autonomy and dependence within the group.
- **Recommended reading:** Ogie, O'Brien, and Federici (2021); O'Mathúna et al. (2020).

Task

1   Students imagine a scenario in which they have identified a local need for the translation of health-related information in a situation not

dissimilar to Covid-19. To meet this need, they have assembled a small group of volunteer translators who will produce translations in several languages to support the local community. The group consists of local "citizen" translators with no training or experience as well as professional translators based in other countries, recruited to ensure coverage of relevant language combinations.

2   Working in small groups, students devise a short set of community rules for participating in the project. These rules should address the following issues:

- identifying and managing expertise (e.g. language, local knowledge, etc.) within the group;
- tone of communications;
- revision processes;
- establishing group approaches to achieve terminological consistency; and
- accessing domain-specific experts.

3   Students identify the types of media and technological support that will aid their collaboration, bearing in mind the need for contingency planning.

4   Extension discussion: on completion of the task, students discuss a scenario in which it becomes clear that there will be an ongoing need for translation throughout the crisis to support the local community. Several members of the group with professional translation experience insist that the local authorities should become more involved by employing professional translators who are remunerated for their work. The group discusses how it might respond to an accusation that its work is undermining paid translation opportunities.

5   Extension discussion: students discuss a scenario in which it becomes clear that one of the translators has been altering text and including religious references based on the view that the target audience would expect such an approach. Some members of the group feel uncomfortable about this. How might the group address this issue in a productive manner? (NB: Think about whether the claims are based on fact or perception, the group's goal of establishing a good reputation with the local community, and whether uniformity of approach is desirable across all translated outputs.)

6   Extension discussion: students discuss a scenario in which the unequal levels of skill and experience within the group have resulted in some aspects of the work taking longer than others, and a lack of resources to support some language combinations have left some of the translators struggling to deliver. How might the group establish positive working relationships to support those with lower levels of skill and experience? Which strategies might be implemented to support translators with fewer resources and concerns about their accuracy?

7   Extension discussion: students discuss a scenario in which the group has started to rely on one experienced, highly skilled member for support and to coordinate its activities. What might the group do to alleviate the pressures of the crisis on group members and ensure a more even distribution of responsibilities? (NB: Think about Ricœur's concept of linguistic hospitality and the implications of it for understanding translation encounters in crisis situations, when both the translator and the recipient experience the crisis at first hand.)

3.5.4 *Wikipedia as a support for translator ethics education*

Wikipedia is a long-established crowdsourced initiative in which article translation (along with article creation and editing) is entirely user-driven (McDonough Dolmaya, 2015, p. 18). Translation on the platform is generally undertaken by non-professionals. As a potential pedagogical resource and translator training environment, the platform has received some attention within translation studies (e.g. Calzada Pérez, 2019), and there is scope to realise this potential within translator ethics education. The platform's rich data – for instance, all amendments to a translation are archived and justifications for the changes are posted on the Revision History or Talk pages – provides a window on interactions about thorny concepts such as difference, worldviews, and translation practice, among many others. The wider platform and the policy environment in which it operates support student engagement with complex issues of language policy, translation policy (including the right to translation), and their intersections with regard to fairness and access to knowledge (McDonough Dolmaya, 2017).

Wikipedia affords three main types of pedagogical resource: a textual resource; a translation environment set within a particular policy universe; and a resource that can support experiential learning.

3.5.4.1 *Wikipedia as a textual resource for exploring ethical issues*

As McDonough Dolmaya (2017, p. 154) observes, Wikipedia encourages people to contribute "whenever and however they can". In terms of translation output, this means that comparative source language and target language versions are not necessarily available, as texts produced in other languages may involve a new piece from scratch on the same topic, or translated content that does not necessarily preserve style, content, and form. Students may study these shifts, which will vary in degree and extent, to explore the relationship between language and power in translation, the concept of history-making and its relation to translation (particularly in the context of Wikipedia's core content policy of editing from a "neutral point of view"), and the binary of "source" and "target" text.

According to Wikipedia, contributors are required, among other things, to "put aside their own opinions" and "describe a controversy rather than partake in it" (Phillips, 2016, p. 533); yet, the open policy on version creation and lack of a clear translation policy (although there are translation guidelines[7]) enable individual translators who also have editor status to court controversy through their ideologically motivated translation decisions, in some cases leading to "edit wars" when one translator edits another's text (Yasseri et al., 2012; Góngora-Goloubintseff, 2020). The aim of investigating the role of translation in maintaining or violating Wikipedia's core content policy is not to determine the ethicality of the practice itself, but rather to allow students to ask broader questions of the Wikipedia project and the role of collaborative translation within it.

Activity

Analysing the "neutral point of view" through translation practices

- **Learning aims:** to develop familiarity with the concept of "neutral point of view"; to facilitate application of different tools to analyse translation practice and discern ideological shifts.
- **Learning outcomes:** by the end of this activity, students will be able to: articulate the concept of "neutral point of view" and how it applies to the Wikipedia project; apply knowledge of translation practice to evaluate policy compliance.
- **Recommended reading:** Góngora-Goloubintseff (2020).

Task

1 Educator or students select one or two examples of translated content from Wikipedia on topics known to generate intense debate (e.g. the use of toponyms such as Derry/Londonderry, environmental issues such as global warming/cooling, the use of unmanned drones during warfare, language rights, etc.). Refer to Wikipedia's own list of topics for further inspiration: https://en.wikipedia.org/wiki/Wikipedia:List_of_controversial_issues.

2 Students analyse selected sections of the text (and visual material, if desired) with the goal of identifying ideologically motivated decisions that may impact on the neutral point of view. Several analytic approaches can be used alone or in combination, including:

- linguistic analysis (following Góngora-Goloubintseff, 2020, p. 3), paying particular attention to over-lexicalisation (proliferation of certain lexemes) and lexical suppression or absence; and
- narrative analysis, drawing on features of narrativity (Baker, 2006), such as selective appropriation, framing, and labelling.

3 Each student writes a report on their findings, using examples from their analysis to support key points.

Activity

Wikipedia Talk pages as a site of ethical encounter

- **Learning aims:** to explore translator agency through online talk about translation decisions; to identify discursive constructions of neutrality in the context of the policy of "neutral point of view".
- **Learning outcomes:** by the end of this activity, students will be able to: evaluate the ethicality of discursive practices in situations of (strong) disagreement and discern examples of effective practice that could be replicated in professional collaborative translation environments; evaluate the structure of pages and the ecology of translation practices on Wikipedia as a model of online collaborative translation and make recommendations for change/enhancement.

Task

This task can be used as a follow-up to the previous task.

1. Students use the same topic and versions they used in the previous activity or select new ones.
2. The focus of this exercise is an analysis of the Talk pages that accompany a translated text to explore the textual history of the version and the discussion and justifications for changes posted on the Talk pages.
3. In particular, students should search for reactions to disputed elements of the translated text, described as "ideological squaring" (following Góngora-Goloubintseff, 2020).
4. When examining the Talk pages, special attention should be paid to rhetorical devices used in justifications of changes and the discursive construction of "neutrality" within the context of "neutral point of view".
5. Consideration should be given to the infrastructure of Wikipedia (including page layout and interactional features, the wider ecology of editing tools, and policies) with a view to determining the site's potential to foster productive interactions as part of an ethically informed approach to communication *about* translation in the digital sphere.
6. Finally, students make recommendations for enhancements or improvements to the site.

3.5.4.2 Experiencing Wikipedia as an educational environment

Wikipedia welcomes student involvement on the platform but highlights the need for appropriate scaffolding and management by educational institutions.[8] For translation educators, it offers a number of learning opportunities as well as an integrated translation tool.[9]

The Wikitrad project, developed by María Calzada Pérez at Universitat Jaume I, Castellón, Spain, has evolved into an established component of the translation curriculum at that institution and elsewhere. Calzada Pérez's (2019) account of the project, which involves students working collaboratively to translate Wikipedia articles (termed as "social translation"), does not explicitly refer to ethics, but it is present in all of the environmental, interactional, and interpersonal layers of Wikitrad. Of particular import to the project in pedagogical terms is the explicit shift away from "the mainstay model of translator competence" (Calzada Pérez's, 2019, p. 180) to a model derived from the emergentist pedagogical paradigm and complexity theory developed by Kiraly (2016) and highlighted in the introduction to this chapter. This model takes a multi-vortex form, helping to emphasise the non-linearity of both translation and learning processes and as something "occasioned surprisingly and unexpectedly from intended and unintended efforts and circumstances" (Kiraly, 2016, quoted in Calzada Pérez, 2019, p. 181).

The pedagogical imperative of taking students "to the edge of chaos" that underpins the project draws on the idea of "complex adaptive systems" (CAS), developed out of complexity theory (Lewin, 1993) and applied to the educational sphere. In CAS, a "system" is understood as a network of individual local entities that interact with each other and the environment. The product of these interactions is "a global property that cannot be limited to the sum of its local parts" (Calzada Pérez, 2019, p. 182) In CAS, systems seek to generate order, but as self-generating and self-organising, the dynamics for generating order come from within, which is why they may move variously between chaos and order and back again when establishing connections with local entities.

Maximum complex activity is said to take place at the edge of chaos. In Calzada Pérez's (2019, p. 186) words, social translation projects offer "meeting points" for students where they must interact with each other, with tools, and with other human agents (instructors and translation professionals), requiring sensitivity to a certain ethics of engagement. These meeting points lead the students to the edge of chaos as they encounter unfamiliar translation situations and working environments and have to navigate their way through to create a credible final translation product. The destabilising effects of the journey are what lead to change.

Wikitrad involves students translating Wikipedia pages in teams, although there is some emphasis on individual contributions, which are expected to be at least 1500 words in length. Students select the topics they wish to work on with guidance from educators, then follow a five-stage process: preparation, draft of the translation, peer revision, professional editing, and publication. They receive a short course from a specialist on Wikipedia tools, guidelines, and methodology, then create their own user-name pages and "sandboxes" where their draft work will appear. After a process of peer revision whereby all teams comment on two other teams' work through relevant Talk pages, external professional editors review the translations before publication. Calzada Pérez (2019, p. 190) notes the importance of the peer-revision stage because it allows students to "show that they can produce comments about others in the requested manner", suggesting that relational ethics is foregrounded in the task. Of course, the final, published versions have an afterlife where editors with no connection to the project can contribute, thereby placing the translation and the learners into another unstable environment.

What potential does this project offer for translator ethics education? In common with the crisis translation situation, Wikitrad helps to create an environment in which ethical thinking and acting evolve through different phases of human and material interaction in a well-delimited context. The interconnected forms of complexity that emerge during the project, listed by Calzada Pérez (2019, p. 193) as the complexity of the classroom environment, the intercultural encounter fostered by that environment, and the complexity of social translation itself, generate situations in which multiple ethical frameworks need to be navigated, sometimes simultaneously, sometimes hierarchically. These include group decision-making around meaning and process, interactions with others to learn and master a new translation environment, reconciling the impact on the self of certain stressors of the task parameters (environmental, interactional and intellectual), and time constraints. If students have already been introduced to different ethics traditions earlier in the programme, they can be encouraged to interrogate their project experience through *post-hoc* reflection in order to identify which frameworks were relevant at various points, as well as what the experience helped them learn about whether and in what ways their translator self-concept has evolved as a consequence.

3.6 Chapter summary

This chapter draws attention to the many and varied ethical implications of translation technologies, including those used in the translation process and those used to disseminate translated outputs. It underscores the importance of developing effective digital ethics practices in the deployment of technologies and in monitoring their impact on translator workflow and remuneration. Finally, it offers practical suggestions for activities to develop ethical awareness and ethical judgement in a range of translation situations, both for-profit and non-profit, which draw on a wide range of source materials.

Notes

1 Bracketing the word "digital" highlights that reflexivity occurs both within and outside of digital environments.
2 The concept of reflexivity has its roots in sociology and social theory (e.g. Durkheim); for a discussion on the relationship between reflexivity and habit, see Archer (2012).
3 www.taus.net/resources/reports/mt-post-editing-guidelines.
4 Following Nitzke (2019).
5 See Sutherlin (2013) for an insightful account of the problems arising from a lack of expert involvement in the design process with regard to Haiti, Egypt, and Libya, the consequences of competing attempts to use data for different purposes (e.g. aid relief

and policy-making), and the lack of feedback loops for users to suggest improvements or report issues.
6 https://cordis.europa.eu/project/id/734211/results.
7 https://en.wikipedia.org/wiki/Wikipedia:Translate_us.
8 See the Wikipedia page on university and school projects (https://en.wikipedia.org/wiki/Wikipedia:School_and_university_projects) for examples that include translation projects, and the page on student involvement in Wikipedia editing (https://en.wikipedia.org/wiki/Wikipedia:Student_assignment).
9 www.mediawiki.org/wiki/Content_translation.

References

Alcina, A., Soler, V., & Granell, J. (2007). Translation technology skills acquisition. *Perspectives*, 15(4), 230–244. https://doi.org/10.1080/13670050802280179.

Archer, M. (2012). *The reflexive imperative in late modernity*. Cambridge University Press.

Asscher, O., & Glikson, E. (2021). Human evaluations of machine translation in an ethically charged situation. *New Media and Society*, 25(5), 1087–1107. https://doi.org/10.1177/14614448211018833.

Baker, M. (2006). *Translation and conflict: A narrative account*. Routledge.

Basalamah, S., & Sadek, G. (2014). Copyright law and translation: Crossing epistemologies. *The Translator*, 20(3), 396–410. https://doi.org/10.1080/13556509.2014.931020.

Bowker, L. (2020). Translation technology and ethics. In K. Koskinen and N. K. Pokorn (Eds.), *The Routledge handbook of translation and ethics* (pp. 262–278). Routledge.

Bowker, L., & Buitrago Ciro, J. (2015). Investigating the usefulness of machine translation for newcomers at the public library. *Translation and Interpreting Studies*, 10(2), 165–186. https://doi.org/10.1075/tis.10.2.01bow.

Bowker, L., & Buitrago Ciro, J. (2019). *Machine translation and global research: Towards improved machine translation literacy in the scholarly community*. Emerald Publishing Limited.

Bowker, L., & Marshman, E. (2010). Toward a model of active and situated learning in the teaching of computer-aided translation: Introducing the CERTT project. *Journal of Translation Studies*, 13(1–2), 199–226. https://doi.org/10.15388/infedu.2008.12.

Cabrera, L. (2022). Babel Fish democracy? Prospects for addressing democratic language barriers through machine translation and interpretation. *American Journal of Political Science*, 18 July. https://doi.org/10.1111/ajps.12728.

Cadwell, P., O'Brien, S., & DeLuca, E. (2019). More than tweets: A critical reflection on developing and testing crisis machine translation technology. *Translation Spaces*, 8(2), 300–333. https://doi.org/10.1075/ts.19018.cad.

Cadwell, P., O'Brien, S., & Teixeira, C. S. C. (2018). Resistance and accommodation: Factors for the (non-)adoption of machine translation among professional translators. *Perspectives*, 26(3), 301–321. https://doi.org/10.1080/0907676X.2017.1337210.

Calzada Pérez, M. (2019). Beyond order and magic: Complexity-based emergentism, social translation and the Wikitrad project. *Translation Studies*, 12(2), 177–195. https://doi.org/10.1080/14781700.2019.1689162.

Canfora, C., & Ottmann, A. (2020). Risk in neural machine translation. *Translation Spaces*, 9(1), 58–77. https://doi.org/10.1075/ts.00021.can.

Christensen, T. P., Bundgaard, K., Schjoldager, A., & Dam Jensen, H. (2022). What motor vehicles and translation machines have in common: A first step towards a

translation automation taxonomy. *Perspectives*, 30(1), 19–38. https://doi.org/10.1080/0907676X.2021.1900307.
Cordingley, A., & Frigau Manning, C. (Eds.) (2017). *Collaborative translation: From the Renaissance to the digital age*. Bloomsbury.
Cronin, M. (2020). Translation, technology and climate change. In M. O'Hagan (Ed.), *The Routledge handbook of translation technology* (pp. 516–530). Routledge.
Daems, J., Vandepitte, S., Hartsuiker, R. J., Macken, L., & Bastin, G. L. (2017). Translation methods and experience: A comparative analysis of human translation and post-editing with students and professional translators. *Meta*, 62(2), 245–270. https://doi.org/10.7202/1041023ar.
DePalma, D. A., & Kelly, N. (2011). Project management for crowdsourced translation: How user-translated content projects work in real life. In K. J. Dunne and E. S. Dunne (Eds.), *Translation and localization project management: The art of the possible* (pp. 379–408). John Benjamins.
Depraetere, I. (2010). What counts as useful advice in a university post-editing training context? Report on a case. *Proceedings of the 14th Annual Conference of the European Association for Machine Translation, Saint Raphaël, France*. https://aclanthology.org/2010.eamt-1.11.pdf.
Desjardins, R. (2017). *Translation and social media: In theory, in training and in professional practice*. Palgrave Macmillan.
Drugan, J. (2019). Ethics. In P. Rawling and P. Wilson (Eds.), *The Routledge handbook of translation and philosophy* (pp. 243–255). Routledge.
Drugan, J., & Tipton, R. (2017). Translation, ethics and social responsibility. *The Translator*, 23(2), 119–125. https://doi.org/10.1080/13556509.2017.1327008.
Enríquez Raído, V. (2013). Teaching translation technologies "everyware": Towards self discovery and lifelong learning approach. *Tradumàtica*, 11, 275–285. https://revistes.uab.cat/tradumatica/article/view/n11-enriquez-raido/pdf.
Esqueda, M. D. (2021). Machine translation: Teaching and learning issues. *Trabalhos em linguística aplicada*, 60(1), 282–299. https://doi.org/10.1590/01031813932001520210212.
European Commission (2017). *European Master's in Translation: Competence framework 2017*. https://commission.europa.eu/system/files/2018-02/emt_competence_fwk_2017_en_web.pdf.
Farkas, A., & Németh, R. (2022). How to measure gender bias in machine translation: Real world oriented machine translators, multiple reference points. *Social Sciences and Humanities Open*, 5(1). https://doi.org/10.1016/j.ssaho.2021.100239.
Flanagan, M., & Christensen, T. P. (2014). Testing post-editing guidelines: How translation trainees interpret them and how to tailor them for translator training purposes. *The Interpreter and Translator Trainer*, 8(2), 257–275. https://doi.org/10.1080/1750399X.2014.936111.
Forcada, M. L. (2017). Making sense of neural machine translation. *Translation Spaces*, 6(2), 291–309. https://doi.org/10.1075/ts.6.2.06for.
García, I. (2015). Cloud marketplaces: Procurement of translators in the age of social media. *Journal of Specialised Translation*, 23, 18–38. www.jostrans.org/issue23/art_garcia.pdf.
Ginovart Cid, C. (2020). The professional profile of a post-editor according to LSCs and linguists: A survey-based research. *HERMES: Journal of Language and Communication in Business*, 60, 171–190. https://doi.org/10.7146/HJLCB.V60I0.121318.
Ginovart Cid, C., Colominas, C., & Oliver, A. (2020). Language industry views on the profile of the post-editor. *Translation Spaces*, 9(2), 283–313. https://doi.org/10.1075/ts.19010.cid.

Góngora-Goloubintseff, J. G. (2020). The Falklands/Malvinas war taken to the Wikipedia realm: A multimodal discourse analysis of crosslingual violations of the neutral point of view. *Palgrave Communications*, 6, Article 59. www.nature.com/articles/s41599-020-0435-2.

González Pastor, D., & Rico, C. (2021). POSEDITrad: La traducción automática y la posedición para la formación de traductores e intérpretes. *Docencia universitaria*, 15 (1), e1213. http://dx.doi.org/10.19083/ridu.2021.1213.

Guerberof, A., & Moorkens, J. (2019). Machine translation and post-editing training as part of a master's programme. *Journal of Specialised Translation*, 31, 217–238. www.jostrans.org/issue31/art_guerberof.pdf.

Hunt, M., O'Brien, S., Cadwell, P., & O'Mathúna, D. P. (2019). Ethics at the intersection of crisis translation and humanitarian innovation. *Journal of Humanitarian Affairs*, 1(3), 23–32. https://doi.org/10.7227/JHA.022.

Jiménez-Crespo, M. A. (2017). *Crowdsourcing and online collaborative translations: Expanding the limits of translation studies*. John Benjamins.

Kadiu, S. (2019). *Reflexive translation studies: Translation as critical reflection*. UCL Press.

Kang, J.-H., & Hong, J.-W. (2020). Volunteer translators as "committed individuals" or "providers of free labor"? The discursive construction of "volunteer translators" in a commercial online learning platform translation controversy. *Meta*, 65(1), 51–72. https://doi.org/10.7202/1073636ar.

Kenny, D. (2017). Introduction. In D. Kenny (Ed.), *Human issues in translation technology* (pp. 1–7). Routledge.

Kenny, D., & Doherty, S. (2014). Statistical machine translation in the translation curriculum: Overcoming obstacles and empowering translators. *The Interpreter and Translator Trainer*, 8(2), 276–294. https://doi.org/10.1080/1750399X.2014.936112.

Kiraly, D. C. (2006). Beyond social constructivism: Complexity theory and translator education. *Translation and Interpreting Studies*, 1(1), 68–86. https://doi.org/10.1075/tis.1.1.05kir.

Kiraly, D. C. (2015). Occasioning translator competence: Moving beyond social constructivism toward a postmodern alternative to instructionism. *Translation and Interpreting Studies*, 10(1), 8–32. https://doi.org/10.1075/tis.10.1.02kir.

Kiraly, D. C. (2016). Authentic project work and pedagogical epistemologies: A question of competing or complementary worldviews. In D. C. Kiraly (Ed.), *Towards authentic experiential learning in translator education* (pp. 53–66). Mainz University Press.

Konttinen, K., Salmi, L., & Koponen, M. (2020). Revision and post-editing competences in translator educator. In M. Kaponen, B. Mossop, I. S. Robert, and G. Scocchera (Eds.), *Translation revision and post editing: Industry practices and cognitive processes* (pp. 187–202). Routledge.

Lewin, R. (1993). *Complexity: Life at the edge of chaos*. Maxwell Macmillan.

Marczak, M. (2018). Translation pedagogy in the digital age: How digital technologies have been altering translator education. *Angles*, 7. https://journals.openedition.org/angles/895.

Marzouk, S., & Hansen-Schirra, S. (2019). Evaluation of the impact of controlled language on neural machine translation compared to other MT architectures. *Machine Translation*, 33, 179–203. https://doi.org/10.1007/s10590-019-09233-w.

McDonough Dolmaya, J. (2011). The ethics of crowdsourcing. *Linguistica Antverpiensia*, 10. https://doi.org/10.52034/lanstts.v10i.279.

McDonough Dolmaya, J. (2015). Revision history: Translation trends in Wikipedia. *Translation Studies*, 8(1), 16–34. https://doi.org/10.1080/14781700.2014.943279.

McDonough Dolmaya, J. (2017). Expanding the sum of all human knowledge: Wikipedia, translation and linguistic justice. *The Translator*, 23(2), 143–157. https://doi.org/10.1080/13556509.2017.1321519.

McDonough Dolmaya, J., & del Mar Sánchez Ramos, M. (2019). Characterizing online social translation. *Translation Studies*, 12(2), 129–138. https://doi.org/10.1080/14781700.2019.1697736.

Melby, A. K. (2020). The future of machine translation: Musings on Weaver's memo. In M. O'Hagan (Ed.), *The Routledge handbook of translation technology* (pp. 419–436). Routledge.

Mellinger, C. D. (2017). Translators and machine translation: Knowledge and skills gaps in translator pedagogy. *The Interpreter and Translator Trainer*, 11(4), 280–293. https://doi.org/ 10.1080/1750399X.2017.1359760.

Mitchell-Schuitevoerder, R. (2020). *A project-based approach to translation technology*. Routledge.

Monk, N., McDonald, S., Pasfield-Neofitou, S., & Lindgren, M. (2015). Portal pedagogy: From interdisciplinarity and internationalization to transdisciplinarity and transnationalization. *London Review of Education*, 13(3), 62–78. https://doi.org/10.18546/LRE.13.3.10.

Moorkens, J. (2018). What to expect from NMT: A practical in-class translation evaluation exercise. *The Interpreter and Translator Trainer*, 12(4), 375–387. https://doi.org/10.1080/1750399X.2018.1501639.

Moorkens, J. (2020). A tiny cog in a large machine: Digital Taylorism in the translation industry. *Translation Spaces*, 9(1), 12–34. https://doi.org/10.1075/ts.00019.moo.

Moorkens, J. (2022). Ethics and machine translation. In D. Kenny (Ed.), *Machine translation for everyone: Empowering users in the age of artificial intelligence* (pp. 121–140). Language Science Press.

Moorkens, J., Castilho, S., Gaspari, F., & Doherty, S. (Eds.) (2018). *Translation quality assessment: From principles to practice*. Springer.

Moorkens, J., & Lewis, D. (2020). Copyright and the re-use of translation as data. In M. O'Hagan (Ed.), *The Routledge handbook of translation technology* (pp. 469–481). Routledge.

Moorkens, J., Lewis, D., Reijers, W., Vanmassenhove, E., & Way A. (2016). Translation resources and translator disempowerment. *Proceedings of ETHI-CA2 2016: ETHics in Corpus Collection, Annotation and Application*, 49–53. www.lrec-conf.org/proceedings/lrec2016/workshops/LREC2016Workshop-ETHICA2_Proceedings.pdf.

Moorkens, J., & O'Brien, S. (2017). Assessing user interface needs of post-editors of machine translation. In D. Kenny (Ed.), *Human issues in translation technology* (pp. 109–130). Routledge.

Munro, R. (2010). Crowdsourced translation for emergency response in Haiti: The global collaboration of local knowledge. *Proceedings of the Workshop on Collaborative Translation: Technology, crowdsourcing, and the translator perspective*. https://aclanthology.org/2010.amta-workshop.1.pdf.

Munro, R. (2013). Crowdsourcing and the crisis-affected community: Lessons learned and looking forward from mission 4636. *Journal of Information Retrieval*, 16(2), 210–266. https://doi.org/10.1007/s10791-012-9203-2.

Neves, J. (2022). Project-based learning for the development of social transformative competence in socially engaged translators. *The Interpreter and Translator Trainer*, 16(4), 465–483. https://doi.org/10.1080/1750399X.2022.2084258.

Nitzke, J. (2019). *Problem-solving activities in post-editing and translation from scratch: A multimethod study*. Language Sciences Press.

Nitzke, J., Hansen-Schirra, S., & Canfora, C. (2019). Risk management and post-editing competence. *Journal of Specialised Translation*, 31. www.jostrans.org/issue31/art_nitzke.pdf.

Nitzke, J., Tardel, A., & Hansen-Schirra, S. (2019). Training the modern translator: The acquisition of digital competencies through blended learning. *The Interpreter and Translator Trainer*, 13(3), 292–306. https://doi.org/10.1080/1750399X.2019.1656410.

Nurminen, M., & Koponen, M. (2020). Machine translation and fair access to information. *Translation Spaces*, 9(1), 150–169. https://doi.org/10.1075/ts.00025.nur.

O'Brien, S. (2002). Teaching post-editing: A proposal for course content. *Proceedings of the 6th EAMT Workshop: Teaching Machine Translation*. https://aclanthology.org/2002.eamt-1.11.pdf.

O'Brien, S. (2011). Towards predicting post-editing productivity. *Machine Translation*, 25(3), 197–215. https://doi.org/10.1007/s10590-011-9096-7.

O'Brien, S. (2012). Translation as human–computer interaction. *Translation Spaces*, 1(1), 101–122. https://doi.org/10.1075/ts.1.05obr.

O'Brien, S. (2022). How to deal with errors in machine translation: Post-editing. In D. Kenny (Ed.), *Machine translation for everyone: Empowering users in an age of artificial intelligence* (pp. 105–120). Language Sciences Press.

Ogie, R. I., O'Brien, S., & Federici, F. M. (2021). Towards using agent-based modelling for collaborative translation of crisis information: A systematic literature review to identify the underlying attributes, behaviours, interactions, and environment of agents. *International Journal of Disaster Risk Reduction*, 68. https://doi.org/10.1016/j.ijdrr.2021.102717.

O'Hagan, M. (2011). Introduction: Community translation: Translation as a social activity and its possible consequences in the advent of Web 2.0 and beyond. In M. O'Hagan (Ed.), *Translation as a social activity: Community translation 2.0* (pp. 11–23). University Press Antwerp.

O'Hagan, M. (2020). Translation and technology: Disruptive entanglement of human and machine. In M. O'Hagan (Ed.), *The Routledge handbook of translation technology* (pp. 1–18). Routledge.

Olohan, M. (2011). Translators and translation technology: The dance of agency. *Translation Studies*, 4(3), 342–357. https://doi.org/10.1080/14781700.2011.589656.

Olohan, M. (2014). Why do you translate? Motivation to volunteer and TED translation. *Translation Studies*, 7(1), 17–33. https://doi.org/10.1080/14781700.2013.781952.

Olohan, M. (2017). Technology, translation and society: A constructivist, critical theory approach. *Target*, 29(2), 264–283. https://doi.org/10.1075/target.29.2.04olo.

O'Mathúna, D. P., Escartín, C. P., Roche, P., & Marlowe, J. (2020). Engaging citizen translators in disasters: Virtue ethics in response to ethical challenges. *Translation and Interpreting Studies*, 15(1), 57–79. https://doi.org/10.1075/tis.20003.oma.

Park, J. (2023). Ethical approach to translation memory re-use: Discussions from copyright and business ethics perspectives. *Translation Studies*, March. https:doi.org/10.1080/14781700.2023.2183248.

Phillips, M. G. (2016). Wikipedia and history: A worthwhile partnership in the digital era? *Rethinking History*, 20(4), 523–543. https://doi.org/10.1080/13642529.2015.1091566.

Pietrzak, P. (2022). *Metacognitive translator training: Focus on personal resources*. Palgrave Macmillan.

Piróth, A., & Baker, M. (2020). Volunteerism in translation: Translators Without Borders and the platform economy. In E. Bielsa and D. Kapsaskis (Eds.), *The Routledge handbook of translation and globalization* (pp. 406–424). Routledge.

Prates, M. O., Avelar, P. H., & Lamb, L. C. (2020). Assessing gender bias in machine translation: A case study with Google Translate. *Neural Computing and Applications*, 36, 6363–6381. https://doi.org/10.1007/s00521-019-04144-6.

Pym, A. (2003). Redefining translation competence in an electronic age: In defence of a minimalist approach. *Meta*, 48(4), 481–497. https://doi.org/10.7202/008533ar.

Pym, A. (2011). What technology does to translating. *International Journal of Translation and Interpreting Research*, 3(1), 1–9. www.trans-int.org/index.php/transint/article/viewFile/121/81.

Pym, A. (2012). *On translator ethics: Principles for mediation between cultures*. John Benjamins.

Pym, A. (2020). Translator ethics. In K. Koskinen and N. K. Pokorn (Eds.), *The Routledge handbook of translation and ethics* (pp. 147–161). Routledge.

Ragni, V., & Vieira, L. N. (2022). What has changed with neural machine translation? A critical review of human factors. *Perspectives: Studies in Translatology*, 30(1), 137–158. https://doi.org/10.1080/0907676X.2021.1889005.

Rico, C., & González Pastor, D. (2022). The role of machine translation in translation education: A thematic analysis of translator educator beliefs. *International Journal of Translation and Interpreting Research*, 14(1), 177–197. doi:10.12807/ti.114201.2022.a010.

Rico, C., & Torrejón, E. (2012). Skills and profile of the new role of the translator as MT post-editor. *Tradumàtica*, 10, 166–178. https://doi.org/10.5565/rev/tradumatica.18.

Ricœur, P. (2007). *On Translation*. Routledge.

Rivas Ginel, M. I., & Theroine, S. (2022). Machine translation and gender biases in video game localisation: A corpus-based analysis. *Journal of Data Mining and Digital Humanities*, special issue: Towards robotic translation? https://dx.doi.org/10.46298/jdmdh.9065.

Rothwell, A., & Svoboda, T. (2019). Tracking translator training in tools and technologies: Findings of the EMT survey 2017. *Journal of Specialised Translation*, 32. https://jostrans.org/issue32/art_rothwell.pdf.

Sakamoto, A. (2019a). Unintended consequences of translation technologies: From project managers' perspectives. *Perspectives: Studies in Translation Theory and Practice*, 27, 58–73. https://doi.org/10.1080/0907676X.2018.1473452.

Sakamoto, A. (2019b). Why do many translators resist post-editing? *Journal of Specialised Translation*, 31. https://jostrans.org/issue31/art_sakamoto.pdf.

Sánchez-Gijón, P., & Kenny, D. (2022). Selecting and preparing texts for machine translation: Pre-editing and writing for a global audience. In D. Kenny (Ed.), *Machine translation for everyone* (pp. 81–103). Language Science Press.

Sánchez-Gijón, P., Moorkens, J., & Way, A. (2019). Post-editing neural machine translation versus translation memory segments. *Machine Translation*, 33(1–2), 31–59. https://doi.org/10.1007/s10590-019-09232-x.

Schön, D. A. (1983). *The reflective practitioner: How professionals think in action*. Routledge.

Shuttleworth, M. (2017). Cutting teeth on translation technology: How students at University College London are being trained to become tomorrow's translators. *Tradução em Revista*, 22, 18–38. https://doi.org/10.17771/PUCRio.TradRev.30595.

Sin-Wai, C. (2016) *The future of translation technology: Towards a world without Babel*. Routledge.

Sumara, D., & Davis, B. (1997). Enactivist theory and community learning: Toward a complexified understanding of action research. *Educational Action Research*, 5(3), 403–422. https://doi.org/10.1080/09650799700200037.

Sutherlin, G. (2013). A voice in the crowd: Broader implications for crowdsourcing translation during crisis. *Journal of Information Science*, 39(3), 397–409. https://doi.org/10.1177/0165551512471593.

Sycz-Opoń, J., & Gałuskina, K. (2017). Machine translation in the hands of trainee translators: An empirical study. *Studies in Logic, Grammar and Rhetoric*, 49(1), 195–212. https://doi.org/10.1515/slgr-2017-0012.

Tomlain, M., Byrne, B., Concannon, S., Saunders, D., & Ullmann, S. (2021). The practical ethics of bias reduction in machine translation: Why domain adaptation is better than data debiasing. *Ethics and Information Technology*, 23(3), 419–433. https://doi.org/10.1007/s10676-021-09583-1.

Van Parijs, P. (2011). *Linguistic Justice for Europe and the World*. Oxford University Press.

Vieira, L. N. (2019). Post-editing of machine translation. In M. O'Hagan (Ed.), *The Routledge handbook of translation and technology* (pp. 319–335). Routledge.

Vieira, L. N. (2020). Automation anxiety and translators. *Translation Studies*, 13(1), 1–21. https://doi.org/10.1080/14781700.2018.1543613.

Vieira, L. N., Alonso, E., & Bywood, L. (2019). Post-editing in practice: Process, product and networks. *Journal of Specialised Translation*, 31. https://jostrans.org/issue31/art_introduction.pdf.

Vieira, L. N., O'Hagan, M., & O'Sullivan, C. (2020). Understanding the societal impacts of machine translation: A critical review of the literature on medical and legal use cases. *Information, Communication and Society*, 24(11), 1515–1532. https://doi.org/10.1080/1369118X.2020.1776370.

Way, A. (2018). Quality expectations of machine translation. In J. Moorkens, S. Castilho, F. Gaspari, and S. Doherty (Eds.), *Translation quality assessment: From principles to practice* (pp. 159–178). Springer.

Willbergh, I. (2015). The problems of "competence" and alternatives from the Scandinavian perspective of Bildung. *Journal of Curriculum Studies*, 47(3), 334–354. https://doi.org/10.1080/00220272.2014.1002112.

Yamada, M. (2019). The impact of Google neural machine translation on post-editing by student translators. *Journal of Specialised Translation*, 31. https://jostrans.org/issue31/art_yamada.php.

Yasseri, T., Sumi, R., Rung A., Kornai, A., & Kertész, J. (2012). Dynamics of conflicts in Wikipedia. *PLoS ONE*, 7(6). https://doi.org/10.1371/journal.pone.0038869.

Zetzsche, J. (2020). Freelance translators' perspectives. In M. O'Hagan (Ed.), *The Routledge handbook of translation technology* (pp. 166–182). Routledge.

Zhang, J., & Wu, Y. (2020). Providing multilingual logistics communication in Covid-19 disaster relief. *Multilingua*, 39(5), 517–528. https://doi.org/10.1515/multi-2020-0110.

Zwischenberger, C. (2021). Online collaborative translation: Its ethical, social, and conceptual conditions and consequences. *Perspectives: Studies in Translatology*, 30(1), 1–18. https://doi.org/10.1080/0907676X.2021.1872662.

4 Ethics and the interpreting curriculum

4.1 Chapter overview

This chapter focuses on teaching ethics in relation to spoken language interpreting in all modes. It foregrounds an integrated and contextualised approach to ethics education (following Biagini, Boyd, and Monacelli, 2017) with practice at its core. In relation to dialogue interpreter education, the chapter highlights the potential of Dean and Pollard's (2013) Demand Control Schema for developing spoken language interpreter ethical decision-making. It also shows how drama-based approaches can complement student learning, which is often anchored around scripted role-plays, opening up new possibilities for classroom participation and ethical responsibility development. With regard to conference interpreting, the chapter suggests ways to incorporate academic research into materials development and classroom activities to target specific decision-making challenges, particularly in political and institutional contexts. The chapter also discusses the affordances and limitations of case-based learning in interpreter ethics education, and offers practical suggestions for ways in which educators can critically review and refine current materials and learning outcomes. Finally, the chapter explores different conceptualisations of interpreter agency through social justice and activist paradigms and their potential for enhancing interpreter decision-making vis-à-vis their wider societal role; it invites critical reflection on the relationship between activism and professional ethics.

4.2 Ethics and the interpreting curriculum

The merits of maintaining a distinction between conference and dialogue interpreting in academic research are increasingly being called into question, since many topics and issues cut across settings and modes (Downie, 2021), with ethics no exception. By way of an introduction to the topic, however, it is useful to examine, if only briefly, approaches to ethics education that have been adopted in both areas of interpreter education. The various factors that have shaped attitudes and pedagogical practices are teased out as a foundation for developing an integrated approach.

DOI: 10.4324/9781003098485-5

4.2.1 Conference interpreting

For a long time in conference interpreting teaching, the topic of ethics received very limited attention, despite "hovering in the background" (Mikkelson, 2000, p. 52). The relative neglect of ethics derives, in part, from a tendency to conflate professional standards and competence with ethical practice – that is, to assume that the competent interpreter is an ethical interpreter – but factors such as limited attention given to the topic in academic research and limited space in the curriculum are also recognised. For some scholars, this neglect is a consequence of the dominance of the metaphoric concept of interpreters as conduits (e.g. Zwischenberger and Bastin, 2015). In conference settings, and particularly those where simultaneous interpreting is used, the physical remoteness of interpreters working in booths, coupled with the desirability of achieving professional detachment, has doubtlessly served to reinforce this metaphor. To some extent, interpreter education has also been influenced by the belief that conference interpreters do not encounter the full range of ethical issues that arise in other contexts, such as public service settings; however, this is perhaps more a reflection of the conference settings that are emphasised in research (i.e. principally conference interpreting in international organisations), to the neglect of other settings and their associated ideologies (e.g. non-governmental or commercial).

Professional standards, under which ethics is often grouped, became an established focus most notably through the European conference interpreting training model. This model is designed to promote the highest standards of interpreter education with the aim of graduate students entering the profession having demonstrated a level of interpreting proficiency that "should allow them to be recruited immediately to work alongside accredited conference interpreters, it being understood that beginners are not normally assigned to the most technical or demanding meetings" (EMCI Quality Assurance Standards).[1] It was founded on a combination of apprenticeship and cooperative partnership work that supports socialisation into the profession (Setton and Dawrant, 2016b).

Setton and Dawrant (2016b, pp. 339–340) propose incorporating a dedicated unit on professional practice in the final semester of a programme, based on topics such as the evolution of the profession and its norms of practice, discussion and analysis of case studies (e.g. of interpreter misconduct), role-playing and simulation, and introduction to the ecosystem of the profession. Professionalism, for these authors, involves intersecting craft, moral, and practical dimensions. Positioning such a unit towards the end of the programme of study is justifiable on the basis that students will be better equipped to take a global view of the interpreting process and the situational factors that impact on decision-making, although its status as a "bolt-on" unit risks underplaying the value of experientially oriented ethics learning across the curriculum. In terms of curriculum design, educators therefore need to identify which profession- and ethics-oriented dimensions can be separated out, and which can be woven into learning across the curriculum or end-loaded.

4.2.2 Dialogue interpreting

Understanding the place of ethics within the dialogue interpreting curriculum presents educators with a different, yet often intersecting, set of questions compared to conference interpreting education. On the one hand, the complexities of position-taking, the affective dimensions of many encounters, imbalances in power relations, and shared cultural understanding place ethics front and centre of the interpreting activity. On the other hand, few programmes of learning, particularly in higher education, are entirely devoted to dialogue interpreting, which diminishes scope for ethics education in the curriculum. Moreover, dialogue interpreting education often takes place outside of tertiary education establishments, with learners who vary significantly in terms of educational levels and social background, and a tendency in many contexts for interpreters to move from informal practice to formal service practice as a professional vocation, carrying through certain dispositions to practice that may not align with professional norms and expectations (Bahadır, 2017, p. 126).

There is greater likelihood of a very cursory approach to ethics-related learning in community-based interpreter courses. Where it is present, there is a quite high possibility of instructor-led prescriptions regarding desired interpreter behaviour and an unquestioning use of codes of ethics (see Baker and Maier, 2011), due to the lack of access to and/or engagement with empirical studies that problematise interpreter decision-making. Consequently, some interpreters in public and community services may be left to rely on intuitive decision-making, underpinned by oversimplistic conceptualisations of interpreter impartiality, which entail different consequences for the parties involved. This does not preclude such interpreters from demonstrating good practice, but the scope for variability is noteworthy.

Furthermore, this variability has consequences for teaching and learning in research-led contexts. The melting pot of attitudes and practices at the level of the local market can be difficult for graduates of research-informed programmes to reconcile and navigate. For instance, different approaches to role boundary-setting can shape expectations of service providers in ways that have ethical consequences, one example of which is a police officer who expects an interpreter to take a witness statement, as opposed to the interpreter interpreting while the officer takes the statement. The ways in which students are taught to assert good practice in interpreting encounters and develop effective interprofessional working relationships therefore becomes a pressing ethical question for educators working in research-led teaching contexts.

Ethics in dialogue interpreter education has evolved in line with insights from empirical research, although, in the classroom, the dominance of codes of ethics as a driver of ethics education has, at least anecdotally, limited scope for developing critical reasoning skills. The concepts of interpreter neutrality and impartiality have dominated much of the academic debate, and hence teaching and learning, for complex reasons.

During the early phases of professionalisation, the idea of interpreter neutrality – that is, a "strong form" of neutrality based on the interpreter-as-conduit model and the goal of "invisibility" – became a dominant norm that was promoted as a counterpoint to anecdotal reports of untrained interpreters speaking on behalf of service users, as opposed to interpreting what the latter actually said. Interpreters who adopted a more liberal approach to accuracy and voice were often prompted to do so by perceived disadvantages of service users in complex institutional encounters in relation to knowledge of the practices, power relations, and discourses within such institutions. This more interventionist approach was not routinely rejected by all in the academy, however, as Barsky's (1994) work on Canadian Convention Refugee hearings shows. While many may be sympathetic to Barsky's position, it places an undue burden on the interpreter to resolve imbalances of power over which other professionals in the process (e.g. immigration lawyers) have some influence, at least in principle.

Later research on interpreters in complex socio-political environments – for instance, in Iraq (Inghilleri, 2010) and post-apartheid South Africa (Wallmach, 2014) – further problematised the interpreter's positioning, shedding light on issues such as the degree of complicity in sustaining morally questionable activities and worldviews, and the limitations of the idea that interpreting (and translation) always operate in spaces "in-between". In other non-service-based settings, such as broadcast interpreting, the interpreter's vulnerability to external pressures in the entertainment sphere also led to questions about the value of metaphors of in-betweenness in framing the interpreting activity, leading to a proposal for an "ethics of entertainment" to account for these pressures (e.g. Katan and Straniero-Sergio, 2001).

Early empirical studies of dialogue interpreting in institutional encounters (e. g. Wadensjö, 1998), based on authentic data, helped to shift the parameters of debate on neutrality and perceived invisibility (see also Angelelli, 2004a), since they showed the extent to which interpreters were active agents in the interaction through the coordination of others' talk. Greater critical engagement with the concepts of neutrality and impartiality ensued, sometimes in ways that unhelpfully conflated professionalism and ethics. Coordination, as an act of professionalism, ensures voices are heard and space is made for the interpretation; it is not an unethical move on the part of the interpreter who temporarily steps out of their interpreting role, although some may see it in those terms.

The overriding goal of the interpreter to interpret "fully" and "faithfully" has never been questioned. However, what constitutes "full" and "faithful" can vary due to institutional requirements, and this variability has been the source of much anxiety for interpreters from an ethical perspective. For instance, while filtering out repeated phrases or false starts is acceptable practice in many settings, it may not be conducive to institutional goal realisation in speech therapy, a criminal trial, or a mental health appraisal, where the service provider must consider the manner of the person's speaking, as well as what they say, in order to make an appropriate assessment. This variability has generated challenges for educators in developing frameworks that build interpreter confidence in discerning what degree of mediation – understood here in Pöchhacker's (2008, p. 14) terms of "contractual mediation": interpreter intervention to resolve or mitigate intercultural conflicts or differences – is warranted in a given situation.

The myriad external pressures on interpreters are reflected in approaches to practice captured in the growing body of empirical studies, which show interpreters enacting degrees of intervention in encounters along a continuum. Examples of such pressures include limited stakeholder understanding of how to work with interpreters, face-threatening acts, vague questions, unreasonable requests for interpreters to take on tasks beyond their role or technical expertise, and safeguarding issues, among many others. In the academic literature, recognition of these external pressures has led some scholars to propose a more fluid conceptualisation of the interpreter's role in the interaction (e.g. Tipton and Furmanek, 2016), but such conceptualisations are not without risk and require further empirical research.

A key point is that if these pressures are not routinely discussed or enacted in teaching and learning, students enter professional practice without robust frameworks in place to support their decision-making. Turning to a professional code of ethics to aid decision-making in these circumstances often yields little support, since such codes are not designed to cover the minutiae of practice. The consequences of this for interpreters can be quite overwhelming and lead to a level of anxiety that is not only professionally but personally damaging. Therefore, a goal of dialogue interpreter ethics education should be to equip students with the knowledge to handle the limits of their expertise and agency, the vocabulary and critical thinking skills to take a balanced approach to decision-making and risk-taking, and the confidence to navigate key interpreting challenges openly with others.

4.2.3 What to prioritise in interpreter ethics education?

An integrated approach to ethics education helps students to "identify shared values, notice when values are in tension, and then develop strategies and behavioural commitments to resolve those tensions" (Baird and McCaig, 2022, p. 203). Part of this work, according to Baird and McCaig, involves educators supporting students to understand the different worldviews present within the discipline, and allowing scope to evaluate their relative strengths and weaknesses, while adopting a neutral stance to the various worldviews themselves. In other words, although students will inevitably engage with discourses about the "rights" or "wrongs" of certain actions, an integrated approach based on the observation of tensions can foster a more open mindset, leading to more effective independent critical reasoning in the longer term.

A key question for educators concerns the sequencing of topics and types of pedagogical input in the curriculum. As Kermit (2019, p. 21) asserts, "Ethics is not something one acquires by reading ethical theories." This does not mean that it should be avoided; rather, as Kermit writes, it can help to clarify ethical positions and support individuals to critically self-examine their positions in terms of consistency. Although it may seem reasonable and logical to adopt a theory-to-practice approach, a "practice-first", experiential approach is suggested in this chapter. This is because, regardless of the mode or the setting of interpreting, interpreters need to develop robust frameworks for enacting discretion with a clear sense of which professional duties and responsibilities shape their role (Skaaden, 2019a). This is best supported through opportunities for experiential learning and structured reflection on practice. The concept of agency, which is central to an ethics education, has the potential to frame the suggested approach effectively. As Skaaden (2019b, p. 715) observes, "the interpreter's agency is realized through the exercise of discretion", but a key challenge, especially in dialogue interpreting, is how interpreters achieve this without "infringing on the professional integrity of those in charge of the institutional encounter" (p. 716).

The way in which a student's interpreter identity develops over the course of the programme of study, if at all,[2] helps to foreground the importance of agency in ethics education. Drawing on the work of Tan, Van der Molen, and Schmidt (2017), Contreras (2022), for example, explores factors relevant to the development of a student's translator identity, which resonates with interpreter identity development. These factors are: knowledge of the occupation, having the professional as a model, and experience of the occupation. Two further factors relate to the student specifically: preference for the occupation (i.e. how the student conceives of and identifies with the occupation) and professional self-efficacy beliefs (i.e. the student's confidence in their ability to perform the task in question). The exercise of agency while on a programme of study will vary among students, impacted by extrinsic and intrinsic factors such as outside pressures and personal motivation, especially if self-efficacy beliefs stall or diminish. The relationship between self-efficacy beliefs and confidence in using discretion in interpreting has yet to be empirically investigated; however, by sensitising students to likely tensions between their student and interpreter identities during their learning, educators can help them to make sense of their learning trajectories in their evolution as ethics-aware practitioners.

The concept of agency, then, is suggested as part of an explicit classroom discourse that engages students from the early phases of the programme in thinking about the potential power they hold as interpreters, the importance of being conscious of this power, and the responsibilities that ensue as the interpreter identity status evolves. In this approach, agency is for the most part separated in the classroom from discourses on interpreter presence or non-presence, which can create confusion (see Diriker, 2011). An agency-oriented ethics pedagogy assumes interpreter presence as a given, couched in terms of responsibility and active decision-making, and applies as much to the conference interpreting classroom as to the dialogue interpreting one.

To support this approach, educators' framing of the "interpreter-as-agent" starts with considering different definitions of agency and how each may be factored into the student interpreter's learning. Agency has been variously viewed as an "intention or capability of an individual to act, initiate, self-regulate or make differences or changes to their situation" (Liddicoat and Taylor-Leech, 2021, p. 1), an exercise of choice (Pickering, 1995), or even act of resistance (Giddens, 1984), taking into account various situational parameters and constraints. Although most of the programme of initial conference and dialogue interpreter education and training will concentrate on developing what Moser-Mercer (2008) terms "routine expertise", interpreters also need to keep one eye on future professional contexts of work in which skills of "adaptive expertise" will come into play and which, for instance, are likely to require increased attention to the ideological contexts of and influences on interpreters' professional practice. An agential shift is implied in these types of expertise.

Foregrounding agency as a basis of ethics education on conference interpreter programmes also speaks to a critical gap highlighted by Baker and Maier (2011) concerning the way interpreters (and translators) think about others: inattention among interpreters (and translators) to changes in all areas of society, from technology to social policy, and to the challenges the changing moral environment presents to their positioning. At the time of writing, this gap has still not been adequately addressed in the interpreting curriculum. With this in mind, the concept of agency can usefully frame learning about the performative dimensions of interpreting and especially the micro-level decisions about content handling (responsibility to the speaker, the audience, and the profession) as well as macro-level decisions about interpreters as agents of change at a broader societal level (responsibility to society).

Finally, a focus on agency can be a useful concept through which to explore different theorisations of the dialogue interpreter's role – from the sociological, largely Goffmanian, emphasis explored by scholars such as Wadensjö (1998), to the socio-political framing of role by scholars such as Bahadır (2017). The triadic grouping in dialogue interpreting, for example, means that "[t]he ethics and the politics of the encounter change; the interpreter becomes an ethical agent of sociopolitical change", in as much as they become a person "divided between high ethical demands and the political (empirical) praxis" (Bahadır, 2017, p. 129). Bahadır makes two compelling calls in terms of a future basis for (dialogue) interpreting pedagogy relating to the teaching of ethics: first, for viewing the interpreter's in-between position and hence one that "disturbs" affirmatively, rather than as something that needs to be mitigated through emphasis on impartiality, and investigation of the empirical moments of suspension of impartiality; and, second, for viewing the ethical interpreter always as a subject-in-becoming and foregrounding the situatedness of ethical subjectivity and therefore the relativity of ethical stance development (p. 136).

4.3 Ethics education through practice

In this section, building ethical discernment among a community of learners is explored through practical interpreting tasks and guided/non-guided reflection on practice. The nature and scope of classroom tasks are examined from several pedagogical perspectives, accompanied by suggested activities as a foundation for educators to develop their own approach.

4.3.1 Dialogue interpreting: frameworks to support ethics education through practice

Dean and Pollard's (2011) emphasis on interpreting as a "practice profession" foregrounds the importance of experiential learning, "knowing how" in addition to "knowing that" (Skaaden, 2017). These authors, along with others (e.g. Angelelli, 2004a; 2004b; 2017), highlight the importance of fostering interpreters' sense of responsibility in interaction, as opposed to mere reaction, thereby minimising the potential for ethical issues to arise in the first place.

Dean and Pollard (2001; 2013) developed the Demand Control Schema, anchored in Karasek's (1979) demand control theory, to help interpreters address the complexities of sign language interpreting, but it also serves as an excellent support for decision-making in spoken language interpreting. "Demands" are grouped under four main categories: environmental (the "where", "who", and "why" of situations), interpersonal (the "what" of situations), paralinguistic (e.g. speech idiosyncrasies, accent), and intrapersonal (e.g. psychological, physical, and philosophical stresses experienced by the interpreter). "Controls" are individual interpreter resources that are deployed to respond to the demands of the encounter during the encounter itself (and can include "assignment" controls, such as prior relationships or codes of ethics), but also extend to pre- and post-assignment controls, such as preparatory terminology work and debriefing. The choice of control during the assignment often has to factor in concurrent demands, and several possible controls can be appropriate for a given situation.

Developing critical thinking and ethical reasoning skills within this schema are anchored around the ability of the interpreter to recognise where their decisions lie on a continuum (between too liberal and too prudent or conservative) in terms of their effectiveness and degree of ethicality, as opposed to a dichotomous "right" or "wrong". In this regard, there is a close link between their thinking and the concept of ethical thresholds introduced by Floros (2011) and discussed in Chapter 1.

An example of a demand (here in sign language interpreting) introduced by Dean and Pollard (2013, p. 103) concerns the question of what interpreters should do if they cannot hear the speaker. Several options (controls) suggest themselves, including: ask for a repetition; let the deaf person know the interpreter cannot hear; move to a better location; or omit the content. The choice of control (i.e. which option is most likely to be effective and ethical) depends on identifying concurrent demands in the situation. For instance, if the control choice is to omit the content, this could be ethical and effective if the comment was intended for another person, or if the other people in the room did not respond to it out of respect for the intended private nature of the comment.

The Demand Control Schema falls within an emerging body of literature that supports holistic situational analysis of interpreter-mediated events in both conference and dialogue interpreting. These studies present various axes of decision-making and presentation of self along different continua (e.g.

Llewellyn-Jones and Lee, 2014; Setton and Dawrant, 2016b, Biagini, Davitti, and Sandrelli, 2017). Their utility when planning ethics education in the interpreting curriculum derives from their ability to support analysis of fragments of interaction (students' own and peers') as well as learner understanding of the complexities of decision-making, without being restricted to binary judgements as to whether a decision is "ethical" or "unethical". Attention is drawn to these frameworks at the start of this section because they support many of the activities suggested later in this chapter.

4.3.2 Role-playing and dramaturgical approaches to pedagogy in dialogue interpreting ethics teaching

The use of role-play is widespread in teaching and learning in dialogue interpreting, as it offers ample scope to support the development of students' moral sensitivity to matters arising from service interactions underpinned by quite radical power imbalances. This subsection examines role-playing as a pedagogical approach and its potential to support skills development in interpreter discretion and professional judgement.

Students often work with scripted role-plays in small groups, or with two instructors playing the roles of the primary parties. These activities are beneficial in terms of exposing students to real-world occupational talk (Hale and Gonzalez, 2017) and controlling the level of difficulty of the language and the complexity of the interaction. However, they also have several drawbacks. For example, it can be difficult for some students to read from a script in a manner that reproduces natural features of talk. Furthermore, when two instructors act as interlocutors or consumers of interpreting services, it is not uncommon for them to act as "pure customers" who pretend not to understand anything said by the other interlocutor. The more varied language repertoire often displayed by interlocutors in public service encounters is underplayed as a consequence, leading to the neglect of certain ethical challenges, such as when a service provider relegates the interpreter to a "stand-by" position and the latter has to determine when to interpret (see Monteoliva-García, 2020).

Furthermore, Wadensjö (2014, p. 447) suggests that "a script-bound role play constitutes a particular challenge when it comes to communicating and understanding shifts in role players' participation status". As she observes, the exchanges in the encounter can all be "perceived as an animation of the script writer's words". Only when the script is abandoned do participants "mean what they say", which impacts on the assessment of elements such as the interpreter seeking a clarification.

Students are sometimes encouraged to adopt a more spontaneous approach to role-playing on the basis of an educator-created scenario that sets out contextual information about the interlocutors and the overall communicative goals of the situation. However, most students will struggle to inhabit certain roles – from an interviewing police officer to a critically ill patient – convincingly (Ozolins, 2017) due to limited performance skills and their lack of socialisation into the discourse practices and protocols of the setting in question. Furthermore, students' intuitions about certain social roles that are likely to manifest in such activities cannot be fully trusted due to the tendency to caricature what happens in reality (Niemants and Stokoe, 2017, p. 297). While interdisciplinary learning can mitigate these issues, it can be difficult to timetable and relies on a good level of compatibility between learning levels in each of the groups involved, as discussed later in this chapter. One alternative approach is to introduce a semi-scripted task in which students are given roles (e.g. the agreer or the arguer) that they have to research prior to the role-play.

Another shortcoming of scripted role-plays, identified by Niemants (2013) and teased out by Merlini (2017, p. 151) in relation to dialogue interpreting during film festivals, is the problem of "didactic framing" – namely, the inescapable reality that the role-play is a game or exercise that precludes effective orientation to interactional contingencies as they arise in actual settings (Stokoe, 2011, cited in Niemants and Stokoe, 2017, p. 299). In teaching and learning terms, this highlights the need for educators to help students overcome a so-called "ethics of conviction" in the classroom and orient towards a real-life "ethics of responsibility", expressed as a difference between "role playing" and "role taking" (p. 299). Reconciling this difference may not be entirely possible through the role-play approach, in part because it permits limited focus on the learner's reaction to the constellation of actors and complexities of the dialogue interpreting interaction (Niemants and Stokoe, 2017), especially if insufficient time is devoted in class to exploring that reaction. The exercise becomes one of merely getting through the material and animating the words; the parties playing roles are unlikely to engage with each other on the terms of the role (in part distanced through the text on the page to be read out), rather than attending to self and other meaningfully. Several of these shortcomings can be mitigated by incorporating complementary approaches such as Conversation Analytic Role-Play, experimental drama, and theatre-based learning into the curriculum.

4.3.2.1 Conversation Analytic Role-Play

Conversation Analytic Role-Play is a means of training professionals for effective communication in workplaces where talk is core to the activities, such as courts and schools. Developed by Elizabeth Stokoe (2011), this method has been applied to interpreter education to help foster interpreter responsibility and decision-making. It involves "progressively presenting anonymized recordings and transcripts of real, recorded conversations in which a particular interactional problem arises, and in which a successful outcome is or is not achieved" (Niemants and Stokoe, 2017, p. 293). Learners listen to several turns of talk in tandem with a transcript (e.g. through a presentation tool such as PowerPoint) and discuss potential difficulties and next turns before being exposed to the actual next turn in the sequence and discussing its implications for the unfolding dialogue. Niemants and Stokoe (2017) provide an excellent starting point in the form of some worked examples of materials used in a dialogue interpreting class on healthcare interpreting.

The method is anchored around discussion and collaborative learning. It relieves the pressure to perform and focuses students' attention on alternative courses of action and their implications for an unfolding dialogue. In so doing, the performative elements of gaze – non-verbal communication that more traditional role-plays can potentially simulate – are lost. That said, if students are working with scripts, it could be argued that these elements are often lost in this type of activity. A strength of Conversation Analytic Role-Play lies in the attention students need to give to all parties in the interaction. The approach also lends itself to applications of the Demand Control Schema to analyse factors impacting on the interaction and decision-making from each party's perspective. Seeing how service providers take responsibility (or not) for certain aspects of talk and adapt to communication through an interpreter offers important insights into distributed responsibility for meaning-making and goal achievement in encounters, rather than presenting interpreter decision-making as an isolated, non-dialogic process, which can skew ideas about the relationship between impartiality and responsibility.

4.3.2.2 Theatre-based approaches

A second complementary approach to (semi-)scripted role-plays concerns the incorporation of theatre- and drama-based methods into the interpreting classroom, whether as curricular or extra-curricular activities. Such approaches have been shown to support better handling of performance-related stress (Cho and Roger, 2010; Arnaiz-Castro and Pérez-Luzardo Díaz, 2016) and non-verbal communication (Bendazzoli, 2009), but they are also often ideologically leveraged to promote problem-posing under a critical pedagogy approach (see Freire, 1970).

Critical performative pedagogies have since evolved from Freire's thinking, most notably through Boal's (2008) Theatre of the Oppressed and Forum Theatre, and are prominent, for example, in healthcare education, which must prepare students to deal with patients, relatives, and colleagues of all ages and backgrounds. Scholars have also taken inspiration from Boal to advance teaching and learning in dialogue interpreting in ways that have excellent potential to support ethics education. For example, Kadrić (2014; 2017) draws on Boal's thinking to help students navigate complex interpersonal power relations, foregrounding its potential to game-play alternative lines of action. As such, alternatives are triggered by a particular "demand", to use Dean and Pollard's term, or, following Boal, an "act of oppression".

Van Bewer, Woodgate, Martin, and Deer (2021, p. 2) describe Boal's Theatre of the Oppressed (TO) as "a form of participatory and interactive education that uses theatre as a method to develop a critical consciousness and as an instrument for social change". Boal was inspired by Freire's (1970) dialogical model of education, in which educator and students are partners in learning, as opposed to the latter being passive recipients of knowledge. This approach is anchored around what Boal (2008, p. 120) terms "rehearsal theatre". In other words, participants do not aim to create a finished and polished spectacle;

142 *Ethics and the interpreting curriculum*

instead, they "explore and practice multiple ways of communicating without resorting to any kind of prescriptive answer for a given situation" (Sevrain-Goideau et al., 2020, p. 1). The rehearsal space gives scope for experimental and experiential action, learning through performing and re-performing.

Boal's (2008, pp. 97–98) approach developed out of a new poetics of the oppressed that focuses on the action itself and challenges the traditional theatrical concept of the passive spectator. Building on Brecht's ideas of the active spectator, rather than limiting activity to the intellectual sphere, Boal aims to activate spectators physically as "spect-actors" (Cohen-Cruz and Schutzman, 2021, p. 5) by enabling them to assume a "protagonic role" and act in a manner that "changes the dramatic action, tries out solutions, discusses plans for change" (Boal, 2008, p. 98). In other words, in this approach, everyone is able to intervene in the action and give new directions and ideas to those who are central to the role-play to see how different scenarios play out.

The culmination of various preparatory phases, Forum Theatre – which entails direct intervention in an acted scene to alter its course – has emerged as a very flexible tool for educators in a wide range of practice-oriented disciplines, including nursing, medicine, social work, and law; it has been described as "a form of embodied reflective practice" (Van Bewer et al., 2021, p. 2). However, there have been some critiques of Boal's Theatre of the Oppressed, such as those that suggest it "oversimplif[ies] complex identities and situations" and positions characters that are "germane to TO scenes" in oppressed groups (Cohen-Cruz and Schutzman, 2021, p. 6).

4.3.2.3 Applying drama-based pedagogies

Implementing drama-based pedagogies can be much more resource intensive than other pedagogical methods. Input from a drama specialist in an initial workshop is crucial if the interpreter educator has no background in this type of approach. Furthermore, without any additional drama training, students may feel so self-conscious about performing that their learning is hampered (Arveklev, Wigert, Berg, and Lepp, 2020). An initial drama-focused workshop will help create the safe space students need to build confidence in experimenting with a Forum Theatre format. Such a workshop will usually be anchored around activities to increase trust and foster collaboration in ways that are rarely found in the dialogue interpreting classroom.

Following Boal's (2008) framework, activities in the initial workshop could start with a focus on "knowing the body" (inhabiting a character, thinking about how bodies of different ages, gender, and so on move through space), "making the body expressive" (e.g. through non-verbal means) in a kind of "wayfaring" (see Chapter 1), and moving on to an appreciation of "theatre as language", with the aim of increasing individuals' confidence to progress from passivity to action or Forum Theatre (here, intervention in the drama). The purpose behind this preparatory work is twofold: to help students put themselves in another's shoes in ways that require total immersion; and to create a shared understanding of creative activity in a safe and non-judgemental space. Designating the teaching area a "rehearsal space" as opposed to a "classroom" shifts students' thinking about the body in that space, opening new possibilities for action and interaction.

Even after extensive input to help students adjust to learning in a new type of educational environment, they may remain reluctant to enter into improvised learning activities directly. A lecturer-modelled approach can be an effective means of overcoming this. The following activity, which takes inspiration from Middlewick, Kettle, and Wilson (2012), shows that students within such an approach do not need to be relegated to passive spectators; instead, they can develop confidence in shaping ideas about interaction and best practice and how it unfolds.

Activity

"Stop" and "go"

- **Learning aim:** introduce students to the learning potential of a dynamic role-play activity in which interactions are played and replayed.
- **Learning outcomes:** by the end of this activity, students will be able to: identify and describe salient differences between the rehearsal space and typical classroom space in dialogue interpreting; articulate rationales for different approaches to the scenario; take stock of the interactional consequences of the various trialled approaches and relate these observations to their understanding of interactional dynamics from the relevant literature and frameworks of interpreter performance analysis.

Task

1. Lecturers create a short, scripted scene based on an interpreter-mediated encounter in a public service. The script ends in an unsatisfactory manner for the service user. Examples include:

    - conversation between a teacher and a parent about careers;
    - conversation with a housing officer about substandard materials used to repair a leak; and
    - conversation with a hospital about physiotherapy services following a leg injury.

2. Lecturers perform the scene for students to observe.
3. Students enter into small groups and discuss what they have observed, exchanging ideas on what they think went well, what went less well, and why (e.g. using the Demand Control Schema as a framework to reflect on the "demands" and "controls").
4. Lecturers perform the scene again. Students may shout "stop" at any point and ask for the interaction or a section of the

> interaction to be re-performed on the basis of a suggestion for a change (language use, face-threatening act, non-verbal communication, etc.). Lecturers repeat the scene so that more students have an opportunity to redirect the interaction.
> 5 Plenary discussion: "stop" points are connected to a wider discussion on the "demands" and "controls" foregrounded in the scene and the key ethical points arising from the different iterations of it.
> 6 Extension activity: students work in small groups using a different scenario, emulating the process.

Variations may include incorporating an "expository approach" to interpreting practice, following Turner and Best (2017, p. 112), through which interpreters are encouraged to expose their thinking and uncertainty in oral annotations to a task. It will take time to develop this skill. Students may feel that it is too obtrusive and therefore a hindrance at certain points, and that it may even undermine consumer trust in their ability to deliver their service if they were to apply it in real-world situations. However, its value as a learning tool merits consideration in groups that are more receptive to drama-based pedagogies.

In a phased approach, lower-stakes scenarios can be followed by more complex situations, such as an asylum-seeking interview (see Kadrić, 2017). In this activity, students were invited to comment on perceived oppressive strategies in the scene and the interpreter's reaction (e.g. did they use any counter-strategies, did they become personally involved?). Kadrić suggests that students should determine whether the interpreter's behaviour can be described as partial, impartial, or independent, but should not judge whether any one of these is "right".

Complementary approaches to this type of task include "back channel pedagogy" and the "fishbowl strategy". In the former approach, educators open up lines of communication among students (e.g. using X (formerly Twitter) or Zoom) in the (on- or offline) classroom to facilitate multiple conversations and comments as the session unfolds, rather than limiting comments to the educator–student dyad, with others remaining passive. In the latter approach, two circles are generated: an inner circle (or "fishbowl"), where a discussion or scenario is acted out, and an outer circle of observers/note-takers. The two circles then swap so that different iterations of the same activity are enacted.[3]

4.3.2.4 Interdisciplinary learning

Situated learning approaches, through which the degree of authenticity of the interpreting task is foregrounded, form a core part of interpreting education and offer excellent potential to develop sensitivity to a range of ethical issues. The degree of situatedness needs careful consideration in the context of the student learning journey and can be managed effectively in a staged approach, such as the one proposed by Miner and Nicodemus (2021).

"Interdisciplinary learning" is one of many labels used to describe collaborative approaches to learning involving more than one group ("interprofessional education" and "joint learning" are also used). The former term is used here to denote learning that takes place at the pre-qualification stage. At its core is interaction: it "promotes *active* learning *with, from and about* others" (Freeth, 2005, p. 11; original emphasis).

Examples of interdisciplinary learning in dialogue interpreting have proliferated in recent years in response to the interpreter-centred nature of much dialogue interpreter education (Krystallidou and Salaets, 2016). Healthcare (Krystallidou et al., 2018; Hlavac and Harrison, 2021) and speech therapy encounters (e.g. Merlini and Favaron, 2005; Saenz and Langdon, 2019; Crezee and Marianacci, 2021) are prominent among the published studies, with somewhat fewer covering other service encounters, such as social work (e.g. Ozolins, 2018). Approaches to interdisciplinary learning vary in terms of the degree of embeddedness within the core curriculum: for instance, Krystallidou et al. (2018) offered a learning opportunity as an extra-curricular activity, whereas Crezee and Marianacci (2021) report on a set of activities that featured in the core curriculum over the course of eight years.

In the dialogue interpreting studies cited above, the potential for interdisciplinary learning to support an ethics education remains largely implicit. Allocating space in interdisciplinary events to discuss such matters should be routine at the level of both role-play activities and interdisciplinary discussions. For instance, interpreters would benefit from hearing more about a medical student's understanding of patient ethics (such as choice and voice) and how they think these could be impacted and navigated effectively in an interpreter-mediated encounter. Interpreting students would also benefit from discussing the ways in which ethics informs certain (clinical and non-clinical) routines across different settings, particularly if working with students from another discipline who have participated in placements where they may have faced certain dilemmas or even observed poor ethical practice. In terms of teaching strategies, Machin et al. (2019) explore how ethics can be incorporated into interdisciplinary learning for health and social care students, highlighting the importance of students developing a clear shared vocabulary for discussing ethical issues. Drawing on Cowley (2005), they suggest that students should "define their own terms, and explore each other's understanding of ethical jargon" (Machin et al., 2019, p. 615), which can be supported through readings of selected resources in each of the disciplines, but would require allocating time for pre-event and/or post-event discussions to achieve this.

The incorporation of interdisciplinary approaches in conference interpreting has also attracted scholarly attention, particularly in relation to simulated or mock-conference events, which are a common feature of conference interpreting curricula. As Defrancq, Delputte, and Baudewijn (2022, p. 42) observe, although approaches to mock-conferences typically range from teacher-centred to learner-centred (e.g. with students invited to play different roles), most of these events involve "interpreting students interpreting for other interpreting students or their trainers", which limits their scope as a learning experience.

146 *Ethics and the interpreting curriculum*

Defrancq et al. (2022) report on an interdisciplinary mock-conference event that has been embedded into the curriculum at the University of Ghent, involving the postgraduate programme in conference interpreting and the Centre for European Studies. The conference takes place towards the end of each academic year, reflecting an incremental approach to situatedness; for the interpreting students, it is the fourth out of five mock-conferences on their programme. The authors point out that role-play is a common element of political science and international relations programmes as a means to deepen knowledge and develop competence in negotiation skills, teamwork, and decision-making (pp. 40–41). The fact that these skills are likely to be employed in multilingual environments means that the interdisciplinary learning event with the conference interpreting students is particularly complementary. This one-off learning event takes place over six hours, with scope for interaction between all participants during breaks.

Mock-conference events anchored around interdisciplinary learning support an ethics education in several ways. For delegates, they support greater self-awareness in communicating for an international and multilingual audience. Moreover, Rünz (2015) stresses that opportunities to promote citizenship are created when participants from different backgrounds are brought together. For interpreters, they provide opportunities to practise retour and relay interpreting, and address complexities involved in a less controlled approach to speech than might be the case in a typical mock-conference that involves only interpreters and their trainers (e.g. in relation to values and ideologies). Finally, delegates have opportunities to discuss interpreting processes, challenges, and specific terminology during breaks, although, as Defrancq et al. (2022) observe, take-up of these opportunities may vary.

> **Prompts for reflection**
>
> *Incorporating ethics education in interdisciplinary learning events*
>
> - Do you already incorporate interdisciplinary learning into your programme? If so, how often, and how do you approach the setting up of events?
> - What are the main ethical issues students involved in interdisciplinary learning could usefully explore? Imagine various scenarios:
>   - nursing students and dialogue interpreting students;
>   - law students and dialogue interpreting students;
>   - international development students and dialogue and/or conference interpreting students;
>   - international relations students and conference interpreting students.
> - What role (if any) do you see technology playing in supporting an interdisciplinary event (e.g. prior to, during, and after)?

- Would you consider assessing student performance in such an event? If so, how might you assess a student in relation to ethics issues (written reflection, class debate, or something else)? (NB: Consider how much access is provided to a speaker before an event, terminology, pre-conference talk, etc.)

4.3.3 Conference interpreting: ethics education through practice

Despite the relative neglect of ethics in conference interpreter education, in recent years some scholarship has emerged offering educators practical guidance and frameworks for incorporating ethics-related topics into practical interpreting tasks. As in dialogue interpreting, reliance on a narrow set of concepts that are discussed chiefly in the abstract belies the scope for incorporating ethical and moral matters into classroom activities. In this subsection, several options for structuring practice and developing materials are explored as part of an integrated approach.

In their student guide to conference interpreting, Setton and Dawrant (2016a, p. 361) suggest that management of the interpreter's role is most thorny where "expectations of neutrality or loyalty may vary, and may alternately license or limit different levels of intervention and optimisation". In distinguishing between "shared" and "affiliated" interpreters, they show how educators can support clearer student understanding of role boundaries and how the concept of "fidelity" is achieved "along a continuum of accepted norms" (Setton and Dawrant, 2016b, p. 343).

The "shared" interpreter is described as an international civil servant, employed by an international or multilateral entity, and who acts without showing any allegiance to a member state of the entity in question. Setton and Dawrant (2016b, p. 378) counsel students to avoid betraying any potential sympathy (e.g. through tone of voice), to suppress any convictions or opinions, and to operate along the lines of what Gile (2009, pp. 33–34) terms "rotating sender-loyalty". They also assert the importance of interpreters not taking any instructions from third parties with regard to style or content of the interpretation.

In the second condition, the "affiliated" interpreter is commonly expected to act in a more partial manner, for instance by serving as a cultural consultant and providing additional services, such as giving cultural advice or reminders and helping to draft points (Setton and Dawrant, 2016b, p. 348); however, they are still "ethically bound to provide default *basic fidelity* to all speakers" (Setton and Dawrant, 2016a, p. 381; original emphasis). The concept of the affiliated interpreter has come to prominence in recent studies on interpreted conference events in China, commonly through corpus-based methodologies. These show how government-affiliated interpreters routinely leverage their position as spokespeople by acting in a partial manner to promote or even enhance the government's image to international audiences (Wang and Feng, 2018; Gu, 2019).

Though not affiliated, similar practices are also evident among interpreters who are "attached" to particular parties in diplomatic or business spheres.

Acknowledging the likely dominance of "proactive idealism" in the conference interpreting sphere and the concomitant expectation that interpreters will be completely neutral at all times, Setton and Dawrant (2016a; 2016b) find that such generalisations are unhelpful at providing guidance and unreflective of the highly variable settings and contexts in which interpreters may work over the course of their careers. Ren and Yin (2020, p. 202) observe that adopting a neutral position may protect (especially freelance) interpreters from criticism and "deflect potential pressure from powerful clients". For Turner (2007), however, such self-limiting approaches to professionalism, termed "defensive interpreting", have a range of consequences for both interpreter and client, and should not be automatically viewed as a problem-free fallback position.

The concepts of fidelity – for Setton and Dawrant (2016a; 2016b) – and accuracy – for Seeber and Zelger (2007) – are central to supporting students' learning about ethical decision-making *in situ*. Conceptually, these authors are building a very similar set of ideas, with Seeber and Zelger using "truth" in place of Setton and Dawrant's emphasis on "fidelity". Setton and Dawrant provide very practical starting points for instructors to move away from the more abstract discussions of fidelity through an emphasis on the form/meaning dichotomy to thinking in concrete terms about what is feasible and appropriate, on the assumption that interpreters have a degree of choice and control. They outline a concept of basic fidelity, akin to the concept of "baseline neutrality" (Tipton, 2008) – namely, the idea that interpreters strive to deliver "an honest and accurate reflection of each speaker's communicative intent, or main point, without distortion or misrepresentation" (Setton and Dawrant, 2016b, p. 353).

Interpreter agency (deliberative and conscious decision-making) is activated when faced with challenges that require the optimisation of communication (e.g. culture-specific items, ambiguity, factual errors, omission). For Setton and Dawrant (2016a; 2016b), conscious optimisation is a point on a continuum of practices, from coping to strong mediation. In order to address a range of what they describe as commonly arising "residual challenges", such as vagueness, ambiguity, and speaker errors, interpreters need to develop conscious awareness of which devices can optimise communication. For instance, content optimisation to improve communication through clarification can be achieved through paraphrasing; oral annotations (adding a few words to explain); correction (in the event of a speaker mistake); and filtering (omission, toning down, or censoring). The topic of censoring merits particular attention, with students encouraged to reflect on occasions in their learning when they have consciously censored their output to save face, and in broader terms on the relationship between free speech and interpreting.

There are two main approaches to skills development for these areas: targeted and non-targeted. The former might involve working on a particular topic (such as vagueness) in isolation, with the educator manipulating a speech to include one or more examples for students to tackle in consecutive and/or simultaneous mode. Students would not necessarily be told what the feature is prior to the exercise, so as not to shift attentional resources in ways that impact on the wider interpreting process.

The non-targeted approach, which relies on students' participation in simulated conference activities, encourages them to work through recordings of their performance to identify "critical points" (e.g. paraphrasing, filtering, and correcting) and select a couple of examples to share with their peers. The presentation of examples is accompanied by analysis of whether they think the approach was justified in the context, the ways in which it impacted the source message (on a continuum of weak–strong) and intention, their subsequent interpreting (i.e. did it mean they fell too far behind the speaker in simultaneous?), and whether they might adopt the same approach in the future. Educators can shape the approach through the incremental introduction of certain features/challenges of varying complexity in line with the students' level of development. For instance, conference delegates might make a point deliberately vague, include a deliberate error, or speak in a way that suggests a face-threatening act.

4.3.4 Materials creation for targeted practice

The activities described in this subsection develop some of the ideas outlined above and draw inspiration from several corpus-driven studies for the creation of materials. Wang and Feng's (2018) study is based on a corpus-driven approach to the analysis of so-called "critical points" in interpreting practice. The authors borrow this term from Munday's (2012), p. 41) analysis of translators' decision-making processes, in which critical points are defined as "those points and lexical features … most susceptible to value manipulation … those that may be most revealing of the translator's values". Drawing on transcriptions of 15 press conferences attended by two Chinese premiers between 1998 and 2012, Wang and Feng analyse the translation of a particular word – 问题 – which can be translated into English as "issue", "problem", "question", or "matter", each of which implies a different attitude. They also point to certain standardised translations into English, such as "Taiwan question" as opposed to "Taiwan issue", which highlights that the matter is in dispute. The different attitudes implied by the interpreter's choice can therefore be seen to take on a degree of ethical importance in the framing of certain political topics.

Drawing on this example and the available materials in the public domain for the press conferences, educators can develop exercises (on-sight translation, consecutive and simultaneous interpreting) using 问题 in different contexts for students to reflect on the parameters that influenced their decisions. Students can then compare their interpretations with the interpreted versions on the day and discuss the interpreters' choices in light of their civil servant status, considering the implications of that status for the event, in contrast with a freelancer at a different type of event (e.g. a business forum) in which similar collocations may be heard. This activity can then be repeated over the course of the programme, building in different layers of complexity and lexical density. It can also be replicated in other language combinations, with educators developing a series of interpreting exercises of an incremental level of difficulty that draw on other available corpora. A key point is that students are exposed to ethical decision-making around items of language that may appear very straightforward to interpret but carry particular weight in political contexts.

Inspiration for topics and materials creation is also taken from research by Beaton-Thome, who draws on plenary debates in the European Parliament via the latter's Multimedia Library website. For instance, one study focuses on debates on the topic of Brexit to shed important light on some of the ethical issues interpreters may face when working with discourse that aims to challenge their employer (Beaton-Thome, 2020). Using extracts from similar materials (on this and other institutionally sensitive topics), interpreters can experience the discourse first-hand and reflect on elements such as tone and positionality. Students' interpretations are recorded before they analyse their work independently, first as a performance in its own right and second against the publicly available recorded version from the institution in question. The interpreters are invited to examine their choices around issues such as lexis, framing, and omission, and the extent to which they believe their interpreting maintains, weakens, or strengthens the institutional discourse. Recordings could then be exchanged with a peer who compares their output with the public record to determine whether there are any discernible differences between their performance and that of the institutional interpreter, especially in relation to institutional bias. Note that publicly available institutional recordings should not be presented as the "model version" (although students might benefit from observing how the interpreters tackled the material in general terms). Instead, the goal is to allow space for reflection on the ethical implications of certain features of discourse, the choices the students made, and their potential consequences.

Another of Beaton-Thome's studies can support the development of more advanced decision-making in interpreting, with specific reference to lexical density and lexical preference (Beaton-Thome, 2013). The research concerns the European Parliament's debates on the contentious issue of individuals held at Guantánamo Bay and how they are labelled in different languages. Beaton-Thome acknowledges that in some pairings (e.g. English and German) there can be significant differences in the lexical richness between the two languages for describing the same phenomenon. As a result, interpreters have to be aware that their lexical choices may have political connotations, and that those choices may be influenced by other factors, such as a more limited lexical range in the target language.

Educators may have to allocate more time for activities that are anchored around a sensitive topic and for which there can be variability in lexical density because the emphasis needs to be on a debate as opposed to a single speech. There is also likely to be a need for greater manipulation of materials to create a credible activity at an appropriate level, as opposed to drawing directly on authentic materials. In this case, the students would engage in group analysis and discussion after completing the exercise, as opposed to comparing output with a publicly available recording of the interpretation.

4.4 Ethics education through case-based learning

This chapter promotes a practice-first approach to ethics education in interpreting before exploring professional dimensions of practice. Between these two phases, however, case-based learning can support skills development in ethical reasoning.

4.4.1 Affordances and limitations of case-based approaches

Case-based (or dilemma-based) approaches to ethics education are used across many different disciplinary areas, including social work, engineering, and nursing. They can sometimes be associated with a "big bang" approach to ethics: a focus on complex, high-stakes situations that, although very engaging, are unlikely to arise in an interpreter's career. Such an approach takes time away from the lower-level but still complex decision-making that interpreters confront in their day-to-day practice. It is a reminder that not all cases are of equal pedagogical value (Bagdasarov et al., 2013). Furthermore, if the scaffolding of the learning activity is not managed appropriately, there is a risk that students will look to their instructor at the end to "reveal all" and provide the optimum solution. While modelling solutions can be useful, the practice has been critiqued for tending towards prescriptivism (Dean, 2014; Howes, 2023).

Following Hill (2004), Dean (2014, p. 61) highlights some of the limitations in using the approach to develop students' moral sensitivity to practice due to the "pre-determined ethically troubling material", which presents an already-framed dilemma for students to consider. If it is assumed that an important part of an ethics education is to support students to identify the ethical issues at stake, a multi-pronged approach is necessary; however, if the students have already been exposed to practice-based ethical discussions, they will come to case-based learning with a reasonable range of critical thinking tools, sensitivity to the issues at play in terms of the speaker/hearer roles of participants in interaction, and a vocabulary that supports higher-order thinking around interpreter agency.

Among the affordances of case-based learning are that "people find it useful to hear others' deliberations about moral cases" (Howes, 2023, p. 3); they also shine a spotlight on real-world encounters and their possibilities; and, in the context of dialogue interpreting, they can serve as a reminder that ethical issues are not necessarily to be found solely in the interaction itself but in the wider administrative and institutional structures that govern provision. Finally, they offer a learning experience in a safe space, since some ethical issues do not lend themselves to learning through direct experience because they are too high stakes (Drugan and Megone, 2011, p. 194).

4.4.2 Constructing a case

Case-based learning typically involves a situated example from a real-world practice setting; however, in interpreter education, these often seem to be short summaries of a situation, include limited contextual information, and, as mentioned above, frequently pre-frame the ethical issue(s) at stake. Bagdasarov et al. (2013) assert that effective case-based learning needs to be underpinned by case-based reasoning and sense-making. This typically involves a learner recalling a similar situation to the case in question and drawing on that prior experience to develop a response (along the lines of the ethical prototype discussed in Chapter 1). In the interpreting classroom, however, what constitutes "prior experience" for learners may be very limited, even if case-based learning accompanies an approach such as the Conversation Analytic Role-Play described earlier.

Good case construction ideally encompasses contextual and individual elements (Bagdasarov et al., 2013). An emphasis on context allows students to consider external environmental and situational cues as opposed to relying wholly on prior experience. Furthermore, if learning and transfer are promoted, cases also need to be "instructional, structurally realistic, relevant to the reader, emotionally evocative and have socio-relational content" (Johnson et al., 2012, p. 63). A case should include a good amount of descriptive information on the social context in which the case is anchored (such as hierarchies and cultural climate), as this will not only enhance authenticity but also support decision-making. Individual elements concern character (personality, motivations, intent), and their inclusion in a case can help students understand not only "the key causes and constraints of the situation" (Bagdasarov et al., 2013, p. 1308) but also why a person might have chosen a particular course of action or made a particular decision.

4.4.3 Supporting learning

Case-based learning does not necessarily lead to the tidy resolution of ethical issues. Rather, as Johnson et al. (2012, p. 65) suggest, the best solution in a particular case may simply be "the mitigation of further problems". These authors reflect on the importance of outcomes or consequences in the creation of case materials based on a study in which the manipulation of "outcome favourability" – that is, the degree to which the outcomes of a case are favourable or unfavourable – has implications for student learning. Including such information in a case can help learners to "develop cause-and-effect relationships between elements of a case". In Johnson et al.'s estimation,

> Positive case outcomes can provide case readers with information regarding opportunities and resources as well as model successful navigation of an ethical issue, while negative outcome information provides readers with valuable information on contingencies, potential consequences and problems, as well as demonstrating potentially disastrous navigation of ethical issues.

There is a need to avoid placing undue emphasis on the question "What would you do in this situation?" in case-based learning, as limited prior experience and variability in ethical maturity will limit the ability to project the self into the situation, and answers are likely to be shaped by social desirability bias – that is, a person gives a response that will be viewed favourably by others. Instead, the approach can be used to build competence in evaluating a situation in all of its dimensions (environmental, interpersonal, intrapersonal, regulatory, and inter-cultural), applying different ethical theories from moral philosophy, and even identifying potential gaps in institutional representatives' education and knowledge in terms of effective inter-professional working, and the implications of these gaps for interpreted encounters.

Case-based learning also offers students a basis for critically examining the concept of role fluidity in interpreting – which manifests through the presentation of self, cultural brokerage, co-diagnosis, and so on – and its ethical implications. Skaaden (2019b) cautions that expanded conceptualisations of role or role fluidity can do more harm than good because they preclude the primary interlocutors from knowing where they stand in terms of the interpreter's communicative approach. Case descriptions could therefore incorporate different degrees of role fluidity for students to work through – for instance, drawing on role-space theory, introduced by Llewellyn-Jones and Lee (2014) – and explore ways in which they may need to limit their agency, use their discretion, and, crucially, think about the ethical responsibilities of the institutional representatives in each case.

4.4.4 Case examples

This subsection presents case examples with suggested discussion points for students. The case descriptions are deliberately very basic and accompanied by a series of prompts for educators to draw on the above discussion on case construction and reflect on ways in which these (and other cases they may already use) can be enhanced to meet a defined set of learning aims and outcomes.

---

1 Court interpreting

An interpreter is performing whispered simultaneous interpreting for a defendant in an English courtroom. The defendant is not being addressed directly. One of the legal representatives mentions to the open court that a witness summons has gone out to a particular individual but there have been some problems in persuading the person to attend court. The interpreter interprets this information using the correct equivalent term for "witness summons" and shortly afterwards is interrupted by the defendant, who asks: "What is that?" The interpreter, concerned that they do not have the legal expertise to provide an explanation and aware that they cannot stop court proceedings to request such an explanation, says to the defendant, "I will ask your legal representative to explain later."

154 *Ethics and the interpreting curriculum*

- **Additional information:** The interpreter knows what a witness summons is and feels confident to provide a short gloss to support the defendant's understanding at that point, but decides against this course of action in the belief that it is beyond their interpreting remit.
- **Discussion prompts for students:**
  - In terms of a hierarchy of priorities, what has driven the interpreter's decision in this case? (Accountability? Loyalty? If so, to whom or what?)
  - What would be the consequences of offering a short gloss? What are the potential consequences for the defendant of not knowing what the term means at that point in the proceedings?
  - What are the "demands" of this interpreting situation and what "controls" are available to the interpreter? What justification would you provide for the implementation of your choice of controls?
  - To what extent do the ethical issues in this case reflect others that you have encountered on your programme of study so far?
- **Prompt for reflection (educators):** How can this case description be enhanced to reflect Bagdasarov et al.'s (2013) emphasis on the importance of contextual and personal information in case construction?

2 Medical interpreting

An interpreter interprets for an encounter involving the birth of a child in a hospital's maternity unit. After a very long labour, the mother gives birth and develops sepsis, a condition that can be life threatening. In the interaction, the interpreter uses the correct term for sepsis, but can see that the mother is not reacting in a way that shows she understands the potential seriousness of the situation. Recognising that the midwife has not picked up on this, the interpreter explains to the midwife how she might explain sepsis to the mother in order to highlight the danger and support her decision-making. The midwife does not treat the interpreter's suggestion as problematic. The mother makes a full recovery.

- **Discussion prompts for students:**
  - What are the potential motivations behind the interpreter's decision?
  - What are the ethical implications of the interpreter continuing to interpret without alerting the midwife to the mother's reaction?
  - Which emotional consequences might this situation generate from the interpreter's perspective?
- **Prompts for reflection (educators):**
  - What are the key points of (ethics) learning deriving from this scenario?

Ethics and the interpreting curriculum 155

- How can this case description be enhanced to reflect Bagdasarov et al.'s (2013) emphasis on the importance of contextual and personal information in case construction?

3 Social work interpreting

A social worker is involved in making an assessment of a mother's relationship with their young infant. In the room, the infant is playing on its own and the mother appears uninterested. The interpreter is aware that this sort of behaviour is very common in the mother's home country (the interpreter grew up in that country and left in their early 20s), but they does not say anything to the social worker. The social worker does not ask any questions about the mother's background or experiences of motherhood pre-migration. The child is eventually taken into care.

- **Additional information:** the social worker is eight years post-qualification. Their initial social work education did not include any specific training on inter-cultural working or working with interpreters. The interpreter is five years post-qualification, but this is their first assignment in a social work context (they mainly work in healthcare settings). There was no briefing between the social worker and the interpreter prior to the interaction.
- **Discussion prompts for students:**
    - What difference might a briefing have made in this scenario?
    - Which new "demands" might the interpreter encounter in this scenario compared to many healthcare scenarios, and might these demands require different "controls"?
    - As the interpreter has never interpreted for this type of encounter before, which cues might they look out for in the situation to support their decision-making?
    - Think about the potential consequences of the interpreter making an unprompted comment to the social worker about the mother–child interaction.
    - How might the interpreter respond to a social worker's request to comment on what they are observing as opposed to just interpreting the mother's responses, given that commenting on matters is explicitly proscribed in the interpreter's code of ethics?
    - Which emotional consequences might this situation generate from the interpreter's perspective?
- **Prompts for reflection (educators):**
    - What are the key points of (ethics) learning deriving from this scenario?

- Which learning outcomes might you write for a session in which this scenario is the focus?
- How can this case description be enhanced to reflect Bagdasarov et al.'s (2013) emphasis on the importance of contextual and personal information in case construction?

4 Business interpreting

In a business negotiation regarding the purchase of a very costly piece of equipment to provide neutron beam radiation therapy, the interpreter makes a conscious decision to tone down elements of the conversation based on their view that maintaining the tone of the primary speaker may be misconstrued as overly aggressive to the other party. They make this decision in the belief that it will increase the likelihood of the purchase going ahead. The purchase does go ahead soon after the conversation.

- **Additional information:** the interpreter has worked for the equipment manufacturer in the context of international sales for several years. They have interpreted at three other meetings prior to this one. The potential buyer speaks the manufacturer's language at a conversational level but would be unable to carry out high-level purchase negotiations.

- **Discussion prompts for students:**
    - To what extent do you think the interpreter's decision-making changes the power dynamics in the interaction?
    - Which factors might have influenced the interpreter's decision to change the tone?
    - To what extent did the interpreter underestimate the purchaser's level of insight into negotiating cultures in that country and hence their ability to accommodate an approach to expression that may be quite different to negotiations elsewhere?
    - What would have been the consequences for the encounter if the interpreter had decided to interpret without making any adjustments?
    - Which emotional consequences might this situation generate from the interpreter's perspective?

- **Prompts for reflection (educators):**
    - What are the key points of (ethics) learning deriving from this scenario?
    - Which learning outcomes might you write for a session in which this scenario is the focus?
    - How can this case description be enhanced to reflect Bagdasarov et al.'s (2013) emphasis on the importance of contextual and personal information in case construction?

Ethics and the interpreting curriculum 157

5 Media interpreting

An experienced media interpreter is employed to interpret for a well-known international writer during a live televised interview as part of International Book Week. The interpreter is visible on screen throughout the interview. The writer has recently announced that they are transgender and has talked openly about this in recent interviews; however, the current interviewer repeatedly misgenders the guest in the conversation. The interpreter adjusts the interviewer's speech when interpreting for the writer to correct these errors in the belief that the interviewer has simply forgotten. Later in the conversation, it becomes clear that the misgendering is deliberate.

- Discussion prompts for students:
  - Which factors may have shaped the interpreter's decision in this case?
  - Which emotional consequences might this situation generate from the interpreter's perspective and those of the other interlocutors?
  - What would have been the consequences if the interpreter had decided not to make any adjustments?

- Prompts for reflection (educators):
  - What are the key points of (ethics) learning deriving from this scenario?
  - Which learning outcomes might you write for a session in which this scenario is the focus?
  - How can this case description be enhanced to reflect Bagdasarov et al.'s (2013) emphasis on the importance of contextual and personal information in case construction?

4.5 Professional dimensions of practice

This section examines selected aspects of practice and their implications for teaching and learning with an emphasis on codes of ethics and self-care.

4.5.1 *Teaching codes of ethics*

Many students' first encounter with ethics in interpreting is through codes of ethics; in a crowded curriculum, this should perhaps come as no surprise. Codes are tangible artefacts anchored in real-world organisational contexts and are often of a length that is conducive to discussing within the average class time. However, as a tool for learning, they can be a rather blunt instrument. It is not uncommon for tasks to involve learners applying a relevant code as an evaluative framework to examine professional interpreters' practice. However, without acknowledging many stakeholders' limited appreciation of the complexities of the task or limits of the interpreter's role (Martín Ruano, 2015, p. 144), this approach is likely to lead to some frustration for learners as they enter professional practice and need to grapple with a wide range of external pressures.

This is why, within an integrated approach, critical reasoning and thinking skills in relation to ethics in interpreting practice are promoted through the practice-first approach and the application of frameworks such as the Demand Control Schema, introduced earlier in this chapter. The value of introducing codes towards the end of a programme of study merits consideration, not least because, "[i]n most professions, a code of ethics complements and reinforces what was learned on a professional course of study" (Hale, 2007, p. 103).

The academic literature contains numerous examples of studies, particularly comparative studies, of codes that distil common principles and values. From these studies, concepts of accuracy, impartiality, and confidentiality are seen to form the bedrock of professional ethical practice (see Baixauli-Olmos, 2018; Bancroft, 2005; Hale, 2007; Mizuno, 2005; Phelan, 2019). However, there is almost no literature on how the findings of academic research on codes can be effectively translated into the classroom. A number of core topics are suggested as a foundation for teaching and learning activities: functions of codes of ethics; sources of codes of ethics; prescriptivism; key concepts in codes; and spirit of codes of ethics. In terms of educator teaching aims, the main priorities lie in helping students to:

- acknowledge tensions between actual practice and codes, and develop positive and constructive dialogue;
- understand how codes and their underpinning assumptions about role evolve over time;
- understand the language and discourse practices in codes;
- develop practical skills of writing and revising codes; and
- understand how codes are used in disciplinary proceedings.

Several scholars acknowledge codes of ethics as a mechanism through which an interpreter's power is controlled (Rudvin, 2019; Skaaden, 2019b), which explains why prescriptivism in codes is often deemed an "inevitable and inherent element" (Phelan, 2019, p. 110). However, as Hale (2007, p. 114) observes, over-reliance on a code to solve professional issues is risky, and effective application needs to be accompanied by robust pre-service training.

Discussions of codes often touch upon two major tensions: the apparent contradiction between the need for fidelity and interpreter facilitation of understanding; and lack of congruence between personal morality and code prescriptions. With regard to the former, which is discussed by Diriker (2004) in relation to conference interpreting, Donovan (2011, p. 112) asserts that such prescriptions respond to two different professional concerns: the need for client reassurance and the need for the profession "to claim authority over the way the message is re-expressed", an authority she perceives as being on a much less stable footing in community interpreting. Setton and Dawrant (2016b) cut through this tension by asserting an ethical commitment to "basic fidelity" to all speakers, which is achieved through interpreter discretion as to what is feasible and appropriate at a given moment. With regard to the latter, Dean and Pollard (2011, p. 170) suggest that helping students overcome this tension lies in enabling them to distinguish between interpersonal and intrapersonal demands and cultivate "disciplined subjectivity". In other words, these authors stress the need for students to acknowledge and address "potential intrapersonal influences" to prevent these from spilling over and tainting their perception of interpersonal dynamics in the interpreting event. Further, as Hale (2007, p. 124) notes, "[d]isagreeing or agreeing with what the parties state does not constitute unethical behaviour and it would be ludicrous for interpreters to feel guilty about any situation".

As suggested above, a practice-oriented approach allows students to unpack these concepts productively, taking account of the positionality, professional ideologies, and knowledge bases of each party within the encounter. As an extension, students may also benefit from undertaking comparative approaches to professional codes themselves as a means to understand how interpreting practice is guided across different contexts, even extending such work to comparisons of codes from other salient professions. Whose professional norms take precedence in a given situation also merits attention in the classroom, and is a layer of reflection that could be incorporated into Conversation Analytic Role-Play (see Subsection 4.3.2.1) or interdisciplinary learning events.

4.5.2 Practical activities

This subsection presents a series of practical activities designed to support teaching and learning in relation to different facets of codes of ethics. There is a deliberate avoidance of activities involving the application of codes to examples of practice, as ethics education in this regard is promoted through the application of other tools, such as Dean and Pollard's Demand Control Schema.

Activity

Historical approaches to the development of codes of ethics

- **Learning aim:** to engage students researching the evolution of codes of ethics.
- **Learning outcomes:** by the end of this activity, students will be able to: locate relevant sources of information on ethical codes; identify differences between labels used for codes and understand their relevance; articulate the merits/demerits of publicising how codes are revised and the individuals involved in the process.
- **Recommended reading:** Angelelli (2006).

Task

1. Outside of the classroom, students chart the evolution of codes and standards in a single country. To do this, they identify current codes, examine the authorities behind the codes and their evaluation, and explore the approach(es) to interpreting they reflect.
2. Students may also consider the labels used for codes (i.e. do different languages and cultures distinguish between codes of ethics and codes of conduct?) and the implications for a code and interpreting practice if the term for "translator" and "interpreter" is the same (as it is, for example, in Polish). They should also be encouraged to consider the extent to which a particular code protects interpreters and their clients.
3. Students try to gather information on how codes have been created and revised if this information is in the public domain. They then discuss the merits/demerits of making such information routinely available.
4. Finally, students report back to the wider group in a class plenary.
5. Extension activity: students explore the symbolic function of codes (following Baixauli-Olmos, 2018). How do different codes seek to establish the legitimacy of the profession (i.e. which discourse strategies are used)?

Activity

Comparing the structure, language, and assumptions about role in codes of ethics

- **Learning aim:** to sensitise students to the way in which codes are structured and written.
- **Learning outcomes:** by the end of this activity, students will be able to: discern patterns in the way codes are structured and topics are prioritised/weighted; draw on their knowledge of academic theorisations of the interpreter's role to examine assumptions about it within different codes; apply a systematic approach to the study of the language of the selected codes.

Task

1. Working in small groups, students gather a corpus of codes from a single domain of interpreting (e.g. healthcare), generic codes, company codes, professional association codes, or a mixture.
2. Each group determines a set of criteria by which to evaluate the codes from the perspective of structure/topic prioritisation.

3   Each group then analyses the language of the codes either manually or using a corpus tool.
4   Each group researches different theorisations of the interpreter's role in the academic literature.
5   Each group discusses the assumptions about and theorisations of role relevant to each code to determine whether there are commonalities and differences.
6   Each group presents its findings to the whole class for discussion.

Activity

Exploring the application of codes of ethics in disciplinary hearings

- **Learning aim:** to engage students in the work of disciplinary panels of professional interpreter associations and the application of professional codes in decision-making.
- **Learning outcomes:** by the end of this activity, students will be able to: identify elements in disciplinary processes (e.g. those of an interpreting service provider and a professional body); articulate the role that a code of ethics plays in a disciplinary process; establish which clauses in codes are most commonly breached and why; make connections between their practice-based learning and the rationale given for a breach of a code.
- **Recommended reading:** Hayes and Hale (2010).

Task

1   Working either independently or in small groups, students examine the different phases of disciplinary procedures in at least two settings (e.g. company and professional association).
2   Drawing on publicly available information on disciplinary procedures, students identify the ways in which codes are used in those procedures.
3   The task continues with one of two approaches:

APPROACH A

- If reports on the outcomes of disciplinary hearings are publicly available, educators or students collect a number of examples.
- Working in small groups, students critically examine the reports to identify how the language of ethics is used (i.e. which ethics traditions are invoked) and which clauses in codes are most commonly breached and why.

- Finally, each group discusses examples of ethics-related issues arising from their practice-based learning and the rationale given for a breach of a code in a disciplinary hearing.

APPROACH B

- If no public information is available, educators invite a representative of an association who sits on a panel to talk through some cases and outcomes, and how the panel works with codes of ethics in disciplinary hearings.
- The discussion could also extend to aspects of hearings that fall into grey areas not specifically covered by a code, and the extent to which knowledge generated through disciplinary hearings for the association supports periodic reviews and revisions of codes.
- Students share their findings with the whole class.

Activity

Developing a code of ethics

- **Learning aim:** to encourage interpreters to reflect on codes from an active learning perspective.
- **Learning outcomes:** by the end of this activity, students will be able to: articulate their understanding of the core concepts they have included in their code; provide a rationale for the order of code's clauses; draw on academic literature to support their articulation of assumptions behind the role of the interpreter in the code; emulate the relevant structure and language of codes found elsewhere.

Task

1. Students imagine that a charity that supports victims of torture has approached them to develop a code of ethics for its interpreters, who provide their services in therapy sessions, during medical check-ups, and at informal social events.
2. Students examine relevant empirical research to understand the complexities of interpreting during the organisation's activities.
3. Students may explore examples of codes that are relevant to these activities to support the drafting of their code.
4. Students develop a code from scratch and provide a rationale for each clause based on their understanding of key concepts. They should also specify how they are theorising the role of the interpreter based on relevant academic reading.
5. The draft code and statement of rationales behind the layout and content are written up and either presented as a single group document to the instructor or shared with the wider group ahead of a plenary discussion.

Activity

Shifts in language in dialogue interpreting and their ethical implications

- **Learning aim:** to encourage students to reflect on possible motivations for a language shift before an encounter has commenced and/or part way through an encounter.
- **Learning outcomes:** by the end of this activity, students will be able to: define a language shift in the context of dialogue interpreting; identify the ethical implications of language shifts for all parties before or part way through an encounter.
- **Recommended reading:** Hlavac (2010).

Task

1. The educator presents students with several scenarios to read either in small groups in class or independently. Examples include:
   - An asylum seeker who has requested an interpreter in the language of a country they have passed through. Their main language is shared with the immigration lawyer, who decides to switch to direct communication after seeing the asylum seeker struggle to answer questions in the requested language.
   - A musician who is being interviewed on live TV with an interpreter present. Part way through the interview, the host realises that the musician has some command of the majority language of the country where the interview is taking place and seeks to communicate directly in that language.

2. For each scenario, students identify who is suggesting the shift in language (service user, service provider, interpreter), for what reason, and the ethical implications of each initiated move for the parties involved and the interpreter's professional conduct.

Activity

Public comment as an ethical issue in interpreting

- **Learning aim:** to sensitise students to the issue of confidentiality in interpreting through the lens of public comment.
- **Learning outcomes:** by the end of this activity, students will be able to: identify why public comment is an ethical issue in interpreting; distinguish between different types of public comment (including whistleblowing); articulate ways in which interpreters can productively draw on their experiences to help shape policy debates.

164 *Ethics and the interpreting curriculum*

Task

1. Students are introduced to the concept of public comment as an ethical issue in interpreting through examples of codes that include this topic (both conference and dialogue interpreting).
2. Students are familiarised with Erik Camayd-Freixas's account of his work as an interpreter during the Postville raid (Camayd-Freixas, 2009).
3. In small groups, students discuss Camayd-Freixas's rationale for going public and the potential role of a code of ethics in shaping an interpreter's decision to do so.
4. Each group shares its thoughts with the rest of the class before exploring other reactions to the case, such as Hennessy (2008).
5. Educators may broaden the debate by encouraging students to reflect on other situations in which interpreters may witness injustice (e.g. due to a service provider not knowing how to work effectively through an interpreter) and their options during or outside of the encounter to ameliorate practice. The literature on interpreting during asylum procedures (e.g. Maryns, 2006) and Baroness Coussins's many interventions in the House of Lords on the subject of interpreters' work on behalf of the British government in Afghanistan (https://members.parliament.uk/member/3829/writtenquestions) are good starting points for this discussion. (NB: Educators might also wish to consider organising language forums for different sectors that bring together professionals and interpreters to discuss key topics and training requirements.)
6. Extension activities/variations: this activity can be replicated with reference to scenarios from conference interpreting settings, such as media outlets asking an interpreter to comment on negotiations, or the publication of interpreters' memoirs.

4.5.3 Self-care as an ethical commitment to interpreting: implications for pedagogy

Interpreters working in public service and community settings with asylum seeker and refugee service users are often exposed to harrowing narratives of war, conflict, persecution, and perilous journeys. While there is evidence to suggest that interpreters often experience a higher level of compassion satisfaction than other professions (Mehus and Becher, 2016), a German study (Kindermann et al., 2017) reported that they also experience higher levels of stress and anxiety than a representative population sample. The toll that this takes on interpreters' mental health and the risk of vicarious trauma have been well documented in interpreting studies, yet scholars have only recently started to discuss these topics in practical terms (Costa, Lázaro Gutiérrez, and Rausch, 2020; Crezee et al., 2015; Tipton and Furmanek, 2016). At present, guidance is limited to fairly generic statements on the importance of maintaining health and wellbeing through the likes of diet, exercise, and mindfulness activities, but such advice could be complemented by more fine-grained learning about different emotional responses and their triggers in the moment of interpreting.

If self-care is promoted as an ethical duty for interpreters in order for them to perform optimally in complex encounters and handle any impact on life beyond those encounters, there is scope to consider where and how it might fit within the curriculum in ways that educators will feel able to manage. Given the impossibility of simulating conditions that will facilitate experiential approaches to self-care, there is a risk that it remains tagged on and presented as something that students "just need to bear in mind" when they start working professionally.

Introducing the topic can be anchored around selected academic readings. For example, in relation to dialogue interpreting, Geiling, Knaevelsrud, Böttche, and Stammel (2021) analyse interpreters' accounts of the effects of their work with refugees, including reports of helplessness, hopelessness, uselessness, anger, guilt, fear, and hyperarousal. Within the triadic exchange, these negative emotional responses may be caused by ambivalent feelings towards service users, attempts to remain neutral to service users, clients who display a lack of respect towards or have unreasonable expectations of interpreters, feeling disrespected by providers, concerns about providers' attitudes, limited provider understanding of the interpreter's work and role, and feeling restricted. Students may use the Conversation Analytic Role-Play method (see Subsection 4.3.2.1) to consider the implications of interactions for emotional responses and how they might develop "disciplined subjectivity".

The concepts of "emotional labour" (Hochschild, 2012) and affect can support a more nuanced approach to understanding how feelings (towards self and other) can influence the interpreting process and subsequent personal life. Students may use the Conversation Analytic Role-Play method to reflect on potential emotional triggers at different points in an interaction (and their order of magnitude) and put them into perspective in terms of how they might impact language choices, tone, or even the decision to continue with an assignment or not. Talking through why an interpreter might experience guilt or anger in a particular situation can help to build emotional resilience in a safe environment, and is a pre-emptive approach to self-care.

In conference interpreting, by contrast, research on interpreter stress can be a useful entry into reflections on self-care (e.g. Kurz, 2003; Korpal, 2016), supplemented by insights and examples from the field. For instance, student interpreters would benefit from hearing about the pressures that can be created by certain (institutional) demands for travel or expectations in terms of the range of agendas they may have to interpret in a single week. The topic of vicarious trauma is discussed by Chief of Language Services Justine Ndongo-Keller and other interpreters in the context of the Voices from the Rwanda Tribunal project,[4] which documents the experiences of various actors in the United Nations' International Criminal Tribunal for Rwanda. Although many interpreters will never experience this kind of event, the public record of reflections can encourage connections between exposure to different forms of content and the potential consequences for health and wellbeing (there are some overlaps between the testimonies heard by the interpreters in Rwanda and those an asylum interpreter may hear), enabling informed decisions in the future.

> **Prompts for reflection**
>
> - In your current teaching practice, to what extent do you include reference to affect (or other related terms, such as "emotional labour") as part of your classroom discourse and/or specific learning activities?
> - At what point do you think the concept of topic could/should be incorporated into the curriculum?

4.6 Social justice and ethics education

This section explores the value of introducing alternative conceptualisations of interpreter agency in the context of interpreter ethics education to promote critical thinking and widen the scope of ethical responsibility to the societal level. It examines the potential for interpreting services to be pressed into the service of different social goals at the behest of interpreters themselves and in ways that promote greater linguistic diversity and voice than many institutional language regimes are able or willing to facilitate. The discussion acknowledges the limitations imposed by the different ideological contexts in which interpreter education takes place.

4.6.1 Activism within ethics education

In recent decades, questions of social justice and the role of translators and interpreters as agents of social change have emerged in the interpreting studies literature (e.g. Wolf, 2012). Within these discussions, activist translation and interpreting have featured prominently and cover a wide range of communicative practices (see Boéri and Delgado Luchner, 2020). In Rudvin's (2019, pp. 62, 66) analysis, activist approaches come under an "outer-oriented public level" of interpreting ethics since the appeal to a higher sense of loyalty – that is, to wider society – means that activist approaches could be viewed as falling outside of the interpreter's core ethical mandate. For Rudvin, the qualitatively different categories of interpreter/activist can make it particularly challenging to embed an activist ethics into the professional realm for the individual to reconcile the two positions. Role hybridity becomes especially problematic if an activist orientation is adopted unilaterally and potentially unevenly, as this risks eroding trust in and legitimacy of the service provided. Although Boéri and Delgado Luchner (2020, p. 265) recognise the potential problem of hybridity, it is reconciled, in their view, through "place finding" – namely, recognising "a positionality that is dynamically constructed in and through translation, for and by fighting injustice".

Ethics and the interpreting curriculum 167

In terms of curriculum planning, it is important for educators to reflect the range of practices that fall under the broad term of "activist interpreting". These may be construed in structural, motivational, and practice terms. For instance, interpreters may provide a service in situations where the role of the activist interpreter is highly visible and made transparent through an organisation's planning processes. Babels, which served the World Social Forum for several years, is a prime example, as interpreters were not only present as both delegate–participants and interpreting service providers but also helped to plan phases of the event (see Boéri, 2008; 2012). Although the mechanisms used to achieve coverage of language needs have been subject to criticism (e.g. Naumann, 2005), Babels is instructive in terms of how a particular "moral posture" (Mosko, 2018, quoted in Boéri and Delgado Luchner, 2020) is translated into practice.

Of course, the nature of engagement can and does vary. Boéri and Delgado Luchner (2020) caution against thinking that all activist approaches necessarily equate to intervention at the level of the text (as promoted in committed approaches, such as feminist translation), highlighting that commitment to a cause or group may be the principal form of activism an individual takes, labelled an "ethics of engagement". This could be manifested, for instance, in a decision to interpret *pro bono* during an asylum case.

4.6.2 Curriculum planning

Since most, if not all, tertiary interpreter education programmes of study are designed to support graduating students into professional careers within the prevailing political and economic system of the country of practice or the international system, activist interpreting is less likely to feature prominently within the curriculum. The level of attention devoted to the topic will also be conditioned by the local political context and/or the composition of students within the group and the sensitivities arising from discussions of alternative modes of practice from a more radical ideological position. Nevertheless, the principles associated with activist interpreting merit attention as part of the interpreting curriculum in the context of ethics. Even though interpreters may not be interested in pursuing this approach in the future, these principles can be teased out in practical activities that provide a set of parameters that shed light on core concepts introduced elsewhere on the programme.

Incorporating activist interpreting into the ethics-oriented curriculum could include all or a selection of the following topics:

- the historical development of activism, putting TI studies research into perspective;
- introduction to different types of activism, including different organisations and communities;
- values common to activism, such as horizontality and participation, diversity and pluralism, advocacy and listening, and the quest for social justice;
- reflection on the relationship between political activism and ethics;

- organisational expectations;
- trajectories of socialisation within activist movements;
- potential flashpoints for interpreters in terms of career planning; and
- forms of textual manipulation in activist contexts of interpreting.

4.6.3 Practical activities

The activities presented in this subsection encourage individual and group reflection based on real-world scenarios. Emphasis is placed on personal values and their potential enactment through interpreting and related activities, such as organising interpreting provisions.

Activity

Future employment opportunities and activist positions

- **Learning aim:** to stimulate reflection on the potential implications of an activist perspective on interpreting in a humanitarian organisation.
- **Learning outcomes:** by the end of this activity, students will be able to: articulate the characteristics of interpreter role hybridity arising in the advertised position; think through the potential consequences of "strong" and "weak" forms of position-taking in this role; and apply an understanding of emotional labour to the role to suggest potential issues and their mitigation.

Task

1   The educator presents the following scenario:

You see an advert for interpreting work with the International Red Cross/Red Crescent (or other humanitarian aid organisation). It is a paid position on a short-term contract. You think that the work looks interesting and rewarding and you have been an active supporter of the organisation for several years, including fundraising in your local area.

2   Students reflect on the following questions:

- If you apply for the role, to what extent do you think you would be professionally positioning yourself as an activist within the humanitarian context?
- To what extent do you think that your personal commitment to the organisation might impact on the way you discharge your duties, if at all?
- How would you feel if you secured the role and arrived to find that you were the only professionally trained interpreter in that

location and that the other interpreters were exhibiting poor practice through a lack of training?
- What positive action might you take after securing the role and discovering that it entails a significant amount of emotional labour that you have not been trained to handle as an interpreter?

Activity

Leveraging interpreting skills to support causes of personal interest

Learning aim: to sensitise students to the ways in which professional skills can support wider personal values and social goals.

Learning outcomes: by the end of this task, students will be able to: identify opportunities to use their professional skills at the service of activities of special personal interest; reflect on the degree of engagement that fits with their personal goals and career aspirations; and articulate strategies for connecting with key interlocutors in organisations to actively engage and/or encourage others to engage.

Task

1. Independently or in small groups, students reflect on social questions in which they have a particular interest (environmental, health, ecological, educational, animal rights, immigration, etc.) and the international dimensions of these issues.
2. In discussion with others, students reflect on their level of interest in and engagement with organisations that seek to draw attention to these issues and/or formulate practical solutions. For instance, level of interest may range from generally concerned public citizen to active engagement with (or even membership of) an association.
3. Students discuss how they might leverage their interpreting skills and knowledge in the future to support various goals in ways that are commensurate with their level of engagement.

Activity

Activism in local organisational contexts[5]

- **Learning aim:** to simulate an activist approach to the organisation of a local event to promote voice and inclusivity.
- **Learning outcomes:** by the end of this activity, students will be able to: plan informal/formal support for multilingual communication at a local event; develop strategies for communicating with key stakeholders and organisers prior to the event; develop strategies to

support marginalised groups' participation during the meeting; and articulate ideas for creating a sustainable multilingual presence at such events in the local area in the future.

Task

1. The educator presents the following scenario: a local council in a large multilingual urban area hopes to persuade more people to participate in local decision-making and organises a series of public forums for discussion of pertinent topics.
2. Students put themselves in the position of a local resident who is interested in supporting this initiative, aware of the complexities of facilitating the participation of residents whose proficiency in the majority language is insufficient to allow meaningful input, and keen for marginalised groups to have their fair say.
3. In groups, students discuss the ways in which they might work with the organisers to address multilingual challenges during the forums. Note that suggestions do not need to be limited to issues relating to the provision of interpreting services. In particular, each group should reflect on:

    - the principles of horizontalism and how these might be promoted through specific interventions;
    - strategies for negotiating access to and engagement with the organisers;
    - call for volunteers (including professionals working *pro bono*);
    - implications for different levels of expertise ("uneven efficacy");
    - contingency plans in the event that majority language speakers become the main voices that are heard;
    - pre- and post-event interventions (including in the digital sphere) to support inter-meeting dialogue and the exchange of ideas;
    - their availability for the series of meetings;
    - if a team of interpreters is to be assembled, its potential composition (i.e. trained or untrained) and the guidance it should be given in light of the council's goals and the stated engagement of the interpreters?

4. Each group presents the outcome of its discussions to other groups before the educator supports follow-on discussion in a plenary. The educator should highlight any shared elements across the groups and any gaps in their thinking (such as contingency planning in the event of a hostile reaction from the meeting organisers).
5. Evaluation extension exercise:

    - Which skills learned from this experience could be usefully employed in commercial interpreting settings?

- To what extent and in what ways has this activity helped you to reflect on traditional discourses of interpreter neutrality?
- What risks (if any) do you see for the interpreter–activists and other participants in the forums as a consequence of your involvement?

4.7 Chapter summary

This chapter examines a wide range of teaching approaches to the development of ethical decision-making and responsibility-taking in the interpreting curriculum. In particular, it seeks to illuminate the ways in which academic research in interpreting studies can be leveraged to develop targeted practice materials for conference interpreters, and how drama-based pedagogies in dialogue interpreting afford different types of classroom participation and engagement with ethical issues. It also explores the potential of case-based learning to develop capacity for critical thinking and cautions against the use of hypothetical questions as to what the student might do in certain situations, instead recommending more robust analytical frameworks such as the Demand Control Schema to optimise student learning.

Notes

1 www.emcinterpreting.org/emci/application/files/1516/3189/1065/EMCI_Quality_Assurance_Standards.pdf.
2 Many students, for various reasons, end their interpreting education not wishing to pursue the activity professionally.
3 See also: https://learninginnovation.duke.edu/blog/2021/07/using-a-course-backchannel-to-supplement-teaching-and-learning/ and www.learningforjustice.org/classroom-resources/teaching-strategies/community-inquiry/fishbowl.
4 www.tribunalvoices.org/.
5 Inspired by Doerr (2018).

References

Angelelli, C. V. (2004a). *Medical interpreting and cross-cultural communication.* Cambridge University Press.
Angelelli, C. V. (2004b). *Revisiting the interpreter's role: A study of conference, court and medical interpreters in Canada, Mexico and the United States.* John Benjamins.
Angelelli, C. V. (2006). Validating professional standards and codes: Challenges and opportunities. *Interpreting*, 8(2), 175–193.
Angelelli, C. V. (2017). Anchoring dialogue interpreting in principles of teaching and learning. In L. Cirillo and N. Niemants (Eds.), *Teaching dialogue interpreting: Research-based proposals for higher education* (pp. 29–44). John Benjamins.
Arnaiz-Castro, P., & Pérez-Luzardo Díaz, J. (2016). Correlation between anxiety and academic self-concept in interpreter trainees. *Círculo de lingüística aplicada a la comunicación*, 67, 57–88.

Arveklev, S. H., Wigert, H., Berg, L., & Lepp, M. (2020). Specialist nursing students' experiences of learning through drama in paediatric care. *Nurse Education in Practice*, 43. https://doi.org/10.1016/j.nepr.2020.102737.
Bagdasarov, Z., Thiel, C. E., Johnson, J. F., Connelly, S., Harkrider, L. N., Devenport, L. D., & Mumford, M. D. (2013). Case-based ethics instruction: The influence of contextual and individual factors in case content on ethical decision-making. *Science and Engineering Ethics*, 19(3), 1305–1322. https://doi.org/10.1007/s11948-012-9414-3.
Bahadır, Ş. (2017). The interpreter as observer, participant and agent of change: The irresistible entanglement between interpreting ethics politics and pedagogy. In M. Biagini, M. S. Boyd, and C. Monacelli (Eds.), *The changing role of the interpreter: Contextualising norms, ethics and quality standards* (pp. 122–145). Routledge.
Baird, C. A., & McCaig, K. (2022). Everyone teaches ethics: An embedded approach to ethics education. In L. M. Fedoruk (Ed.), *Ethics and the scholarship of teaching and learning* (pp. 199–218). Springer.
Baixauli-Olmos, L. (2018). Ethics codes as tools for change in public service interpreting: Symbolic, social and cultural dimensions. *Journal of Specialised Translation*, 28. www.jostrans.org/issue28/art_baixauli.php.
Baker, M., & Maier, C. (2011). Ethics in interpreter and translator training: Critical perspectives. *The Interpreter and Translator Trainer*, 5(1), 1–14.
Bancroft, M. (2005). *The interpreter's world tour: An environmental scan of standards of practice for interpreters*. National Council on Interpreters in Health Care.
Barsky, R. F. (1994). *Constructing a productive other: Discourse theory and the Convention Refugee hearing*. John Benjamins.
Beaton-Thome, M. (2013). What's in a word? Your enemy combatant is my refugee: The role of simultaneous interpreters in negotiating the lexis of Guantánamo in the European Parliament. *Journal of Language and Politics*, 12(3), 378–399. https://doi.org/10.1075/jlp.12.3.04bea.
Beaton-Thome, M. (2020). Flagging the homeland: Interpreting Brexit à la Nigel Farage in the European Union. In K. Strani (Ed.), *Multilingualism and politics: Revisiting multilingual citizenship* (pp. 105–128). Springer.
Bendazzoli, C. (2009). Theatre and creativity in interpreter training. In M. I. Fernández García, M.-L. Zucchiatti, and M. G. Biscu (Eds.), *L'esperienza teatrale nella formazione dei futuri mediatori linguistici eculturali* (pp. 153–164). Bologna University Press.
Bendazzoli, C., & Pérez-Luzardo, J. (2022). Theatrical training in interpreter education: A study of trainees' perception. *The Interpreter and Translator Trainer*, 16(1), 1–18. https://doi.org/10.1080/1750399X.2021.1884425.
Biagini, M., Boyd, M. S., & Monacelli, C. (2017). Introduction. In M. Biagini, M .S. Boyd, and C. Monacelli (Eds.), *The changing role of the interpreter: Contextualising norms, ethics and quality standards* (pp. 1–4). Routledge.
Biagini, M., Davitti, E., & Sandrelli, A. (2017). Participation in interpreter-mediated interaction: Shifting along a multidimensional continuum. *Journal of Pragmatics*, 107, 87–90. http://dx.doi.org/10.1016/j.pragma.2016.11.001.
Boal, A. (2008). *Theatre of the oppressed* (new ed.). Trans. C. A. Leal McBride, M.-O. Leal McBride, and E. Fryer. Pluto Press.
Boéri, J. (2008). A narrative account of the Babels vs. Naumann controversy: Competing perspectives on activism in conference interpreting. *The Translator*, 14(1), 21–50. https://doi.org/10.1080/13556509.2008.10799248.

Boéri, J. (2012). Translation/interpreting politics and praxis: The impact of political principles on Babels' interpreting practice. *The Translator*, 18(2), 269–290. https://doi.org/10.1080/13556509.2012.10799511.

Boéri, J., & Delgado Luchner, C. (2020). Ethics of activist translation and interpreting. In K. Koskinen and N. K. Pokorn (Eds.), *The Routledge handbook of translation and ethics* (pp. 245–261). Routledge.

Camayd-Freixas, E. (2009). Interpreting after the largest ICE raid in US history: A personal account. *Latino Studies*, 7(1), 123–139. https://doi.org/10.1057/lst.2008.54.

Cho, J., & Roger, P. (2010). Improving interpreting performance through theatrical training. *The Interpreter and Translator Trainer*, 4(2), 151–171. https://doi.org/10.1080/13556509.2010.10798802.

Cohen-Cruz, J., & Schutzman, M. (2021). *A concise introduction to Augusto Boal: Guide*. Digital Theatre Ltd.

Contreras, N. S. (2022). The development of translator identity: An interpretative phenomenological study of Chilean translation students' experiences amid local and global crises. Unpublished doctoral dissertation, University of Manchester.

Costa, B., Lázaro Gutiérrez, R., & Rausch, T. (2020). Self-care as an ethical responsibility: A pilot study on support provision for interpreters in human crises. *Translation and Interpreting Studies*, 15(1), 36–56. https://doi.org/10.1075/tis.20004.cos.

Cowley, C. (2005). The dangers of teaching medical ethics. *Journal of Medical Education*, 31(12), 739–742. https://doi.org/10.1136/jme.2005.011908.

Crezee, I., Mikkelson, H., & Monzon-Storey, L. (2015). *Introduction to healthcare for Spanish-speaking interpreters and translators*. John Benjamins.

Crezee, I., & Marianacci, A. (2021). "How did he say that?" Interpreting students' written reflections on interprofessional education scenarios with speech language therapists. *The Interpreter and Translator Trainer*, 16(1), 19–38. https://doi.org/10.1080/1750399X.2021.1904170.

Dean, R. K. (2014). Condemned to repetition? An analysis of problem-setting and problem-solving in sign language interpreting ethics. *International Journal of Translation and Interpreting Research*, 6(1), 60–75.

Dean, R. K., & Pollard, R. Q., Jr. (2001). Application of demand-control theory to sign language interpreting: Implications for stress and interpreter training. *Journal of Deaf Studies and Deaf Education*, 6(1), 1–14.

Dean, R. K., & Pollard, R. Q., Jr. (2011). Context-based ethical reasoning in interpreting: A Demand Control Schema perspective. *The Interpreter and Translator Trainer*, 5(1), 155–182. https://doi.org/10.1080/13556509.2011.10798816.

Dean, R. K., & Pollard, R. Q., Jr. (2013). *The Demand Control Schema: Interpreting as a practice profession*. CreateSpace.

Defrancq, B., Delputte, S., & Baudewijn, T. (2022). Interprofessional training for student conference interpreters and students of political science through joint mock conferences: An assessment. *The Interpreter and Translator Trainer*, 16(1), 39–57, https://doi.org/10.1080/1750399X.2021.1919975.

Diriker, E. (2004). *De-/re-contextualizing conference interpreting: Interpreters in the ivory tower?* John Benjamins.

Diriker, E. (2011). Agency in conference interpreting: Still a myth? *Gramma*, 19, 27–36. www.enl.auth.gr/gramma/gramma11/Diriker.pdf.

Doerr, N. (2018). *Political translation: How social movement democracies survive*. Cambridge University Press.

Donovan, C. (2011). Ethics in the teaching of conference interpreting. *The Interpreter and Translator Trainer*, 5(1), 109–128. https://doi.org/10.1080/13556509.2011.10798814.

Downie, J. (2021). Interpreting is interpreting: Why we need to leave behind interpreting settings to discover comparative interpreting studies. *Translation and Interpreting Studies*, 16(3), 325–346.

Drugan, J., & Megone, C. (2011). Bringing ethics into translator training: An integrated, inter-disciplinary approach. *The Interpreter and Translator Trainer*, 5(1), 183–211. https://doi.org/10.1080/13556509.2011.10798817.

Floros, G. (2011). "Ethics-less" theories and "ethical" practices: On ethical relativity in translation. *The Interpreter and Translator Trainer*, 5(1), 65–92. https://doi.org/10.1080/13556509.2011.10798812. Freeth, D. (2005). *Effective interprofessional education: Development, delivery and evaluation*. Blackwell.

Freire, P. (1970). *Pedagogy of the oppressed*. Trans. M. Bergman Ramos. Herder and Herder.

Geiling, A., Knaevelsrud, C., Böttche, M., & Stammel, N. (2021). Mental health and work experiences of interpreters in the mental health care of refugees: A systematic review. *Frontiers in Psychiatry*, 12. https://doi.org/10.3389/fpsyt.2021.710789.

Giddens, A. (1984). *The constitution of society: Outline of the theory of structuration*. Polity Press.

Gile, D. (2009). *Basic concepts and models for interpreter and translator training* (revised ed.). John Benjamins.

Gu, C. (2019). Interpreters' institutional alignment and (re)construction of China's political discourse and image: A corpus-based CDA of the premier-meets-the-press. Unpublished doctoral dissertation, University of Manchester.

Hale, S. B. (2007). *Community interpreting*. Palgrave Macmillan.

Hale, S. B., & Gonzalez, E. (2017). Teaching legal interpreting at university level: A research-based approach. In L. Cirillo and N. Niemants (Eds.), *Teaching dialogue interpreting* (pp. 199–216). John Benjamins.

Hayes, A., & Hale, S. B. (2010). Appeals on incompetent interpreting. *Journal of Judicial Administration*, 20, 119–130.

Hennessy, E. B. (2008). Whistle-blowing and language professionals: The case of Postville and Professor Erik Camayd-Freixas. *Translation Journal*, 12(4). https://translationjournal.net/journal/46ethics.htm

Hill, A. L. (2004). Ethical analysis in counseling: A case for narrative ethics, moral visions, and virtue ethics. *Counseling and Values*, 48(2), 131–148.

Hlavac, J. (2010). Ethical implications in situations where the language of interpretation shifts: The AUSIT code of ethics. *International Journal of Translation and Interpreting*, 2(2), 29–43.

Hlavac, J., & Harrison, C. (2021). Interpreter-mediated doctor–patient interactions: Interprofessional education in the training of future interpreters and doctors. *Perspectives*, 29(1), 1–19. https://doi.org/10.1080/0907676X.2021.1873397.

Hochschild, A. R. (2012). *The managed heart: Commercialisation of human feeling* (updated ed.). University of California Press.

Howes, L. M. (2023). Ethical dilemmas in community interpreting: Interpreters' experiences and guidance from the code of ethics. *The Interpreter and Translator Trainer*, 17(2), 1–18. https://doi.org/10.1080/1750399X.2022.2141003.

Inghilleri, M. (2010). "You don't make war without knowing why": The decision to interpret in Iraq. *The Translator*, 16(2), 175–196. https://doi.org/10.1080/13556509.2010.10799468.

Johnson, J. F., Bagdasarov, Z., Connelly, S., Harkrider, L., Devenport, L. D., Mumford, M. D., & Thiel, C. E. (2012). Case-based ethics education: The impact of cause complexity and outcome favorability on ethicality. *Journal of Empirical Research on Human Research Ethics*, 7(3), 63–77. https://doi.org/10.1525/jer.2012.7.3.63.

Kadrić, M. (2014). Giving interpreters a voice: Interpreting studies meet theatre studies. *The Interpreter and Translator Trainer*, 8(3), 452–468. https://doi.org/10.1080/1750399X.2014.971485.

Kadrić, M. (2017). Make it different! Teaching interpreting with theatre techniques. In L. Cirillo and N. Niemants (Eds.), *Teaching dialogue interpreting: Research-based proposals for higher education* (pp. 275–292). John Benjamins.

Karasek, R. A. (1979). Job demands, decision latitude, and mental strain: Implications for job design. *Administrative Science Quarterly*, 24, 285–308.

Katan, D., & Straniero-Sergio, F. (2001). Look who's talking: The ethics of entertainment and talkshow interpreting. *The Translator*, 7(2), 213–237. https://doi.org/10.1080/13556509.2001.10799102.

Kermit, P. S. (2019). Introduction. In M. Phelan, M. Rudvin, H. Skaaden, and P. S. Kermit, *Ethics in public service interpreting* (pp. 1–23). Routledge.

Kindermann, D., Schmid, C., Derreza-Greeven, C., Huhn, D., Kohl, R. M., Junne, F., Schleyer, M., Daniels, J. K., Ditzen, B., Herzog, W., & Nikendei, C. (2017). Prevalence of and risk factors for secondary traumatization in interpreters for refugees: A cross-sectional study. *Psychopathology*, 50, 262–272. https://doi.org/10.1159/000477670.

Korpal, P. (2016). Interpreting as a stressful activity: Physiological measures of stress in simultaneous interpreting. *Poznan Studies in Contemporary Linguistics*, 52(2), 297–316.

Krystallidou, D., & Salaets, H. (2016). On interprofessionality in interpreter training: A few thoughts and two stories. *Dragoman*, 4(6), 5–21. http://hdl.handle.net/1854/LU-8052972.

Krystallidou, D., Van De Walle, C., Deveugele, M., Dougali, E., Mertens, F., Truwant, A., Van Praet, E., & Pype, P. (2018). Training "doctor-minded" interpreters and "interpreter-minded" doctors: The benefits of collaborative practice in interpreter training. *Interpreting: International Journal of Research and Practice in Interpreting*, 20(1), 126–144. https://doi.org/10.1075/intp.00005.kry.

Kurz, I. (2003). Physiological stress during simultaneous interpreting: A comparison of experts and novices. *The Interpreters' Newsletter*, 12, 51–67. www.openstarts.units.it/handle/10077/2472.

Liddicoat, A. J., & Taylor-Leech, K. (2021). Agency in language planning and policy. *Current Issues in Language Planning*, 22(1–2), 1–18. https://doi.org/10.1080/14664208.2020.1791533.

Llewellyn-Jones, P., & Lee, R. G. (2014). *Redefining the role of the community interpreter: The concept of role space*. SLI Press.

Machin, L. L., Bellis, K. M., Dixon, C., Morgan, H., Pye, J., Spencer, P., & Williams, R. A. (2019). Interprofessional education and practice guide: Designing ethics-orientated interprofessional education for health and social care students. *Journal of Interprofessional Care*, 33(6), 608–618. https://doi.org/10.1080/13561820.2018.1538113.

Martín Ruano, M. R. (2015). (Trans)formative theorising in legal translation and/or interpreting: A critical approach to deontological principles. *The Interpreter and Translator Trainer*, 9(2), 141–155. https://doi.org/10.1080/1750399X.2015.1051767.

Maryns, K. (2006). *The asylum speaker: Language in the Belgian asylum process*. St Jerome.

Mehus, C. J., & Becher, E. H. (2016). Secondary traumatic stress, burnout, and compassion satisfaction in a sample of spoken-language interpreters. *Traumatology*, 22, 249–254. https://doi.org/10.1037/trm0000023.

Merlini, R. (2017). Developing flexibility to meet the challenges of interpreting in film festivals. In L. Cirillo and N. Niemants (Eds.), *Teaching dialogue interpreting: Research-based proposals for higher education* (pp. 137–158). John Benjamins.

Merlini, R., & Favaron, R. (2005). Examining the "voice of interpreting" in speech pathology. *Interpreting*, 7(2), 263–302. https://doi.org/10.1075/intp.7.2.07mer.

Middlewick, Y., Kettle, T. J., & Wilson, J. J. (2012). Curtains up! Using Forum Theatre to rehearse the art of communication in healthcare education. *Nurse Education in Practice*, 12, 139–142.

Mikkelson, H. (2000). Interpreter ethics: A review of the traditional and electronic literature. *Interpreting*, 5(1), 49–56.

Miner, A., & Nicodemus, B. (2021). *Situated learning in interpreter education: From the classroom to the community*. Palgrave Macmillan.

Mizuno, M. (2005). Contents and philosophy of codes of ethics in conference, community, legal and health care interpreting. *Interpretation Studies: The Journal of the Japan Association for Interpretation Studies*, 5, 157–172.

Monteoliva-García, E. (2020). The collaborative and selective nature of interpreting in police interviews with stand-by interpreting. *Interpreting*, 22(2), 262–287. https://doi.org/10.1075/intp.00046.mon.

Moser-Mercer, B. (2008). Skill acquisition in interpreting: A human performance perspective. *The Interpreter and Translator Trainer*, 2(1), 1–28. https://doi.org/10.1080/1750399X.2008.10798764.

Mosko, M. A. (2018). Emancipatory advocacy: A companion ethics for political activism. *Philosophy and Social Criticism*, 44(3), 326–341. https://doi.org/10.1177/0191453717723188.

Munday, J. (2012). *Evaluation in translation: Critical points of translator decision-making*. Routledge.

Naumann, P. (2005). Babels and Nomad: Observations on the barbarising of communication at the 2005 World Social Forum. *AIIC Webzine*, 27 May. https://aiic.org/document/604/AIICWebzine_Summer2005_8_NAUMANN_Babels_and_Nomad_Observations_on_the_barbarising_of_communication_at_the_2005_W_EN.pdf.

Niemants, N. (2013). From role-playing to role-taking: Interpreter roles in healthcare. In C. Schaeffner, K. Kredens, and Y. Fowler (Eds.), *Interpreting in a changing landscape: Selected papers from Critical Link 6* (pp. 305–320). John Benjamins.

Niemants, N., & Stokoe, E. (2017). Using the Conversation Analytic Role-Play method in healthcare interpreter education. In L. Cirillo and N. Niemants (Eds.), *Teaching dialogue interpreting: Research-based proposals for higher education* (pp. 293–322). John Benjamins.

Ozolins, U. (2017). It's not about the interpreter: Objectives in dialogue interpreting teaching. In L. Cirillo and N. Niemants (Eds.), *Teaching dialogue interpreting: Research-based proposals for higher education* (pp. 45–62). John Benjamins.

Ozolins, U. (2018). Social workers, the law and interpreters. In S. Rice, A. Day, and L. Briskman (Eds.), *Social work in the shadow of the law* (pp. 456–474). The Federation Press.

Phelan, M. (2019). Codes of ethics. In M. Phelan, M. Rudvin, H. Skaaden, and P. S. Kermit, *Ethics in public service interpreting* (pp. 85–146). Routledge.

Phelan, M., Rudvin, M., Skaaden, H., & Kermit, P. S. (2019). *Ethics in public service interpreting*. Routledge.

Pickering, A. (1995). *The mangle of practice: Time, agency and science*. University of Chicago Press.

Pöchhacker, F. (2008). Interpreting as mediation. In C. Valero-Garcés and A. Martin (Eds.), *Crossing borders in community interpreting* (pp. 9–26). John Benjamins.

Ren, W., & Yin, M. (2020). Conference interpreter ethics. In K. Koskinen and N. K. Pokorn (Eds.), *The Routledge handbook of translation and ethics* (pp. 195–210). Routledge.

Rudvin, M. (2019). Situating interpreting ethics in moral philosophy. In M. Phelan, M. Rudvin, H. Skaaden, and P. S. Kermit, *Ethics in public service interpreting* (pp. 24–84). Routledge.

Rünz, P. (2015). Beyond teaching: Measuring the effect of EU simulations on European identity and support of the EU. *European Political Science*, 14(3), 266–278. https://doi.org/10.1057/eps.2015.23.

Saenz, T. I., & Langdon, H. W. (2019). Speech-language pathologists' collaboration with interpreters: Results of a current survey in California. *Translation and Interpreting*, 11(1), 43–62. https://doi.org/10.12807/ti.111201.2019.a03.

Seeber, K., & Zelger, C. (2007). Betrayal – vice or virtue? An ethical perspective on accuracy in simultaneous interpreting. *Meta*, 52(2), 290–298. https://doi.org/10.7202/016071ar.

Setton, R., & Dawrant, A. (2016a). *Conference interpreting: A complete course*. John Benjamins.

Setton, R., & Dawrant, A. (2016b). *Conference interpreting: A trainer's guide*. John Benjamins.

Sevrain-Goideau, M., Gohier, B., Bellanger, W., Annweiler, C., Campone, M., & Coutant, R. (2020). Forum Theater staging of difficult encounters with patients to increase empathy in students: Evaluation of efficacy at the University of Angers Medical School. *BMC Medical Education*, 20(1), Article 58. https://doi.org/10.1186/s12909-020-1965-4.

Skaaden, H. (2017). "That we all behave like professionals": An experiential-dialogic approach to interpreter education and online learning. In L. Cirillo and N. Niemants (Eds.), *Teaching dialogue interpreting: Research-based proposals for higher education* (pp. 323–340). John Benjamins.

Skaaden, H. (2019a). Ethics and profession. In M. Phelan, M. Rudvin, H. Skaaden, and P. S. Kermit, *Ethics in public service interpreting* (pp. 147–201). Routledge.

Skaaden, H. (2019b). Invisible or invincible? Professional integrity, ethics, and voice in public service interpreting. *Perspectives*, 27(5), 704–717. https://doi.org/10.1080/0907676X.2018.1536725.

Stokoe, E. (2011). Simulated interaction and communication skills training: The "Conversation-Analytic Role-Play method". In C. Antaki (Ed.), *Applied conversation analysis* (pp. 119–139). Palgrave Macmillan.

Tan, C. P., Van der Molen, H. T., & Schmidt, H. G. (2017). A measure of professional identity development for professional education. *Studies in Higher Education*, 42(8), 1504–1519. https://doi.org/10.1080/03075079.2015.1111322.

Tipton, R. (2008). Interpreter neutrality and the structure/agency distinction. Paper presented at the 3rd International Congress on Translation and Interpreting for the Public Services: Challenges and Alliances in PSIT Research and Practice, University of Alcalá de Henares, Madrid, Spain.

Tipton, R., & Furmanek, O. (2016). *Dialogue interpreting: A guide to interpreting in public services and the community*. Routledge.

Turner, G. H. (2007). Professionalisation of interpreting in the community. In C. Wadensjö, B. Englund Dimitrova, and A.-L. Nilsson (Eds.), *The critical link 4: Selected papers from the 4th International Conference on Interpreting in Legal, Health and*

Social Service Settings, Stockholm, Sweden, 20–23 May 2004 (pp.181–192). John Benjamins.

Turner, G. H., & Best, B. (2017). On motivational ethical norms: From defensive interpreting to effective professional practices. In M. Biagini, M. S. Boyd, and C. Monacelli (Eds.), *The changing role of the interpreter: Contextualising norms, ethics and quality standards* (pp. 102–121). Routledge.

Van Bewer, V., Woodgate, R. L., Martin, D., & Deer, F. (2021). Exploring the Theatre of the Oppressed and Forum Theatre as pedagogies in nursing education. *Nurse Education Today*, 103. https://doi.org/10.1016/j.nedt.2021.104940.

Vansteenkiste, M., Simons, J., Lens, W., Sheldon, K. M., & Deci, E. L. (2004). Motivating learning, performance, and persistence: The synergistic effects of intrinsic goal contents and autonomy supportive contexts. *Journal of Personality and Social Psychology*, 87(2), 246–260.

Wadensjö, C. (2014). Perspectives on role play: Analysis, training and assessments. *The Interpreter and Translator Trainer*, 8(3), 437–451. https://doi.org/10.1080/1750399X.2014.971486.

Wallmach, K. (2014). Recognising the "little perpetrator" in each of us: Complicity, responsibility and translation/interpreting in institutional contexts in multilingual South Africa. *Perspectives*, 22(4), 566–580. https://doi.org/10.1080/0907676x.2014.948893.

Wang, B., & Feng, D. (2018). A corpus-based study of stance-taking as seen from critical points in interpreted political discourse. *Perspectives*, 2, 246–260. https://doi.org/10.1080/0907676X.2017.1395468.

Wolf, M. (2012). The sociology of translation and its "activist turn". *Translation and Interpreting Studies*, 7(2), 129–143. https://doi.org/10.1075/tis.7.2.02wol.

Zwischenberger, C., & Bastin, G. L. (2015). Simultaneous conference interpreting and a supernorm that governs it all. *Meta*, 60(1), 90–111. https://doi.org/10.7202/1032401ar.

5 Teaching research ethics

5.1 Chapter overview

This chapter promotes an integrated approach to the teaching of research ethics with a goal of balancing procedural and situational practices. Specifically, it advocates embedding research ethics in research methods education, as opposed to teaching it as a discrete bolt-on to the curriculum for the purpose of institutional ethics approval processes.

The chapter contextualises shifts in the way ethics is approached in arts and humanities research. It encourages systematic examination of concepts such as integrity and risk across the research process, from design to data collection and data storage, and highlights the influence of different moral philosophical perspectives on research ethics. Finally, it recommends increasing scope in the curriculum for students to explore ethical issues in different qualitative data-collection methods through a focus on experientialism and prospectivism – that is, the ability to draw on the imagination and project ideas onto future research activities (Beardon and Wilson, 2013) through hands-on activities. In common with the overarching approach to this book, the chapter does not provide a checklist approach on what action to take when presented with a particular ethical issue in research; rather, it presents frameworks that can support students to identify and evaluate appropriate responses.

5.2 What is research ethics and why does it matter?

According to von Unger (2016, p. 88), research ethics can be understood as an overarching term that "addresses the social, political and moral dimensions of empirical research and captures a range of questions concerning the values that govern the research process". They are important since "no research proceeds without ethical dilemmas" (van den Hoonaard, 2002, p. 9) and, further, "[b]y caring about ethics and by acting on that concern we promote the integrity of research" (Israel, 2014, p. 3). Research ethics as a concept, however, is constantly evolving and continually impacted by local institutional contexts and wider social and cultural change.

DOI: 10.4324/9781003098485-6

Much of the available literature on research ethics reflects the influence of the Western liberal tradition, although some scholarship has started to unpack the largely deontological and consequentialist approaches to research ethics that are broadly associated with Western value systems (Israel, 2014; Tickly and Bond, 2013). Silverman (2017, p. 23), for instance, draws attention to the principle of autonomy as an example of something that is often viewed as problematic by students from non-Western cultures, due to the individualism that is implied in the Western view of autonomy and the challenge this can present in terms of establishing ethical hierarchies.

Helping students reconcile local institutional research ethics requirements with the values and expectations of researchers and project participants who may be based in a very different cultural environment presents a level of complexity that merits open discussion at graduate level. Critiquing epistemologies and methodologies used in the field in question and developing awareness of local institutional practices help to clarify research ethics and, more importantly, what they mean for individual researchers. Most of the time, this work is an individual endeavour; therefore, in research ethics education, social dialogue's potential to address what it means to "know responsibly" is often undervalued.

5.3 Challenges of teaching research ethics on TI programmes

Across disciplines in tertiary education, most researchers come into contact with research ethics through an apprenticeship route as master's or doctoral candidates, rather than through a structured programme of learning (Macfarlane, 2009). Where such programmes do exist, they are often underpinned by a highly instrumental approach to ethics education, largely driven by an institutional requirement to apply for – or provide a justification for not requiring – ethics approval for research projects. Applications for approval are usually scrutinised by a research ethics committee (also known as institutional review boards or IRBs) at the departmental or institutional level.

Supervisors of student research projects often play a supporting role in the ethical approval process, providing oversight in the preparation of documentation and opportunities to discuss specific ethical issues. Students may also receive dedicated institutional training in research ethics. However, anecdotal evidence suggests that TI programmes allow minimal space for students to engage with the ethical frameworks that underpin the approval process, or indeed to discuss in-field ethical challenges and how best to handle them. In other words, space is often limited to the supervisor–supervisee relationship. Although learning through experience with minimal institutional input (i.e. the apprenticeship model) has some merits, the rise in institutional ethical scrutiny of research in the humanities, arts, and social sciences suggests a pressing need for a more structured approach to teaching and learning not only for the development of short-term skills but also for the long-term good of the discipline.

Creating the conditions for dialogue and discussion outside of the supervisor–student relationship is desirable in the research ethics curriculum, not least because much more is at stake than merely navigating institutional ethical approval. There is a risk that exclusive reliance on supervisor–supervisee conversational spaces will unduly foreground procedural issues in a research project in order to convince an ethics committee that the research meets institutional standards. Timing may be an issue here, however. For example, supervision may begin at the point where the student is already well advanced in their research plans, having developed their project design as part of a taught course unit and now requiring immediate attention to obtain approval. Furthermore, Iphofen's (2011, p. 445) observation that novice researchers often expect ethical issues to be resolved for them may also be due to the need to meet an institutional deadline for submission to the ethics committee. Students' tendency to rely on the epistemic authority of the supervisor to resolve key issues may therefore be governed by factors that go beyond their capacity to work through such issues themselves.

Educators are tasked with creating the learning conditions that foster ethical curiosity and the confidence to accept that ethical quandaries that require a degree of improvisation (reflexivity) will arise. For Israel (2014, p. 2), moving "beyond merely assuaging the concerns of regulators and focus[ing] on thinking creatively and intelligently about ethical conduct" is a central concern for researchers; however, for students who are new to research, this can be fostered only with the right educator planning and input.

Prompts for reflection

The supervisor–supervisee relationship

- Approximately what proportion of your supervision time (of MA and doctoral dissertations) is devoted to ethical issues?
- Do you typically focus on issues requiring attention as part of the institutional ethics approval process, or do you have input on broader matters at an earlier stage of the research design through various coursework and classroom interventions? (NB: Consider issues such as citation ethics, self-plagiarism, publication ethics, co-authorship – including ensuring each author is fairly accounted for when publishing with students – and the use of AI in drafting phases, among many others.)
- What scope is there for you to model good research behaviours by drawing on your own experience?
- What implications (if any) does the linguistic and cultural diversity of your supervisees have for your approach to research ethics?
- Is there anything you would like to improve in terms of the way you approach research ethics with your supervisees and/or liaise with other educators in your discipline on this topic?

182 *Teaching research ethics*

In curriculum development terms, balancing input around procedural and situational matters can be problematic, and not only for reasons of space and time; devising a coherent programme that foregrounds the experiential (including the improvisational) over the theoretical and the hypothetical is needed if students are to be sufficiently sensitised to research ethics *in practice*. Such issues are not exclusive to translation and interpreting studies, but the breadth of topics, methodologies, and research relationships potentially present in a single cohort of master's and/or doctoral students can make targeted pedagogical intervention particularly difficult.

We may imagine a cohort (not unlike one at the author's home institution at the time of writing) of doctoral students who are variously undertaking projects involving online communities, commercial agents, archives, and marginalised groups in community settings, all of which entail different research relationships, risks, and data-collection methods. Some may argue that, beyond teaching courses on the principles of research ethics outside of the home department or even through a generic online learning package, there is limited scope to develop experiential approaches in situations where projects are so diverse. However, diversity can be leveraged as a strength if creative solutions anchored around peer dialogue, demonstration, and reflection are employed. The frequent cries of "They don't mention that in the literature!" from students new to in-field research show the value of developing discipline-specific teaching and learning activities.

Below is one suggestion for a student-led activity anchored in social dialogue and experiential learning on a doctoral programme. (NB: This activity is based on a three-year doctoral programme, not on programmes that involve regular attendance at taught courses in the first couple of years.)

Activity

Peer presentation event: "becoming an ethical researcher"

- **Timing:** mid-point in the academic year.

Task

- **Year 1** students deliver a short presentation to outline the ethical issues arising in their proposed projects and the resources they are using to address them. This can involve all students, regardless of whether the research involves working with human participants, since personal statements can focus on other relevant concepts, such as research integrity (including identifying the need for appropriate training, care for cultural objects, possible risks of using certain types of publicly available information as data, etc.).
- **Year 2** students' presentations focus on ethical issues that arose/are arising in the institutional ethics approval process and in fieldwork, and those that have arisen unexpectedly. Students then lead an activity with peers based on one issue they have experienced. Students not

> working with research participants can discuss their evolving understanding of research ethics in the context of their projects.
> - Year 3 students deliver presentations on how and to what extent ethical issues will be included in the writing up of their theses and on what they might have done differently in their first and second years of study.

The above activity, which is underpinned by the principle of cascading knowledge, creates a virtuous feedback loop through the collaboration of others. It places second-year doctoral students in the position of "facilitator", generating the conditions for them to explore how to engage others who are not directly involved in their research, manage contributions, and summarise, all of which are valuable transferable skills.

At master's level, by contrast, there is likely to be greater scope on taught programmes to incorporate ethics issues into the curriculum more broadly, especially in courses on research methods; however, depending on the size of cohort, it might be possible to invite master's students to attend doctoral events, such as the one outlined above, in addition to dedicated discussions on ethics in the context of research methods teaching.

The timing of pedagogical input on research ethics may also be shaped by the format of the master's or doctoral dissertation. Increasingly, doctoral students are doing a thesis by publication to help establish a research track record and improve their chances of securing employment in academia soon after completion. Master's dissertations also often include an option to leverage experience gained on work placements or internships through a format that consists of a theoretically informed report about such experiences. The potential exploitation of students on placements and internships also forms an important part of research ethics both prior to and during the work experience, and in the writing-up process.

> Prompts for reflection
>
> *Curriculum design and the place of ethics*
> - Does research ethics form part of the taught part of your programmes of study at graduate level? If so, how satisfied are you with the timing and the pedagogical approach adopted? If not, what might be the benefits of adopting a more structured approach to research ethics teaching on your programmes of study?
> - What scope do you generally afford to research ethics topics in your one-to-one supervision of graduate student dissertations? How do you measure the success of your approach? What could you do differently?
> - How were you introduced to research ethics in your academic training and how (if at all) has your understanding of the topic evolved as your research career has developed (e.g. through working in cross-cultural research teams)?

> **Activity**
>
> *Opening up debate about research ethics in TI studies*
>
> Task
>
> 1 Students are asked to read a recommended text, such as Mellinger and Baer (2021).
> 2 Working independently or in small groups, students annotate the article, formulate a series of questions for an interview with an academic about their TI research ethics practice, and select a particular quote for discussion or debate.

5.4 Mapping and responding to change in research ethics expectations in tertiary education

A review of the scholarship on research ethics from recent decades suggests an emerging consensus around perceptions of "ethics creep" in research in the humanities and social sciences, especially in North America and Western Europe (Boden et al., 2009; Haggerty et al., 2004). This is largely considered a consequence of marketisation in higher education and increased accountability to users of its services (Busher and Fox, 2019; see Israel, 2014, ch. 4, for an overview of developments in research ethics in different regions of the world).

Tension emerges when researchers are directly accountable for research practice but have little scope to define what is ethical (Boden et al., 2009, p. 737), as this can have significant implications for the research ethics review process and consequences for the timing and schedule of the proposed research (see Monaghan et al., 2013, for a vivid account of such tensions in practice). Other critiques point to the prevalence of "precautionary" decision-making (Haggerty et al., 2003) that may seem disproportionate and can be particularly difficult to predict in ethnographic research. Indeed, Haggerty et al. (2004, p. 396) assert that research ethics committees in the social sciences are often tasked with mitigating for harms that "are generally of a considerably lower magnitude" in reality.

Common to many critiques of this shift is the compatibility and appropriateness of bureaucratic models and regulatory processes imported chiefly from (Western) biomedical research contexts, which are often "highly scripted" (Boden et al., 2009, p. 734), struggle to accommodate "typically messy and unpredictable fieldwork" (Monaghan et al., 2013, p. 67), and require premeditated ethical responses. Yet, as van den Hoonaard (2002, p. 3) observes, although researchers may bemoan the encroaching influence of the biomedical sciences approach to ethics, this shift has led to deeper reflection on the range of issues that arise in research in the humanities and social sciences, and greater agreement that ethics review is an important educative experience (see also Iphofen, 2009; Wiles, 2013).

Educators seeking to support students to develop a structured approach to the ethical questions raised by their research need to address both procedural and situational issues. Wiles (2013, p. 12) identifies several factors shaping ethical decision-making in research that serve to structure the planning process: ethical frameworks; individual moral frameworks; legal regulation; ethical regulation; professional guidelines; and disciplinary norms. In addition, however, she stresses the emergent nature of many of the ethical issues arising in academic research, draws attention to the available resources (literature, professional codes, disciplinary norms, laws) that can guide researchers' thinking, and acknowledges the importance of an individual's own moral beliefs in their attempts to resolve ethical issues. The emergent nature of many issues is a reminder of the importance of developing ethical reflexivity in graduate researchers, as discussed later in this chapter. As time to acquire knowledge and apply it to practice is likely to be limited, educators will need to prioritise certain tasks over others. Addressing foundational philosophical questions (such as "What is integrity?") directly towards the start of research education can stimulate productive debate and critical thinking in groups, but much of the basic knowledge-acquisition work relating to guidelines can be undertaken independently. One activity that could be incorporated into this phase of learning is outlined below.

Activity

Research ethics and language choice

Language inevitably influences a researcher's perception of the nature of the relationships that will underpin their study. As Williamson and Smyth (2004, p. 4) assert, the choice of language not only has implications for knowledge construction and methodological approach but is also an indication of the values that inform research practice.

Task

1. Working independently or in small groups, students consider the labels they intend to use in their applications to ethics committees when describing the people they hope to recruit for their research projects. As a starting point, each group could discuss the ethical implications of each of the following terms in English and/or relevant terms in other languages: "subject", "participant", "co-researcher", "cohort", "informant", "expert".
2. Questions to guide the discussion:
    - What does each term mean and which values are associated with it?
    - What power relationship between the researcher and researched is implied by each term?
    - Consider the extent to which each term invites a particular approach to protection of the individual.

- Which label best fits the relationship that you, as a researcher, hope to develop with the people in your proposed research project or a hypothetical research plan? Why?
- Which mitigations can researchers implement if the relationship evolves in unanticipated ways that have an unintended impact on the research?

5.5 Core concepts in research ethics and some implications for TI researchers

This section encourages structured reflection on several aspects of research that are core to the planning phase, contact with the field, and the handling of data after collection, most notably risk, consent, and confidentiality. It also considers ethical matters arising from the translation of documentation used to obtain consent from potential participants.

5.5.1 Avoiding harm

Avoiding harm (i.e. the principle of nonmaleficence) in academic research has been fundamental to research ethics ever since the experiments conducted by Nazi doctors in the Second World War and the consequent development of the Nuremberg Code in 1947 (Charbonneau, 1984) and subsequent codes (e.g. the World Medical Association's Declaration of Helsinki and the Belmont Report). Harms in research commonly fall into the following categories: physical, non-physical, social, legal, and economic. Non-physical harms include loss of privacy, psychological trauma, damage to reputation, loss of employment, and breakdown in trust between researchers and participants, and between institutions and society.

Historically, non-physical risks, such as those that might arise in humanities and social science research, were often considered unproblematic. Reflecting on his experience as a member of an institutional ethics review board, Oakes (2002, p. 449) argues that this view stemmed largely from the fact that very little was known of the risks associated with collecting oral histories or conducting anthropological investigations. Unsurprisingly, erring on the side of caution leads to an emphasis on worst-case scenarios and to demands for mitigations for such scenarios (e.g. collecting contact details of a participant's physician ahead of the research in case a difficult memory is triggered), which may discourage potential participants.

One way to identify potential harms is by co-designing research questions and the overall research design with research participants. While this is unlikely to be feasible at master's level, it is a possibility at doctoral level. *Nihil de nobis, sine nobis* (nothing about us without us) has become a powerful slogan that underpins research design and the research process, especially on projects involving (usually minoritised) groups that aim to shape future public policy or training interventions (sometimes known as community-led research; see, e.g., Rawlings, Flexner, and Riley, 2021).

Activity

Understanding harms and risk in research

- **Learning outcomes:** by the end of the seminar, students will be able to: articulate different categories of risk in research; assign different types of data collection to a relevant risk category; identify harms from hypothetical scenarios in relation to several categories (physical, non-physical, social, legal, and economic); and reflect on the range of mitigations the researcher might need to implement, weighed against the perceived level of risk.
- **Delivery:** using a "flipped classroom" approach, materials are made available to students asynchronously through a virtual learning platform in the form of a short video by an educator who introduces the concept of harm, accompanied by recommended reading.

Tasks (in class)

UNDERSTANDING CATEGORIES OF RISK

1 Students read the following definitions of low-, medium-, and high-risk research:

Low risk:
  The research engages healthy adults or children (the latter in an accredited setting such as a cultural institution, school or youth club and accompanied by a carer or professional with a duty of care) who are able to give informed consent via opt-in. The research follows standard procedures and established research methodologies, is carried out online or in a public setting that does not present risks to the researcher or research participants beyond what is normal in that setting, and does not require research participants to provide personal and sensitive information likely to compromise them, or to lead to distress (the research topics are not contentious or sensitive, such as asking about religious beliefs, sexual preferences, political views or illegal activities, or a reasonable person would agree the topic may only result in distress in extremely rare instances).

Medium risk:
  The research engages adults and/or children (the latter in an accredited setting such as a cultural institution, school or youth club and accompanied by a carer or professional with a duty of care), follows standard procedures and established research methodologies, is carried out in a public setting that does not present risks to the researcher or research participants beyond what is normal in that setting, and does not require research participants to provide personal and sensitive information likely

to lead to significant levels of distress (the research topics are either not contentious or sensitive, or a reasonable person would agree the topic is of legitimate interest and may result in distress in *rare* instances).

High risk:
The research focuses on groups within society in need of special support, is carried out in an unstable or volatile setting, involves non-standard methodologies or approaches, presents risks to the personal safety of the researcher or research participant beyond what is normal in the setting, or where there is a possibility the research may be distressing to the researcher or research participant in one or more ways.
(School of Arts, Languages and Cultures, University of Manchester, 2020; original emphasis)

2 Students discuss the following questions:
- What are the salient differences between the low- and medium-risk categories?
- What sort of groups may be included in the high-risk category?

APPLYING KNOWLEDGE ABOUT RISK AND HARMS TO HYPOTHETICAL TI RESEARCH PROJECTS

1 In small groups, students discuss one of two scenarios:
- Translation scenario: the research project aims to identify responses and adjustments made over time by new translators to workflow in a busy translation office. The research will involve three months of workplace observation, focus groups, and individual interviews with new translators, mentors, and project managers.
- Interpreting scenario: the research project aims to collect personal experiences of language and communication support provided by a statutory social service to former unaccompanied minors (now young adults, aged 18–20) from different countries of origin. The research will involve individual online interviews with both social service staff and the recipients of support.

2 Students identify the potential risks and harms for research participants and researchers in their given scenario using the following categories: physical, non-physical, social, legal, and economic.
3 On the basis of these discussions, students categorise the research as low, medium, or high risk.
4 Against each risk/harm, each group brainstorms possible mitigations for researchers and participants before data collection begins, during data collection, and following data collection.

In their enthusiasm to get out into the field, new researchers may underestimate the risks of harm that can arise through even the most apparently straightforward study protocols: lone working, unwarranted disclosures, and requests from gatekeepers and participants are just three of the considerations that may be overlooked. In public service interpreting research in particular, some projects may also benefit from trauma-informed research training to promote the safeguarding of research participants (e.g. minimise the risk of retraumatisation) and the researcher. The following activity is designed to encourage reflection on the differences between low- and medium-risk projects.

Activity

Understanding nuance in research risk

Task

1   Students are presented with the following scenario: a doctoral student wishes to observe a cohort of master's-level conference interpreting students in the classroom over a couple of months as an ethnographic component of a wider study on simultaneous interpreting.
2   Students discuss the following questions in small groups or reflect on them individually:

- Why might a research ethics committee categorise this proposal as medium risk as opposed to low risk?
- What are the potential harms and risks for the participants, and how might the researcher mitigate them?
- What are the risks/harms for the researcher?

5.5.2 Informed consent

(Signed) informed consent is often viewed as the cornerstone of academic research conducted in the Western liberal democratic tradition. However, this tradition privileges the autonomy of the individual to provide consent, which can be at odds with other social formations in which collective decision-making prevails (Silverman, 2017; van den Hoonaard, 2002). Even when working within an individualist paradigm, educators need to sensitise students to a broad range of factors that can impact on the process of obtaining informed consent, such as literacy levels (e.g. might an "easy read" version be required) and issues of anonymity associated with signing a consent form.

Particular consideration should also be given to obtaining consent from individuals who are unable to make wholly voluntary decisions about becoming research subjects (e.g. due to age or capacity) and may qualify for specific protection under the law or some other authority. These include children and young people (whether healthy, unhealthy, or at risk), migrants and refugees, prisoners, older people, vulnerable adults (e.g. with learning difficulties), and people undergoing end-of-life care. Certain high-stakes research involving such groups may be institutionally proscribed, particularly at master's level.

Regardless of whether students are required to go through a formal ethical review before commencing a research project, they will need to plan carefully to recruit and obtain permission from individuals to participate in the research. This usually means providing a "participant information sheet" that should help an individual make an informed decision as to whether they wish to participate or not, guidance on how they can withdraw from the study after it has started, and, in most cases, a consent form for them to sign. When working with vulnerable groups, additional considerations, such as including a trusted adult or relative in the decision-making process and allowing sufficient time for a decision to be taken, will be necessary. In this regard, close contact with institutional research ethics committees can be particularly helpful and, indeed, an invaluable source of support and guidance as a research project unfolds. Hale and Napier (2013, pp. 48–50) provide a useful checklist for interpreting studies researchers on the subject of seeking informed consent, which can be extended to the recruitment of human participants in translation studies research more broadly.

In learning and teaching terms, informed consent raises several ethical issues that can be usefully supported by structured learning activities. Drafting a statement of what a study aims to achieve, what an individual's participation would entail, and what will happen to their data is a first stage that requires awareness of institutional regulatory frameworks with regard to data protection, and clarity with regard to whether personal identifiable data will be collected and stored, and, if so, where and for how long. As this process will be couched within a local institutional framework, the following activity focuses on some common issues that may arise in the planning phase (identifying and interacting with gatekeepers) and when obtaining consent.

Activity

Negotiating access and recruiting (healthy adult) participants

- **Learning aim:** to introduce students to the ethical principles of identifying and interacting with research gatekeepers.
- **Learning outcomes:** by the end of this activity, students will be able to: identify gatekeepers and articulate their role in obtaining informed consent; plan the information needed before approaching a gatekeeper about a research project; articulate a range of strategies to help persuade gatekeepers of the value of the research; and identify ways in which gatekeepers might impact on research plans and intended research participants.

Task

1 Students are presented with the following scenario: a researcher intends to interview volunteers at an NGO who work with interpreters to deliver services. The NGO has a large national presence, but the research will be limited to just one local branch near to the researcher's home institution. The researcher already knows a volunteer at the branch who has agreed to be interviewed.

2 In small groups, students discuss the following questions based on the above scenario:

- Which gatekeeper(s) would the researcher need to contact to obtain organisational permission to conduct the research?
- Would it be ethical for the researcher to contact their friend directly to set up interviews if the latter had cleared it with their local branch manager? (NB: Consider the potential risks and harms associated with this action.)
- Imagine that the researcher's university ethics review committee makes it a condition of approval that the researcher seeks permission from the head of the NGO about the organisation's participation in the research and recommending staff with the relevant expertise and experience as participants.
- Draft a letter to the head of the NGO to seek approval and make a case for the relevance of the research to the organisation.

Reflect on the researcher's options if:

- several weeks after sending the letter to the head of the organisation, they have heard nothing back;
- after receiving a list of individuals to contact, it turns out that some of them do not have the relevant expertise for the study; and
- some of the named individuals who have supposedly agreed to be interviewed are not really interested in participating.

Finally, imagine that the gatekeeper agrees to the organisation's involvement on condition that the researcher provides some free staff training at the end of the project. How would/should the researcher respond?

Activity

Negotiating access and recruiting participants in online worlds

Task

1 Students are presented with the following scenario: a researcher intends to investigate expertise development and group identity by

> interviewing members of a closed fansubber discussion forum. The researcher's knowledge of the forum predates their academic research in this area as they have visited it as an interested member of the public over the course of several years.
>
> 2   In small groups, students reflect on the ethical issues raised by the above scenario from the perspective of the potential for exploitation and/or coercion, role boundaries, and anonymity, before discussing the following questions:
>
> - Based on your discussions of the ethical issues arising from this scenario, do you think it would be ethical for the researcher to try to recruit participants from this forum or would it be preferable to approach a different group?
> - If continuing with the same forum, how should the researcher identify and approach the gatekeeper(s)?
> - What action could be taken in mitigation if the researcher received consent to proceed from the gatekeeper of a very active subset of members, but only some of that subset agreed to participate?

5.5.2.1 Process consent

For many studies, obtaining consent at the start of data collection is a one-time act, usually because involvement is limited to a single event (e.g. interview or focus group). However, in some studies, "process consent" (Ellis, 2007) will be required, which means that the researcher needs to be mindful that consent may change over the course of a participant's involvement in a study. Participants can find it difficult to withdraw from a study once they have given consent at the start; eliciting consent on an ongoing basis and making it clear that this process will be followed will provide a clearer steer to participants that they can cease involvement at any time if they wish.

Process consent usually applies in qualitative longitudinal research (QLR), in studies in which a participant is involved in several event types (e.g. keeping a diary and attending an interview), and when a single event type is repeated (e.g. a series of oral history interviews conducted over several sessions). It encourages reflection on the need to think about the space(s) created by the researcher for negotiating participants' involvement. For example, consider a researcher who believes that they should protect potential participants by guaranteeing their anonymity in the participant information sheet: that is, the guarantee is essentially passed down to the potential participants as a *fait accompli*. This raises the question of how spaces are created within the process for (re-)negotiating the relationship of the researched to the data. In other words, as van den Hoonaard (2002, p. 14) asks, what if participants do not want to be anonymised down the line and instead wish to claim their voice in publications? Where would such a development leave the process of informed consent? In other situations, issues of time may require the support of a third-party transcriber for interview data, requiring additional consent from participants.

5.5.2.2 Translating consent

In some research projects, recruiting participants may require the translation of information about the project and data protection protocols into different languages. This requires careful consideration as the translation needs to do more than merely convey propositional content; it also needs to support understanding of the research culture. Added to this is the issue of translation expertise. A participant information sheet is a mixed genre of text containing practical information on what each participant will be asked to do, how many times, and in what order, but it also encompasses information of a legal nature on data protection.

Prompts for discussion

Translation and the student researcher

- What are your institution's expectations about translation in the recruitment process? Professional/non-professional/student-translated?
- How will you fund the translation?
- What level of translator training is available in the local area suitable for this text type?
- Who controls the quality of the translation and do you need to provide evidence of quality assurance to the ethics review committee?
- How will the researcher know that the translated text has been understood by the participant, and that the participant is able to provide informed consent? Which safeguards could the researcher put in place for this purpose?

5.5.3 Confidentiality

Research involving human participants requires putting in place certain safeguards regarding how the confidentiality of research data will be maintained, how individuals' personal identifiable information will be handled, and how their status as research participants will be protected. At its core, confidentiality concerns questions of privacy and anonymity, but it is a highly contested area in research ethics. Tensions can arise, for example, between the research and reporting phases, and it should not be assumed that all participants are equally concerned about confidentiality issues. For instance, some may want a topic to receive wide societal attention, whereas others may want more control over how the research is reported out of fear of some form of traceability (e.g. if they are a member of a minoritised group in a particular institutional context). "Deductive disclosure" or "internal confidentiality" are terms used to describe the identification of research participants (either individuals or groups) through particular traits (Kasia, 2009). Ellis's (1986) account of fisher folk in Chesapeake Bay is a good example of issues that can arise in this regard. Redacting transcripts ahead of dissemination of research findings is therefore a skill that requires development.

Safeguards to maintain confidentiality are required for all phases of the research cycle, from recruitment through to data collection, data analysis, dissemination of findings, storage, and disposal. They take various forms: physical (e.g. using private rooms for interviews), administrative (e.g. restricting access to personal information), technical (e.g. password-protected files and encryption), and project design (e.g. storing de-identified data separately from coding lists, undertaking transcription of raw data promptly after collection, etc.).

Researchers should also be aware of – and ensure that their plans comply with – local legal frameworks governing data protection (e.g. the General Data Protection Regulation in the European Union). This is to avoid a situation in which a researcher promises unlimited confidentiality to potential research participants without taking account of the broader legal context in which the research will take place. For instance, the duty to protect the privacy and confidentiality of participants' information may be outweighed by external factors, such as a legal requirement for the researcher to disclose information if a third party becomes aware of its existence (see, e.g., Palys and Lowman, 2012, on a complex case involving Boston College's archives of oral histories relating to the Troubles in Northern Ireland).

Many of these issues are procedural in nature, and students will be guided through them as part of the institutional ethics approval process. However, there are several areas in which students would benefit from targeted pedagogical input: research design, in-field work, data transcription/redaction, and dissemination.

5.5.4 Data management, storage, and retention

Good data management and handling is integral to ethical research involving human participants. Institutional research ethics approval processes usually require a clear plan for data storage and management over the course of the project and potentially beyond, depending on the data retention policy of the institution and/or the funder concerned. Locking information away in filing cabinets has diminished as technological storage solutions have come into wider usage, which means that researchers need to familiarise themselves with local institutional data storage options, legal frameworks for data security, and retention policies. In practical terms, student researchers may need to address questions of device encryption, data securitisation, data export (e.g. from surveys), data anonymisation and pseudonymisation, among other issues.

Activity

Data management orientation (online asynchronous)

Task

1 Students read the relevant institutional research data protection policy (e.g. via a virtual learning environment).
2 Students research the various options for storing data (e.g. on personal computers and/or on computer systems) within the institution and familiarise themselves with relevant services for addressing practical issues, such as applying for additional data storage.
3 Extension activity: small student discussion groups exchange information at various stages of their research. Students who are about to submit and those who are awaiting viva examinations are likely to provide particularly helpful advice for those who are less advanced in their projects.

Activity

Data management planning

Task 1

1 Students can draw on their own research for this activity, or on the following hypothetical research projects:

- Hypothetical Project 1: a survey among professional translators about experiences of post-editing.
- Hypothetical Project 2: interviews with military personnel about their experiences of working with civilian interpreters in a theatre of war.
- Hypothetical Project 3: archival research on the translation of a well-known author's work.

2 For each project, where relevant, students reflect on:

- the type of personally identifiable information (PII) that might be needed for the research project (i.e. information that could be used to identify a specific individual from the research);
- the information that must be provided to participants regarding what will happen to their data once it has been collected (including reference to relevant data protection requirements in law);
- any limits on the participant's ability to withdraw from the study (e.g. before the data is analysed);

- information that must be provided to participants regarding how PII will be stored;
- the extent to which any data will need to be anonymised or pseudonymised, and how a key to the information will be stored in case a participant wishes to withdraw their data during the project; and
- the action that should be taken if a person discloses information about poor professional practice/misconduct or current or future illegal activities.

Task 2

1 In an adaptation of Task 1, educators start by sharing sample data management statements for groups to discuss before reflecting on potential adaptations to other types of research project, including their own, where relevant. Two examples are provided below.

EXAMPLE TEXT 1

This example text provides information on the use of recorded Zoom interviews for participants in a UK study:

> Your participation in this research will be recorded in Zoom and your personal data will be processed by Zoom. This may mean that your personal data is transferred to a country outside of the European Economic Area, some of which have not yet been determined by the European Commission to have an adequate level of data protection. Appropriate legal mechanisms to ensure these transfers are compliant with the UK General Data Protection Regulation are in place. The recordings will be removed from the above third-party platform and stored on University of X's managed file storage as soon as possible following the completion of data collection. Also there is a Zoom privacy policy: https://zoom.us/privacy.

EXAMPLE TEXT 2

This example text provides information on the collection of PII for participants in a UK study that involves filmed role-plays:

> In order to participate in this research project we will need to collect information that could identify you, called "personal identifiable information". Specifically, we will need to collect:
>
> - Name
> - Email contact details
> - Gender
> - Ethnicity

- Language(s) spoken
- Your professional background (where relevant)
- Given that you will take part in a group discussion, we might need audio-visual information from you as you participate on Zoom. Video input is compulsory if you speak British Sign Language. Otherwise, it is possible for you to take part in this study with your camera turned off.
- Contact details. If you are interested, we will ask for your email address if you wish to be involved in future research and/or want to be informed of findings. This is not mandatory, and you can refuse to provide this information.
- The video recordings will include recordings of participants' voices and images of the head and shoulders of those participants who opt to keep their camera turned on during the observation and discussion.

2 Students read the two example texts then reflect on any adjustments that might be necessary prior to their use in other hypothetical research projects (such as those outlined in Task 1 or others).

5.6 Ethical traditions in research ethics

This section illuminates aspects of moral philosophy that shape ethical thinking in academic research in relation to data collection as well as practical issues relating to data handling and data sharing. Attention is given to the relational ontology underpinning an "ethics of care", which is becoming increasingly influential as an alternative normative ethical theory in the context of research involving human participants.

5.6.1 *Consequentialism/non-consequentialism*

Consequentialism theory concerns reflection on the potential consequences of actions for individuals and/or groups of people (see Chapter 1). Within this theoretical approach, "the moral status of an action is evaluated by evaluating the balance of its good and bad consequences" (Israel, 2014, p. 10). The feasibility of considering the consequences of every action for everyone who may be impacted has been widely debated, especially by those who orient towards non-consequentialism (deontology) as a normative ethical theory. The latter holds that some actions are good in and of themselves and that determining whether behaviour is ethical depends on considerations other than harmful consequences (Israel, 2014).

In research ethics, consequentialism is related to the ethics of responsibility, which supports researcher response to potential consequences arising from the research environment, research questions, and so on. For instance, while a researcher may determine that a project is in the public interest and that the

198   *Teaching research ethics*

benefits for certain constituencies outweigh any negatives, protocols relating to safeguarding or distress (for researchers and participants) can help to prepare the ground for actions to be taken should the research process prove problematic in any way.

Another aspect of research to which consequentialism theory has been applied is data sharing (e.g. Kim, 2021). Public data sharing is now widely considered as an obligation, supported by many journals' insistence that research articles must be linked to data repositories to allow greater transparency and reproducibility. However, the level of data sharing varies widely across different disciplines, and the deliberate withholding of data remains quite prevalent, not least because of researchers' fear of losing exclusive rights over the data and publication opportunities (Kim, 2021; Kim and Stanton, 2012; Savage and Vickers, 2009). Younger scholars may feel particularly vulnerable in this regard, which is why the topic merits some attention in research training.

Activity

Data sharing

Task

Individually or in groups, students:

- survey a number of translation and interpreting studies journals to identify data sharing policies and practice;
- investigate one or two online data sharing repositories (e.g. figshare);
- reflect on the importance of data sharing for their individual research projects from the perspectives of research ethics and perceived benefit for the researcher and the field of translation and interpreting studies;
- reflect on the risks of sharing data informally with acquaintances or colleagues;
- think about sources of information that will help develop a reasoned approach to data sharing in the future; and
- share the outcomes of these investigations and reflections with the wider group.

5.6.2 Virtue ethics

Virtue-based approaches to research ethics have attracted attention from scholars interested in exploring the concept of research integrity from the perspective of the person who does the research (the research practitioner) as opposed to the research practice (e.g. Banks, 2018).

For Banks (2018, p. 25), the concept of virtue relates to the moral disposition of moral agents to act in ways that "promote human and ecological flourishing".

Responding to so-called "situationist critiques" of virtue ethics, which question the fixity of virtues in the human character, Banks (2018) asserts that virtue ethics in research requires ongoing work. She explores the relationship between virtue and research integrity by distinguishing between "thin" and "thick" integrity. While the former emphasises conduct and compliance, which Banks argues is too managerialist in orientation and fails to consider the researcher as a critical actor, the latter is character oriented and allows focus on the researcher as a critical, reflexive, respectful, and courageous actor, among other characteristics (pp. 28–29). Banks suggests that researchers of integrity tend to display three main characteristics: a situated understanding of the ideals, values, and virtues of a good researcher; a critical and emotional commitment to these ideals, values, and virtues; and a well-developed capacity for ethics work (p. 35). In terms of research integrity education, the last of these characteristics is emphasised.

Finally, for Banks (2018), cultivating researchers of integrity takes many forms, from supervision discussions to case deliberations with others and "neo Socratic" dialogue, following an approach developed by Leonard Nelson in 1940. The latter involves starting a discussion with a philosophical question, such as "What is integrity?", which participants debate by reflecting on examples from their own research.

5.6.3 Critical approaches

Critical approaches to ethics are concerned with relations of power. Ethical discourses, in the words of Tickly and Bond (2013, p. 423), are "more than simply words or language"; they serve a legitimising function (e.g. with regard to social practices) and have material effects in the world.

An "ethics of care", which derives from a feminist philosophical perspective, is an example of a critical approach to research ethics. It is considered as a distinct (normative) moral theory that foregrounds the moral significance of an individual's private sphere (Held, 2006) and "uses a relational and context-bound approach to morality and decision-making" (Burton, Dunn, and Petruzzello, 2013). Initially developed by Carol Gilligan (1982), this approach to research ethics involves a focus on ethical decision-making in ways that benefit the individual or the group at the centre of the research. As such, it recognises "the relationality and interdependency of researchers and research participants" (Wiles, 2013, p. 15) and also values emotion (e.g. sympathy, empathy, etc.), which, according to Held (2006, p. 11), is often "rejected in rationalistic moral theories". Held stresses the importance of an ethics of care, as opposed to simply valuing care, since emotions can become misguided. She also distinguishes between an ethics of care and care as a virtue in the sense that the former focuses on relations as opposed to character (p. 19).

An ethics of care can be applied to all types of research involving human participants. For instance, it has been extensively applied in research involving participatory methodologies, including those connected to emancipatory and decolonising research agendas. Enacting an ethics of care in research can take many forms, which can be the focus of classroom discussions and practical activities, such as those outlined later in this chapter (e.g. research interviewing). As a general set of principles, research underpinned by an ethics of care will be informed by a number of values (following Brannelly, 2018): developing longer-term responsible partnerships with communities; enabling the participation of marginalised groups; fostering participation from multiple positions and identities held by individuals; examining research practices with participants; and co-negotiating locally produced action for change.

Another critical approach concerns postcolonial ethics, which emerged from theories that support critical interrogation of Western rule. The prefix "post" has been widely critiqued, leading some scholars to view postcolonialism as a process involving the gradual "disengagement of formerly colonised countries from European colonisation and classical imperialism and their reinsertion into the flows and networks that characterise contemporary globalisation" (Tickly and Bond, 2013, p. 423).

Postcolonial thinking requires critical engagement with Western conceptualisations of ethics, particularly those that emerged during the Enlightenment and led to the subordination of other ethical traditions. Tickly and Bond (2013, p. 425) describe the dominance of Western ethics as manifesting *inter alia* through an emphasis on modern science and high culture as the sole criteria for truth and aesthetic quality, economic growth as the chief measure of development and progress, and a linear view of time. What may be understood as postcolonial ethics takes many forms, but a common thread concerns the need to recognise alternative forms of knowledge, promote interdependence between scientific and non-scientific knowledge, and accommodate distinctive conceptualisations of human dignity.

In terms of research process, Tickly and Bond's (2013) understanding of postcolonial ethics foregrounds emancipation, situatedness, and dialogue. The first of these concerns giving a voice to people impacted by colonial encounters; the second emphasises the importance of attending to the significance of culture and context in deriving ethical practices at the local level; and the third, which is closely connected to situatedness, stresses the importance of cross-cultural dialogue within research teams and between researchers and research participants in ways that address questions of power in postcolonial research settings.

Prompts for (small group) discussion

- To what extent has your approach to research ethics been shaped by Western influences and ethical discourses?
- How would you articulate the relationship between epistemological choice and ethics in research?
- Are there any examples of epistemological approaches developed in translation and interpreting studies that you think have been particularly successful in accommodating different views on knowledge production?

- Which steps (if any) have you taken to explore alternative epistemologies in your own research?
- To what extent do codes of research that you are familiar with, or your local institutional ethics approval process, reflect a Western bias?

5.7 An integrated approach to teaching research ethics

This section makes a case for integrating research ethics into the curriculum specifically through the teaching and learning of research methods. It provides practical suggestions as to how students can work through certain ethical dilemmas that are known to arise in different data collection methods in a safe space, prior to entering the field. It also examines the importance of accounting for ethical experiences in the writing-up process.

5.7.1 Developing ethical reflexivity in research

Developing researcher ethics and individual understandings of what constitutes an ethics of research confronts the individual with questions about researcher subjectivities and the ways in which these influence the research design, execution, and reporting phases. Education in research methods will likely introduce concepts of insiderhood and outsiderhood, but seldom appears to allow space for reflection on the range of emotional responses both positions can generate for researchers or the potential presence of multiple and overlapping subjectivities. Doctoral students may even be in the final stages of their thesis development before their supervisor encourages them to think about researcher positionality, subjectivities, and how these have impacted the research. Looking back over the full doctoral journey with the benefit of the lived experience to support such reflection is doubtlessly beneficial; however, research processes can be tangibly improved if this form of reflection is encouraged throughout the learning journey.

Hsiung (2008, p. 212) defines reflexivity in research as "a process that challenges the researcher to explicitly examine how his or her research agenda and assumptions, subject location(s), personal beliefs, and emotions enter into their research". It is often considered as a key distinguishing feature of qualitative and quantitative research that, for Hsiung, rests on a conceptualisation of the researcher as an active participant in knowledge (re)production. Willig (2001, cited in Macfarlane, 2009) distinguishes between personal and epistemological reflexivity, with the former concerning reflection on how the research process impacts the individual researcher in terms of (re-)shaping beliefs about research, and the latter involving critically engaged reflection on the process of truth-seeking in the research process at every stage.

Hsiung's work, which is anchored in social science research, addresses some of the challenges of fostering reflexivity in ways that can be extended to translation and interpreting studies. Broadly speaking, reflexive practice involves researchers "interrogating the constitutive role of the researcher in researcher decision-making, data collection, analysis and knowledge production" (Hsiung, 2008, p. 212). Reflexivity is not inherently ethical, but the two are viewed as closely intertwined during research (Warin, 2011). Furthermore, for Michel Foucault, the process of the researcher consciously seeking to attend to their thoughts is a necessary ethical practice (Rabinow, 1997, p. xxxix). Within a virtue ethics framework, Macfarlane (2009, p. 126) argues that reflexivity can be viewed as both an intellectual and a moral virtue; in other words, it is a skill but also a mindset of remaining open to criticism from the start.

What might usefully be termed "ethical reflexivity", then, encompasses researcher vigilance – or "ethical mindfulness" (Warin, 2011) – about ethical issues at every stage of the research cycle. Awareness concerns the self and positioning as a researcher, as well as impact of the self on others, at particular points and cumulatively over the whole research process. For example, as a research interview unfolds, reflexivity can be employed by maintaining vigilance with regard to the dialogic dynamics of the interview (including power relations between researcher and researched) and to any contingencies that may be required if an unexpected ethical quandary occurs. Systematic review of researcher performance after each research event will ensure that vigilance is maintained and attended to throughout the research project. Critical incidents – or "ethically important moments" (Guillemin and Gillam, 2004) – can be an effective focus of discussion during supervision and with peers, and some may be included in the final thesis write-up as evidence of good research practice.

Improvisation is allied to the concept of reflexivity to the extent that it is pursued in and of the moment of action. Fancourt, Foreman-Peck, and Oancea (2022, p. 3) call for an acknowledgement of the value of improvisation in research ethics and insist that it should not be considered as an "unfortunate compromise or deviation", although (following Sawyer, 2011) they do stress the importance of "disciplined improvisation". Thus, improvisation can be viewed in the context of virtue ethics as an example of researcher courage that underpins a critically engaged approach to research process and is a hallmark of what Banks (2018) terms a "developed capacity for ethics work".

Activity

Cultivating disciplined improvisation

This activity encourages students to think about the forms that disciplined improvisation might take (prospective learning) when developing topic guides and questions for interview and focus-group research.

Task

1 Students select a sample of interview questions from their own or a hypothetical project then think through interviewees' possible

> responses along different axes (e.g. highly emotional–indifferent; apolitical–highly political) and what these might mean for the way in which the researcher responds and/or frames subsequent questions.
> 2 Students share their thoughts and ideas for strategies with their peers.
> 3 Extension activity: students engage in short role-plays around one or two of the questions to trial their use of language and strategies in a safe environment.

5.7.2 Integrating ethics into research methods teaching

An environmental scan of the literature on research methods in translation and interpreting studies confirms that greater emphasis is placed on the steps needed for ethical approval than ethics in practice. In this subsection, selected research ethics issues in qualitative research education are discussed with specific reference to interviews, focus groups, surveys, and ethnographic research. This discussion is supported with practical suggestions for pedagogical approaches that maximise experiential learning through the teaching of research methods.

5.7.2.1 Interviews and focus groups

Interviews are sites of interpersonal communication in which the co-presence of researcher and researched brings the intimacy of the relationship, and the importance of trust and rapport, into sharp relief. Hsiung (2008, p. 214) highlights the epistemological shift that reflexive work entails for individuals, namely "the conscious and deliberate effort to interrogate the subjective self in relation to the research subject". Developing competence in this task is challenging, as Hsiung acknowledges. She advocates "a deliberate pedagogical intervention that challenges the tendency to privilege the technical aspects of interviewing skills, while overlooking their epistemological foundation" (p. 214). She has developed this intervention into a two-pronged approach: analysis of others' interactions (e.g. through examples of published transcripts, fieldwork notes, autoethnographies, etc.) and direct experience of interactions. Using excerpts of interview data from the educator's own research or research with which they are very familiar can help to scaffold student learning, encouraging students not to follow an interview topic guide too rigidly and to remain alert to possible unchecked assumptions or beliefs.

Educators need to consider how they might support students to develop ethical reflexivity *in situ*, which may necessitate different approaches for on- and offline interviewing. In this regard, Hsiung's (2008) work is instructive. She draws on the concept of "conceptual baggage" in developing student skills in this area, prompted by her observations that when students are asked to reflect on their own positionalities in relation to their research interests, they often lapse into general and generic discussions around class, gender, and so on, which yield only superficial engagement with the interview process. Hsiung's pedagogical approach helps students interrogate their own worldviews, assumptions, and personal biographies, and understand the extent to which each of these can substantively impact the interview process.

Researchers in translation and interpreting studies often engage with participants from very different backgrounds, with different life experiences, and of different ages. For example, Contreras (2022) explored undergraduate students' development of translator identity through a primarily interview-based longitudinal project that evolved against an unforeseen backdrop of social upheaval and crisis. The interviewing process therefore demanded significant researcher reflexivity, not least because the interviews were conducted in an online environment, but also because of the multiplicity of subjectivities and positions involved. (Contreras is researcher and educator at one of the institutions in the research.)

In this study, it was important for Contreras to ensure that the participating students viewed the interview space as a safe space where they could speak freely without any fear of negative repercussions on their own studies. The students' motivation for focusing on their studies and participating in Contreras's project inevitably varied over time, which had significant implications for their evolving sense of translator identity. This led to Contreras's decision to allow students to talk through experiences that were unrelated to the study but important for understanding their attitudes to issues such as work placements and thesis writing. It may be said that Contreras's experience as a university educator provided a grounding that facilitated ethics work at an advanced level, and skills that not all (graduate) students will necessarily be able to employ in their interviews. It is worth reflecting on what the impact might have been on the research had the interviewer decided to shut down interviewees' attempts to go "off topic".

Developing researcher reflexivity for interviews requires the educator to sensitise students to the fact that the researcher is an integral part of the interview narrative, regardless of whether they see it in that way. For instance, interviewee verbalisations such as "I'd never thought about [a particular topic] like that" constitute golden moments for researchers as they realise that they are receiving unscripted and intuitive insights generated in that instant. However, such moments can also raise ethical questions for interviewers, especially when responses are unexpected or include unwarranted disclosures.

Discussion activities

Handling unwarranted insights as an ethical issue in interview and process research

Discussion activity 1

Scenario: a researcher contacts a participant by email to arrange an interview; in response, the participant reveals that they have recently lost a close family member. How might/should this impact the interview process and/or the subsequent data analysis, if at all?

Students should discuss this situation in relation to two different research scenarios: in the first, the research focus is on the development of a student's translator identity; in the second, the focus is on software efficiencies in translation project management. In the first scenario, students should consider the issues of timing and the possible impact on motivation to study (and hence translator identity). Would the interviewee's responses be substantively different if the interview were postponed? In the second scenario, students should again consider the issue of timing as well as the possibility of mentioning the loss during the interview. What behaviours or verbalisations might the researcher look out for before suggesting a postponement?

Discussion activity 2

Scenario: in a study of mental health interpreting involving a focus group of former service users in a simulation of an interpreter-mediated assessment, one of the participants contextualises their reflection on an aspect of the simulation in relation to their personal experience, and in so doing discloses very distressing information.

Should the researcher respond to the personal information provided and, if so, what sort of responses would be ethically viable (e.g. an acknowledgement of the experience with a statement such as "That must have been very difficult for you")? Should the researcher attempt to shut down such personal disclosures due to the possibility that they might make others in the focus group feel uncomfortable? What are the implications for the group of both approaches? What additional action (if any) could/should the researcher take after the event to ensure the participant's wellbeing?

Discussion activity 3

Scenario: in a study involving undergraduate students employing think-aloud protocols in a translation assignment, a student who is engaged in a *post-hoc* interview about the task makes several comments that strongly suggest they are feeling overwhelmed by the demands of their programme of study and fears of personal academic failure.

Should the researcher respond directly to these comments either during or after the interview? What rationale could be given for responding? For not responding?

5.7.2.2 Survey research ethics

Survey research is a popular research methodology and method in translation and interpreting studies, although survey response rates can be low and survey fatigue high due to the relatively limited pool of professionals to survey, compared to other professions. In fact, declining survey response rates are observed more widely throughout academia, which raises the possibility of increased fraud through falsified data creation and reporting.

There is a wealth of literature on good questionnaire design for students to access independently. In this regard, educator support should be necessary only further down the line, such as when reviewing a draft questionnaire or discussing approaches to bias, where appropriate. One example of bias is presenting questions in ways that support the research hypothesis or are likely to produce results desired by the sponsor or client (Oldendick, 2012, p. 30). Students also need to think carefully about what sort of personal identifiable information (if any) they will need to collect via the questionnaire, and where such information should be positioned in the wider survey.

Representativeness and sample selection are ethical issues for all researchers. As Oldendick (2012, p. 30) points out, "Any 'sample' that depends on volunteers or on individuals who select themselves into the study cannot ethically be reported as representing some larger population." This raises a practical issue for students – namely, the steps they should take to increase the possibility of survey completion without engaging in coercion. There are three aspects to consider: the language used to persuade potential participants of the benefits of completing the survey (whether for themselves, for a wider group of professionals, or for wider society); the number of reminders potential participants should be sent; and whether it is ethically responsible to offer incentives (e.g. gifts or tokens) in return for participation (although this may be a moot point as some institutions proscribe such practices). Educators can usefully model this process, drawing on example texts from projects that have received ethical approval within the institution, and point students in the direction of institutional guidelines on issues such as incentivisation.

Online surveys are now probably the most common form of questionnaire. There are numerous platforms to support their creation; however, students should check with their institutions which are permitted, as not all of them offer the level of data protection and security needed to meet institutional requirements. Survey design will need to factor in informed consent before a participant can access the survey. This is commonly achieved through a survey landing page, which contains information about how the data will be handled, with a button for participants to click if they are happy to proceed.

Students may also benefit from discussing ethical issues that can arise when writing up survey results. Such conversations will be anchored around the principles of transparency and honesty so that enough information is provided for others to evaluate and replicate the survey, including full text of questions, description of the sample, response rate, and representativeness. Given the increased insistence on data sharing in academic research, educators should consider devoting some curriculum space to supporting students in managing data for depositing in relevant research repositories.

5.7.2.3 Ethnographic research ethics

Many students planning ethnographic research will need support to navigate both the ethics approval process and challenges in the field. From a proceduralist perspective, ethnographic research does not commonly meet the standard ethical requirements for social science research because of the impossibility of setting out all stages of the project prior to entering the field; even the way in which problems are conceptualised can evolve over time (Beach and Eriksson, 2010; Traianou, 2019). This does not preclude researchers from conducting ethnographic research, but they may need to be prepared for requests for ethical approval on an ongoing basis if aspects of the research present particular risks to participants and/or the researcher.

The need for constant (re-)negotiation of access to the field, and in some cases for participant consent on an evolving basis, the safety and security of the researcher and participants, the ways in which power relationships are navigated, and the representation of participants in written outputs are among the most prominent ethics-related matters in ethnographic research. Ideally, therefore, the ability to enact ethical reflexivity in ethnographic research should be foregrounded in researcher skills development. By breaking down the research process into identifiable components, researchers can start to anticipate those aspects of fieldwork that will require vigilance and ongoing ethical work to ensure the continued integrity of the approach.

Discussion activity

Cultivating researcher reflexivity in (face-to-face) participant observation

- **Consent.** Which strategies can researchers adopt to deal with matters of consent in environments where some of those present have not consented to the research? At what point might participant observation be considered unviable from the perspective of consent?
- **Entering the field.** Which steps might researchers take to establish themselves in the field? How might a project's research questions shape the decisions taken at this point?
- **Navigating the physical environment.** Where will you position yourself to observe? Will you occupy the same location throughout the project? Will you vary the length of observations and the locations? Where will you go to take a break from observing others and others observing you?
- **Forming and managing relationships in the field.** Will it be important to create opportunities for informal discussions of your research with other members of your institution (e.g. to provide an overview, receive feedback, etc.)? How will you respond if others seek to engage you in institutional activities that are unrelated to your research? How will you react if others continuously ask for information about

your project, assuming you do not wish to reveal all aspects of your research in order to avoid influencing the behaviour of the participants?
- **Fieldnotes.** Consider the potential impact (on participants and the research relationship) of taking notes *in-situ*. What are the implications (for the researcher and the participants) of taking notes during or after the observation? How will you organise your notes in ways that help you reflect on matters relating to representation, voice, and power? In what language will you write your notes? If you are capturing fragments of conversation, will you translate these on-site or afterwards? What are the potential implications for the representation of participants' voices of translating fieldnotes?
- **Leaving the field.** What will be the impact of your presence in the fieldwork site after your period of observation has ended? Do you think it is important to manage this? Will you return to the fieldwork site to present your findings? How might this benefit you and/or the participants? What are the risks?

Extension activity

After identifying a selection of ethnographic studies in the translation and interpreting studies literature, students discuss the extent to which the above discussion points are reflected in the texts' accounts of the research design and/or research process (collection and analysis).

Discussion activity

Scenario 1

A researcher plans to undertake ethnographic work over several weeks in a school to observe how sign language interpreting is used in a mixed classroom of deaf and hearing children under the age of ten.

- How might the researcher approach the issue of consent in this project?
- How might the researcher respond if a child's parents have given consent for the child to participate in the research, but the child shows signs of not wishing to engage?
- How might the researcher respond if certain children interact or present problems to be solved (e.g. a child falls over – or falls out with – another child)?
- What other ethical issues might arise as the project unfolds?

Extension activity

Imagine this research is conducted in a university environment. What are the implications of the different environment and the different age of the participant(s) for the questions above? An additional set of questions could concern a situation in which a graduate student is doing some teaching and wishes to conduct research on the class(es).

Scenario 2

A researcher plans to conduct an ethnographic study of a literary translation summer school from the perspective of participant translator and researcher.

- How might the researcher approach the issue of consent in this project?
- What are the implications of the researcher's participant status for the way in which relationships are formed with other members of the group?
- Which other ethical issues could arise as the project unfolds?

Scenario 3

A researcher plans to examine language and communication policy and its implementation (including translation and interpreting) in two non-governmental organisations. The research will involve extended periods of observation in the organisations' head offices and two in-country offices.

- How might the researcher approach the issue of consent in this project?
- What impact might the researcher's lack of local language knowledge have on relationship-building in the field?
- What would be the impact on the research (if any) of the researcher volunteering to support organisational activity during the project?

5.7.2.4 Digital research

A considerable amount of research involving digital technologies and environments – commonly known as "Netnography" – falls within the category of ethnographic research (Kozinets, 2020). Increasing numbers of master's and doctoral projects involve engagement with online populations, for instance to examine professional and non-professional translation practices in online environments (e.g. technical expertise, team communications, quality assessment) and responses to translation as a product in commercial and non-commercial online spaces.

Sensitising students to ethical issues relating to publicly available online information is an important aspect of researcher development education, as many of them will be unaware of these issues, viewing all publicly available information as fair game for research. In part, this is due to the complex interactions students have with software and devices on a daily basis – interactions that require critical interrogation when leveraged for research purposes. Educators need to be aware that the regulations governing the ethical use of social media data and other online information vary from institution to institution and country to country; hence, students who have undertaken research projects in one country may be surprised to discover that research practice must comply with a different set of rules in another.

Additionally, students may have been active participants in communities that they wish to study, or view participation as a precursor to investigation and sign up before negotiating researcher access. In each of these scenarios, transparency should be encouraged from the earliest possible point as part of research integrity. Of course, grappling with the concepts of privacy, covert activity, and coercion is important in all academic research, but digital research presents a unique set of challenges in this regard.

In terms of educator input and scaffolding, a combination of structured discussion in supervision and peer-to-peer conversations through a case-based learning approach can be useful. Tiidenberg (2018, p. 469) suggests shifting the focus away from research collectables to research process when developing strategies to address ethical issues in digital research. Specifically, this means reflecting on what she terms "internet-specific tensions" that arise in the different phases of data collection.

The following activities are designed for: 1) supervisor–supervisee/student–student peer discussion; and 2) case-based learning through small-group discussion.

Discussion activity

Sensitising students to ethical issues in digital research

- **Consent.** How will you determine potential participants' ability to consent in terms of their autonomy, competence, and ability to understand risk? Which safeguards can you put into place in the event of someone making a false claim?
- **Public/private spaces.** What are the implications for your research of defining certain types of online data as public or private?
- **Anonymity/confidentiality.** Is it reasonable to try to offer subject protection in digital research as you would in non-digital research? How might you factor in matters of exposure, ownership, and authorship into your research process?

> Discussion activity
>
> *Case-based learning*
>
> This activity is based on research from outside of translation and interpreting studies. Three articles from the journal *Research Ethics* – Mason and Singh (2022), Stommel and de Rijk (2021), and Willis (2019) – are recommended, but educators and students can find their own examples.
>
> *Prompts for discussion*
> - Which ethical issues are reported as salient in each text?
> - Which recommendations (if any) are made to improve research practice from an ethical perspective?
>
> *Extension activity*
>
> Students identify two TI studies journal articles or book chapters that focus on different types of digital research. They should observe how much space the texts devote to ethical considerations and discuss with a peer any ethical questions relating to data collection, analysis, and writing up that have not been fully or adequately addressed.

5.7.3 Ethics and the writing-up process

For many researchers generally, and student researchers in particular, the writing-up process often includes a reference to ethics in procedural terms: that is, acknowledgement of the project's approval by the relevant institutional ethics committee. Moreover, academic journals often require this to ensure research integrity. As mentioned in Subsection 5.7.2, case-based learning can support researchers to navigate complex ethical issues in their work. However, all too often, doctoral (and master's) students overlook the potential value to the field of providing a fuller account of ethical issues and how they impacted on data collection and analysis. In some cases, this may be more to do with the limitations of word count than any reluctance to share experiences. Educators are well placed to advise students about publishing options and the importance of addressing this issue.

To some extent, the neglect of ethical matters when writing up research reflects the lack of an integrated approach to ethics in research education. This can lead students to the misguided belief that this is not part of the "ethics work" of research. Researchers find accounts of the messiness of research encounters useful in helping them plan their entry to sites of data collection and draft potential responses to unforeseen events that generate ethical dilemmas. Therefore, they can play a valuable role in developing approaches to research with human participants.

Another aspect of writing up concerns representational ethics and the value of researchers reflecting on their obligations to participants. For example, Schneider (2006, p. 83) considers whether participants should be able to review researchers' representations of them prior to publication. This decision needs to be balanced against the participants' ability to cope with the language of academic research and the time needed to engage with the work. Sending extracts with straightforward contextual descriptions might be a more effective way to initiate a dialogue than sending a full draft journal article. When deciding whether to share preliminary findings, the researcher should also consider that some research participants may be able to identify colleagues or peers in anonymised extracts, which may cause conflict.

The general principle of reporting findings to participants is considered a basic courtesy, if not a requirement of many contemporary research practices, especially in the biomedical sciences. Educators can support students to think about non-academic publication routes for disseminating their findings and highlighting their relevance to society. Writing up research findings for lay audiences is a skill that can support later grant-writing processes, since those who review grant applications are unlikely to be experts in the field.

Activity

Exploring ethical requirements for authors in academic publishing and peer review

Task

1   Students identify two TI studies journals and examine the guidance given to authors with regard to research ethics (e.g. ethics checklist).
2   Students explore the website of the COPE (Committee on Publication Ethics): https://publicationethics.org/.
3   In both cases, students critically examine the discourse practices and the ethical traditions that they appear to reflect.
4   Students reflect on the process of peer review and the ethical issues that might arise. If their own work has been peer reviewed, they should reflect on what they have learned from the process. They should also consider how they would observe ethical reviewing if asked to undertake a review.

5.8 Chapter summary

This chapter highlights the influence of the biomedical sciences on research ethics development in the humanities and social sciences and encourages educators to situate reflection on research ethics within their local institutional contexts. In addition, it advocates active reflection on the approach to research ethics in the supervisor–supervisee relationship in order to avoid focusing exclusively on procedural matters. It suggests that more time should be devoted to developing ethical practice in relation to specific data collection methods, either within courses on research methods or through dedicated curriculum events. Finally, the chapter's practical activities are designed to support researcher reflexivity in ways that enhance ethical responsibility in research and encourage social dialogue between peers at various stages of the research process.

References

Banks, S. (2018). Cultivating researcher integrity: Virtue-based approaches to research integrity. In N. Emmerich (Ed.), *Virtue ethics in the conduct and governance of social science research*, Advances in research ethics and integrity, Volume 3 (pp. 21–44). Emerald Publishing Limited.

Beach, D., & Eriksson, A. (2010). The relationships between ethical positions and methodological approaches: A Scandinavian perspective. *Ethnography and Education*, 5(2), 129–142.

Beardon, C., & Wilson, J. P. (2013). *Experiential learning: A handbook for education, training and coaching*. Kogan Page.

Boden, R., Epstein, D., & Latimer, J. (2009). Accounting for ethos or programmes for conduct? The brave new world of research ethics committees. *Sociological Review*, 57(4), 727–749.

Bosk, C. (2004). The ethnographer and the IRB: Comment on Kevin D. Haggerty, "Ethics creep: Governing social science research in the name of ethics". *Qualitative Sociology*, 27(4), 417–420.

Brannelly, T. (2018). An ethics of care research manifesto. *International Journal of Care and Caring*, 2(3), 367–378.

Burton, B. K., Dunn, C. P., & Petruzzello, M. (2013). Ethics of care. In *Encylopaedia Britannica*. www.britannica.com/topic/ethics-of-care.

Busher, H., & Fox, A. (Eds.) (2019). *Implementing ethics in educational ethnography: Regulation and practice*. Routledge.

Charbonneau, R. (1984). Ethics in human research. *The IDRC Reports*, 13(1), 20–21.

Contreras, N. S. (2022). The development of translator identity: An interpretative phenomenological study of Chilean translation students' experiences amid local and global crises. Unpublished doctoral dissertation, University of Manchester.

Ellis, C. (1986). *Fisher folk: Two communities on Chesapeake Bay*. University Press of Kentucky.

Ellis, C. (2007). Telling secrets, revealing lives: Relational ethics in research with intimate others. *Qualitative Inquiry*, 13(1), 3–29.

Fancourt, N., Foreman-Peck, L., & Oancea, A. (2022). Addressing ethical quandaries in practitioner researcher: A philosophical and exploratory study of responsible improvisation through hermeneutical conversation. *Teaching and Teacher Education*, 116. https://doi.org/10.1016/j.tate.2022.103760.

Gilligan, C. (1982). *In a different voice: Psychological theory and women's development*. Harvard University Press.

Guillemin, M., & Gillam, L. (2004). Ethics, reflexivity and "ethically important moments" in research. *Qualitative Inquiry*, 10(2), 261–280. https://doi.org/10.1177/1077800403262360.

Haggerty, K. D. (2003). From risk to precaution: The rationalities of personal crime prevention. In R. V. Ericson and A. Doyle (Eds.), *Risk and morality* (pp. 193–214). University of Toronto Press.

Haggerty, K. D., Becker, H. S., & Bosk, C. (2004). Ethics creep: Governing social science research in the name of ethics. *Qualitative Sociology*, 27(4), 391–420.

Hale, S. B., & Napier, J. (2013). *Research methods in interpreting: A practical resource.* Bloomsbury.

Held, V. (2006). *The ethics of care: Personal, political, global.* Oxford University Press.

Hsiung, P.-C. (2008). Teaching reflexivity in qualitative interviewing. *Teaching Sociology*, 36(3), 211–226.

Iphofen, R. (2009). *Ethical decision-making in social research.* Palgrave Macmillan.

Iphofen, R. (2011). Ethical decision making in qualitative research. *Qualitative Research*, 11(4), 443–446. https://doi.org/10.1177/1468794111404330.

Israel, M. (2014). *Research ethics and integrity for social scientists.* Sage.

Kasia, K. (2009). Protecting respondent confidentiality in qualitative research. *Qualitative Health Research*, 19(11), 1632–1641. https://doi.org/10.1177/1049732309350879.

Kim, Y. (2021). An empirical study of research ethics and their role in psychologists' data sharing intentions using consequentialism theory of ethics. *Journal of Librarianship and Information Science*, 54(2), 251–263. https://doi.org/10.1177/09610006211008967.

Kim, Y., & Stanton, J. M. (2012). Institutional and individual influences on scientists' data sharing practices. *Journal of Computational Science Education*, 3(1), 47–56.

Kozinets, R. V. (2020). *Netnography: The essential guide to qualitative social media research.* Sage.

Macfarlane, B. (2009). *Researching with integrity: The ethics of academic enquiry.* Routledge.

Mason, S., & Singh, L. (2022). Reporting and discoverability of "tweets" in published scholarship: Current practice and ethical implications. *Research Ethics*, 18(2), 93–113.

Mellinger, C. D., & Baer, B. J. (2021). Research ethics in translation and interpreting studies. In K. Koskinen and N. Pokorn (Eds.), *The Routledge handbook of translation and ethics* (pp. 365–380). Routledge.

Monaghan, L. F., O'Dwyer, M., & Gabe, J. (2013). Seeking university research ethics committee approval: The emotional vicissitudes of a "rationalised" process. *International Journal of Social Research Methodology*, 16(1), 65–80. https://doi.org/10.1080/13645579.2011.649902.

Oakes, J. M. (2002). Risks and wrongs in social science research: An evaluator's guide to the ERB. *Evaluation Review*, 26(5), 443–479. https://doi.org/10.1177/019384102236520.

Oldendick, R. W. (2012). Survey research ethics. In L. Gideon (Ed.), *Handbook of survey methodologies for the social sciences* (pp. 23–35). Springer.

Palys, T., & Lowman, J. (2012). Defending research confidentiality "to the extent the law allows": Lessons from the Boston College subpoenas. *Journal of Academic Ethics*, 10, 271–297. https://doi.org/10.1007/s10805-012-9172-5.

Pritchard, M. (2005). Teaching research ethics and working together: Commentary on "Pedagogical objectives in teaching research ethics in science and engineering". *Science and Engineering*, 11(3), 367–371. https://doi.org/10.1007/s11948-005-0005-4.

Rabinow, P. (1997). Introduction. In P. Rabinow (Ed.), *Michel Foucault ethics: Essential works of Foucault (1954–1984)* (pp. xi–xlii). Penguin Books.

Rawlings, V., Flexner, J., & Riley, L. (Eds.) (2021). *Community-led research: Walking new pathways together.* Sydney University Press.

Savage, C. J., & Vickers, A. J. (2009). Empirical study of data sharing by authors publishing in PLoS journals. *PloS One*, 4(9). https://doi.org/10.1371/journal.pone.0007078.

Sawyer, R. K. (Ed.) (2011). *Structure and improvisation in creative teaching*. Cambridge University Press.

Schneider, B. (2006). Ethical research and pedagogical gaps. *College Composition and Communication*, 58(1), 70–88.

School of Arts, Languages and Cultures, University of Manchester (2020). *Ethical research risk levels*. Unpublished document available on the University of Manchester's intranet.

Silverman, D. (Ed.) (2017). *Research ethics in the Arab region*. Springer International.

Stommel, W., & de Rijk, L. (2021). Ethical approval not sought: How discourse analysts report ethical issues around publicly available online data. *Research Ethics*, 17(3), 275–297.

Tickly, L., & Bond, T. (2013). Towards a postcolonial research ethics in comparative and international education. *Compare: A Journal of Comparative and International Education*, 43(4), 422–442. https://doi.org/10.1080/03057925.2013.797721.

Tiidenberg, K. (2018). Ethics in digital research. In U. Flick (Ed.), *Sage handbook of qualitative data collection* (pp. 466–479). Sage.

Traianou, A. (2019). Phrónesis and the ethical regulation of ethnographic research. In H. Busher and A. Fox (Eds.), *Implementing ethics in educational ethnography: Regulation and practice* (pp. 19–31). Routledge.

van den Hoonaard, W. C. (2002). Introduction: Ethical norming and qualitative research. In W. C. van den Hoonaard (Ed.), *Walking the tightrope: Ethical issues for qualitative researchers* (pp. 3–16). University of Toronto Press.

von Unger, H. (2016). Reflexivity beyond regulations: Teaching research ethics and qualitative methods in Germany. *Qualitative Inquiry*, 22(2), 87–98. https://doi.org/10.1177/1077800415620220.

Warin, J. (2011). Ethical mindfulness and reflexivity: Managing a research relationship with children and young people in a 14-year qualitative longitudinal research (QLR) study. *Qualitative Inquiry*, 17(9), 805–814. https://doi.org/10.1177/1077800411423196.

Wiles, R. (2013). *What are qualitative research ethics?* Bloomsbury.

Williamson, E., & Smyth, M. (2004). *Researchers and their "subjects": Ethics, power, knowledge and consent*. Policy Press.

Willig, C. (2001). *Introducing qualitative research in psychology: Adventures in theory and method*. Open University Press.

Willis, R. (2019). Observations online: Finding the ethical boundaries of Facebook research. *Research Ethics*, 15(1), 1–17.

Index

accessibility 30; activities 100–1; MT 99–100
accommodations 35
accountability 11
activism 6; activities 168–71; and curriculum planning 167–8; in ethics education 166–7
activities: accessibility 100–1; activism 168–71; children's fiction 66–7; codes of ethics 159–64; codes of ethics in literary translation 70; collaborative translation 111, 113–14; community-led research 117–19; copyright issues 98–9; crisis translations 116–19; crowdsourced translation 112–13; data management 195–7; data security discourse 96–7; data sharing 198; digital ethics 95–6; disciplined improvisation 202–3; emotional labour 166; freelance work, digital ethics 97–8; hashtag translation 76–7; improvisation 202–3; interpreting skills development 169; language choice in research ethics 185–6; monolingual revision 52–3; negotiating MTPE use with client 107–9; neutrality in translation 120–1; post-editing 105–6; research ethics 182–3, 212; risk research 187–9; role playing 143–4; sensing gender bias in MT 93–4; sensitisation to user needs in MPTE 106–7; social bias in MT 93–4; text preparation for neural MT 92–3; translator-client negotiations 68–9; Utilitarianism 22–3; witness texts 62–3
adaptive expertise 84, 137
agency 26; interpreter 148; and interpreting 136–7
Ali, Monica, *Brick Lane* 63, 65
aligned curriculum 13, 32–3

alterity 10
assessment 33; and feedback 34–5; and inclusion 35
assessment literacy 34
ATs (Assessment Tasks) 32

Babels organisation 167
back channel pedagogy 144
biomedical sciences influence: research ethics 184, 212
Boochani, Behrouz, *No Friend but the Mountains* 60
Brick Lane (Ali) 63, 65

CAS (complex adaptive systems) 122
case building: case-based learning 152
case-based learning 6, 21; benefits 151, 152; business interpreting 156; case building 152; competence building 153; court interpreting 153–4; dialogue interpreting 151; ethics education 151–7; examples 153–7; limitations 151; media interpreting 157; medical interpreting 154–5; prescriptivism 151; scaffolding 151; social work interpreting 155–6
CAT (Computer Assisted Translation) tools 84
character virtues 15
children's fiction 65; activities 66–7; *see also* translation for children
classroom: vs real world 26
classroom narrative 10, 11
CLOUT (Controlled Language for Optimized Uniform Translation) 92
codes of ethics 3, 6; activities 159–64; development 159–60, 162; harm avoidance 186; in literary translation 69–71; teaching 157–9

Index

collaborative learning 27, 88; *see also* interdisciplinary learning
collaborative translation 109–23; activities 111, 113–14; approaches 110; crisis situations 6, 114–16; ethics education 109–11; exploitation 111–12; online 110
commercial translation: and ethical competence development 71–9
communitarianism 14; *see also* Confucianism; Ubuntu
community-led research: activities 117–19
competence building: case-based learning 153
conceptual baggage 203
conference interpreting 132; ethics education 147–9; interdisciplinary learning 145–6; proactive idealism 148
confidentiality: research ethics 193–4
Confucianism 14
consent: process 192–3; translating 193; *see also* informed consent
consequentialism 14
consequentialism theory 197–8; *see also* data sharing
constructivism 26–7
controlled language *see* CLOUT
Conversation Analytic Role-Play 140–1, 165
copyright issues: activities 98–9
cosmopolitanism 14
court interpreting: case-based learning 153–4
crisis situations: collaborative translation 6, 114–16
crisis translations 123; activities 116–19; *see also* INTERACT
critical pedagogy 28, 141
critical points: interpreting 149
crowdsourced translation 109–10; activities 112–13
cultural dimension framework 75
cultural relativism 16, 17
curriculum planning 4, 9, 21, 26; and activism 167–8; *see also* translation curriculum

data management: activities 195–7; research ethics 194
data protection: research ethics 194
data security discourse: activities 96–7
data sharing: activities 198
data use/reuse: MT 91, 94
DEFT (Developing Engagement with Feedback Toolkit) 36

Demand Control Schema 131, 141, 158
deontology 12, 13, 14, 69; Kantian 15
dialogue interpreting 6, 11, 131, 133–5, 165; and agency 136; case-based learning 151; drama-based pedagogies 171; and ethics education 138–9, 141; interdisciplinary learning in 145; language shift 163; law students 146; nursing students 146; role playing 139–40
didacticism 84; and retranslation 66–7
digital ethics 83; activities 95–6; freelance work 97–8; good practice 94–9; and MT 91; scope 94
digital reflexivity 83, 85–7; and pedagogical theory 88–9
digital research (netnography) 209–11
disability: biomedical models 30; reflection prompts 30–1; social model 30
disciplined improvisation 202; activities 202–3
diversity 30; *see also* EDI

EDI (equality, diversity, and inclusion) 4, 29–32
educational environment: Wikipedia as 121–3
emergentist pedagogy 6
emotional labour 165, 168, 169; activities 166
EMT (European Master's in Translation) 18–19, 102
epistemologies: research ethics 180
EQF (European Qualifications Framework) 19
ethical commitment 2; reinforcement 25
ethical competence 3–4, 18–20; development through commercial translation 71–9; *see also* TEDC
ethical decision-making 5, 13; neurocognitive model 19
ethical issues: identification 21, 24; literary translation 53–5; translation for children 65–9
ethical judgement: enhancing 24–5
ethical knowledge 2, 22–4; reflection prompts 23–4
ethical maturity 2, 4, 9, 15, 33, 37, 153
ethical priorities: patient information leaflet **49**; and text profiling 48–9; *see also* patient information leaflet
ethical prototypes 19; development 19–20
ethical relativism 4, 9, 16–17
ethical responsibility 4, 12, 79; experiential approach 48; and translator identity status 45

ethical sensitisation: multilingual texts 63–5
ethical sensitivity 5, 21–2
ethical traditions: research ethics 197–201
ethical vigilance 2, 12
ethics: and interpreting 131–7; and machine translation 90–1; survey research 205; in translation curriculum 43–6, 71–2, 90–1; and translation technologies 89; and Wikipedia 119–20; and Wikitrad project 123; writing-up process 183, 201, 211–12; *see also* digital ethics; research ethics; virtue ethics
ethics of care 199–200
ethics of conviction 140
ethics creep 184
ethics education: activism in 166–7; case-based learning 151–7; conference interpreting 147–9; and dialogue interpreting 138–9, 141; and social justice 166–71
ethics of entertainment 134
ethics of responsibility 197–8
ethics sensitisation: pre-translation tasks 46–53
ethics teaching 9–20
ethnographic research ethics 207–9
experiential learning circle 27
exploitation: collaborative translation 111–12
expository approach: interpreting 144

feedback: activity development 36–7; and assessment 34–5; dynamic 35; forms of 35; reflection prompts 36
Finnegans Wake (Joyce) 63; Dutch edition 64; multilingualism 64
fishbowl strategy 144
focus groups 7, 188, 203
folk theorising 10
Forum Theatre 142
freelance work: digital ethics 97–8

gatekeepers 189, 190, 191, 192
gender bias in MT 93–4
Goldstein, Rebecca, *The Mind Body Problem* 20
Google Cloud Translation 95
Google Translate 95
Gorman, Amanda, *The Hill We Climb* 59–60

harm avoidance: codes of ethics 186; and research ethics 186–9

hashtag translation 5, 74–7; activities 76–7
health campaigning 48–9; *see also* patient information leaflet
hidden curriculum 9, 33; reflection prompts 34
Holocaust studies: and translation 61–2
hospitality 54; linguistic 58, 116, 119

ILOs (Intended Learning Outcomes) 32
improvisation: activities 202–3; research ethics 202
inclusion 31; and assessment 35; *see also* equality
informed consent: activities 190–2; and individual autonomy 189; as process 192–3; research ethics 189–92; survey research 206; translating 193
integrity and thoroughness: and translation curriculum 43–5; and virtue ethics 199
INTERACT (International Network on Crisis Translation) 115
interdisciplinary learning 6, 145–7; conference interpreting 145–6; in dialogue interpreting 145; ethics, reflection prompts 146–7; ethics in 145; *see also* collaborative learning
interpreter, affiliated 147–8; agency 148; identity status 136; shared 147; stress 164–5
interpreting, and agency 136–7; broadcast 134; critical points 149–50; defensive 148; and ethics 131–7; expository approach 144; fidelity 148; lexical choices 150; *see also* conference interpreting; dialogue interpreting
interpreting skills development 148–9; activities 169
intersectionality 31
interviews: research ethics 203–4

Kang, Han, *Chaesikjuuija* (*The Vegetarian*) 55–8
Kant, Immanuel: absolutist interpretations 14–15; and deontology 15; *Metaphysics of Morals* 15
Kaza, Madhu, *Kitchen Table Translation* 58

language shift: dialogue interpreting 163
law students: dialogue interpreting 146
learning: storied approach 20; *see also* case-based learning; collaborative learning; constructivism; interdisciplinary learning

Index 219

lexical choices: interpreting 150
linguistic hospitality 58, 116, 119
linguistic justice 101
literary translation: *Brick Lane* 63; case studies 55–60; classroom activities 60–1; codes of ethics in 69–71; ethical issues 53–5; *Finnegans Wake* 63–4; planning ethics 54; reflection prompts 55, 56; *The Hill We Climb* 59–60; *The Vegetarian* 55–8
Lu, Qiouyi, "Mother Tongues" 63, 65

Matilda (Dahl): edited version 68
mattering map 20
medical interpreting: case-based learning 154–5
memory: prosthetic 62
meta-language 79
mock conference events 145–6
monolingual revision 51–3; activities 52–3; inconsistencies 51; spelling 51
MOOCs (Massive Open Online Course providers) 112
moral identity 25
moral imagination 4, 17–18
moral philosophy 13–15; reflection prompts 15
moral reasoning: skill development 24
MT (machine translation) 6, 90–102; accessibility 99–100; data use/reuse 91, 94; definition 90; digital ethics 91; and ethics 90–1; social bias 93–4; *see also* neural machine translation
MTPE (machine translation, post-editing) 103; negotiating use with client 107–9; sensitisation to user needs 106–7; student learning 104–5
multilingual texts, ethical sensitisation 63–5
multilingualism *Finnegans Wake* (Joyce) 64
multimodality 43

narrative theory 12; *see also* storied approach
netnography *see* digital research
neural machine translation 84, 91; text preparation 91–3
neurocognitive model: ethical decision-making 19
neutrality in translation: activities 120–1
NPM (New Public Management) 29
nursing students: dialogue interpreting 146

online: collaborative translation 110
online machine translator 90, 93, 94, 96, 100
online survey research 206
outcome favourability 152

patient information leaflet: text producer's ethical priorities 49, 50; text recipient's ethical priorities 50; translator's ethical priorities 50
pedagogical resource: Wikipedia as 119–23
pedagogical theory: and digital reflexivity 88–9
pedagogies: drama-based 142–4
peer review 48, 122–3
personally identifiable information 195
planning prompts 12
post-editing 102–3; activities 105–6; course topics 102–3; forms 102; ISO standard 102
postcolonial ethics 200
postcolonialism: definition 200
process consent 192–3
professional ethics 12, 14

QLR (qualitative longitudinal research) 192
questionnaire design: bias 206

reading: as ethical activity 46–7; reflection prompts 47
reading levels 166
real world: vs classroom 26
reality-shaping: and translation 12
reflection prompts: disability 30–1; ethical knowledge 23–4; feedback 36; hidden curriculum 34; interdisciplinary learning ethics 146–7; literary translation 55, 56; moral philosophy 15; reading 47; research ethics 183; supervisor-supervisee relationship 181; syllabus development 32; teaching ethics 29; translator identity status 45–6
reflection-in-action 24
reflection-on-action 2, 24, 25
reflective practice 25
reflexivity 2, 6; definition 86; ethical 185; research ethics 201–3; *see also* digital reflexivity; reflection prompts; self-reflexivity
relational ethics 79
relativism *see* cultural relativism; ethical relativism
representational harms 93

220 Index

research ethics 7; activities 182–3, 184, 212; biomedical sciences influence 184, 212; change 184–6; confidentiality 193–4; core concepts 186–97; critical approaches 199–200; data management 194; data protection 194; definition 179; epistemologies 180; ethical traditions 197–201; ethnographic 207–9; and harm avoidance 186–9; improvisation 202; informed consent 189–92; integrated approach to teaching 201–12; interviews 203–4; and language choice 185–6; precautionary decision-making 184; reflection prompts 183; reflexivity 201–3; significance 179; teaching 180–4; Western view 180
research integrity 7
risk 12
risk research: activities 187–9
role hybridity 166
role playing: activities 143–4; Conversation Analytic Role-Play 140–1; dialogue interpreting 139–40; limitations 139–40; and role taking 140; theatre-based approaches 141–2
role taking: and role playing 140
routine expertise 137
Routledge Handbook on Translation and Ethics 3

scaffolding 21–2, 27, 78; case-based learning 151
Schimel, Lawrence: on translation 67–8
secondary witnesses: translators as 59, 61–3
self-care 164–6
self-efficacy 27
self-reflexivity 2, 3, 10, 16, 17
sender-loyalty 147
Shelley, Mary, *Frankenstein* 54
sign language interpretation 6
situatedness 26, 144, 146
skills development: interpreting 148–9
Smith, Deborah (translator), *The Vegetarian* 55–8
social bias: MT 93–4
social justice: and ethics education 166–71
social work interpreting: case-based learning 155–6
spelling: monolingual revision 51
SR (social responsibility) 28, 29
storied approach: learning 20; *see also* narrative theory
stress: interpreter 164–5

student-centred learning 10–11, 28
subjectivity: disciplined 159, 165
supervisor-supervisee relationship: reflection prompts 181
survey research: ethics 205; informed consent 206; online 206
Susam-Saraeva, Şebnem 59, 60
Swift, Johanthan, *Gulliver's Travels* 54
syllabus development: reflection prompts 32

teacher-centred learning 28
teaching ethics 4, 21, 28–37; contextual challenges 28–9; reflection prompts 29
TEDC (translational-ethical decision-making competence) 19
teleology 13
TEP (translate-edit-proofread) model 109
text preparation: neural machine translation 91–3
text profiling 21; and ethical priorities 48–9
theatre-based approaches: role playing 141–2
thoroughness *see* integrity and thoroughness
TI (Translation and Interpreting) 1; consequentialism 11; research ethics teaching 180–4; theory 10, 11
TLAs (Teaching and Learning Activities) 32
TM (translation memory) metadata 94–5
transcreation 71, 77–8, 79
translating consent 193
translation: and Holocaust studies 61–2; and reality-shaping 12; Schimel on 67–8; social 122; as wayfaring 17–18, 20, 62; *see also* collaborative translation; crowdsourced translation; literary translation; MT
translation for children: ethical issues 65–9; *see also* children's fiction
translation curriculum: competence-based 44; ethics in 43–6, 71–2, 90–1; and integrity and thoroughness 43–5
translation curriculum technologies: discussion points 85; *see also* CAT tools
Translation Studies journal 59
translation technologies: and ethics 89
translator identity status 205; and ethical responsibility 45; reflection prompts 45–6
translator self-concept 45, 83, 103, 110, 115, 123

translator-audience relationship 56–7
translator-author relationship 5, 56, 57–8
translator-client negotiations: activities 68–9
translators: as (secondary) witnesses 59, 61–3
trust 12, 22, 24, 116, 142, 144, 166, 186, 203

Ubuntu 14, 38n1
Utilitarian ethics: definition 14
Utilitarianism: activities 22–3

virtue ethics 13, 15, 198–9; and integrity 199
VLEs (virtual learning environments) 28
vulnerability 5, 48

wayfaring: translation as 17–18, 20, 62, 78
web localisation: activities 72–4; approaches 72
Western view: research ethics 180
Wikipedia 6; as educational environment 121–3; and ethics 119–20; as pedagogical resource 119–23
Wikitrad project 122; and translation ethics 123
witness texts 5, 61–2; activities 62–3
writing-up process, ethics 183, 201, 211–12

ZPD (Zone of Proximal Development) 27